Theory of Natural Selection and Population Growth

THEORY OF NATURAL SELECTION and POPULATION GROWTH

Lev R. Ginzburg
State University of New York at Stony Brook

THE BENJAMIN/CUMMINGS PUBLISHING COMPANY, INC.
Menlo Park, California · Reading, Massachusetts
London · Amsterdam · Don Mills, Ontario · Sydney

Series in Evolutionary Biology
Institute of Ecology
University of California, Davis

Francisco J. Ayala, Editor

Sponsoring Editor: James Behnke
Production Editor: Mimi Hills
Book Designer: Greg Hubit

The cover shows an analog-computer simulation of a common gastropod shell form. D. M. Raup and A. Michelson. Theoretical morphology of the coiled shell. *Science* 147:1294–1295 (March 12, 1965). Copyright 1965 by the American Association for the Advancement of Science.

Copyright © 1983 by The Benjamin/Cummings Publishing Company, Inc. All rights reserved. No part of this publication may be reproduced, stored in a retrieval system, or transmitted, in any form or by any means, electronic, mechanical, photocopying, recording, or otherwise, without the prior written permission of the publisher. Printed in the United States of America. Published simultaneously in Canada.

Library of Congress Cataloging in Publication Data
Ginzburg, Lev R.
  Theory of natural selection and population growth.

  Includes index.
  1. Population biology. 2. Population biology—Mathematical models.
3. Natural selection. 4. Natural selection—Mathematical models.
I. Title. QH352.G56   1983   575.1'5   82-17904
ISBN 0-8053-3180-8
ABCDEFGHIJ–AL–89876543

The Benjamin/Cummings Publishing Company, Inc.
2727 Sand Hill Road
Menlo Park, California 94025

To my father,
Ruvim Isaacovich Ginzburg

Foreword

The most outstanding challenge in population biology is the integration of population genetics and population ecology. Evolutionary processes cannot be understood without heeding the ecology as well as the underlying genetics of organisms. Yet the two disciplines had separate origins and have developed mostly in independence.

Population genetics appeared and rapidly bloomed into a mature corpus of theoretical knowledge in the 1920s and 1930s. The theory is based on Mendelian heredity, natural selection, and other processes and parameters, such as mutation rate, population size, and gene flow, which are easy to conceptualize. It was an unusual situation in science. A fully developed theory had emerged without being preceded by a body of empirical information. Population genetics had its Newton—the three giants, Ronald A. Fisher, Sewall Wright, and J. B. S. Haldane—before it had its Copernicus, its Tycho Brahe, or its Kepler. Empirical research followed in short course, guided by the theory, but not always successful at testing it. This was because the theory deals with single genes and simple interactions, whereas the experiments have to use whole organisms; it is rarely feasible to isolate one or a few factors as the only relevant variables. In addition, little attention, if any, was paid to the ecological realities of natural populations: the variegated and ever changing environments, the interactions between organisms of different species, the effects of population density.

The birth of population ecology was less grand. Empirical studies came first, slowly and inconspicuously, as an outgrowth of natural history. The mathematical theories of Alfred J. Lotka and Vito Volterra have been there since around 1930, but these theories are limited in scope and for many years contributed modestly at best towards inspiring and guiding experimental research. Only in the 1960s, spearheaded by Robert H. MacArthur and a few others, would population ecology become a theoretical science. That theory preceded experiment in population genetics but not in population ecology is not just a historical oddity: ecological relationships are not underlain by a simple process like Mendelian heredity.

Theoretical population ecology has flourished in the last two decades. The large number of publications, as well as the insightful advances, have made it highly visible among biological disciplines. The same period has witnessed a renaissance of research in population genetics. Theoretical models have explored ecological problems, such as density-dependent and frequency-dependent selection, but the accomplishments have fallen quite short from a satisfactory integration of population genetics and population ecology, which is required to understand the evolution of natural populations. For there is feedback between the ecology and genetics of populations: ecological processes determine genetic changes but are themselves modified by the changing genetic composition of populations.

The Theory of Natural Selection and Population Growth explores theoretically the interplay between the leading process of genetic change, natural selection, and the most fundamental of ecological phenomena, population dynamics. Ginzburg formulates, in Chapter 2, an original model of population growth, which straddles the precise but simplistic Lotka-Volterra equations and the very general but vague Kolmogorov-type models. Chapters 3 and 4 investigate the genetics of natural selection, with special consideration of the stability of polymorphisms. Most original and relevant, in my view, are the final three chapters, dedicated to the intercausality between ecological and genetic processes, and to the evolutionary consequences of this interplay. The book seeks less than a full integration of population genetics and population ecology, but it is an exciting and significant step towards that endeavor.

This volume is the second of the Series in Evolutionary Biology sponsored by the Institute of Ecology at the University of California, Davis, and published by Benjamin/Cummings. The first volume, David Sloan Wilson's *The Natural Selection of Populations and*

Communities, has received considerable attention. I trust that the present book, like Wilson's, will be effective in promoting theoretical and experimental investigations which will further our understanding of biological evolution.

Francisco J. Ayala
Davis, California

Preface

Population genetics and ecology have been separate branches of biology for a long time, particularly with respect to their theoretical aspects. Mathematical models that describe processes of population growth and interactions have been quite separate from the equations that were designed to describe evolution. The people working in theoretical population biology have had a tendency to specialize either in population genetics or in theoretical ecology. The artificial and undesirable barrier between these fields is disappearing at too slow a pace; I hope to contribute further to its removal with this book.

The state of the art in theoretical population biology is such that it is still very much in a transient state; many basic concepts have not been fully stabilized. It is thus exciting to work in this field, but discouraging to write a "fundamental" book. Who would wish to write such a work knowing that most of the material will not survive more than a decade of scientific evolution? I believe, therefore, that short, narrow-subject-oriented books are beneficial at present.

This book is an attempt to combine materials related to some of the most active parts of theoretical population biology—the interface area between ecology and genetics. Both fields are actively growing disciplines in their own rights, and important theoretical results are being published steadily. I have tried, however, to select for this book the results most relevant to the interaction between evolutionary and ecological theories. We have many more problems in this area than answers. I would prefer that this book be judged by the number of questions it raises and by the approaches it suggests rather than by the number of conclusions it reaches. I have formulated some unresolved problems with extended discussions at the end of each chapter, and I hope that they will stimulate thoughts on some important and often controversial issues. The choice of the problems is necessarily subjective.

For a number of years I have used the material of this book for my graduate courses and seminars in theoretical population biology. Although it will not suffice as the only textbook for a graduate course in either population genetics or theoretical ecology, it could serve as a reference for the specific portion of a course devoted to connecting these two traditionally distinct areas of theoretical biology.

Different parts of this book were written at different periods during the last few years while I was a member of the Department of Ecology and Evolution at the State University of New York at Stony Brook. I received helpful comments from a number of my colleagues during this time. Simon Levin (Cornell) edited a significant portion of Chapter 2 and Robert Sokal (Stony Brook) provided similar help with respect to Chapter 4. Peter Petraitis (University of Pennsylvania) edited parts of Chapters 2 and 6. Jim and Margaret Frauenthal and Craig Sargent (Stony Brook) helped in editing the first draft of the full manuscript. Steve Peterson (Stony Brook) helped read the galley proof and compiled the index. I had a number of extremely helpful discussions with my former students, Carlos Braumann (Evora, Portugal) and R. Woodrow Setzer (Stony Brook). They are also coauthors of Section 4.5.

The evolutionary chapters have been discussed extensively with Lawrence Slobodkin, Richard Koehn, Douglas Futuyma, and James Rohlf (Stony Brook). I received helpful criticism from Marc Feldman, Samuel Karlin (Stanford), and Richard Lewontin (Harvard). I'd like to express special thanks to Francisco Ayala (University of California at Davis) for excellent editorial comments. I have probably missed someone on this list, and I apologize if I did.

Although the actual writing took place over the last few years, the work which led to this book started in the early 1970s in Leningrad. I benefited then from discussions with Ratmir Poluektov (Leningrad), Alexander Gimelfarb (Ann Arbor, Michigan), Grigory Epelman (Norfolk, Virginia), Alexander Basykin (Moscow),

Vadim Ratner (Novosibirsk), and—in particular—Igor Shvytov (Leningrad).

The manuscript was typed and retyped a number of times by Shirley Felicetti, who also corrected a number of errors in spelling and style.

Although I have lived apart from my father, Ruvim Isaacovich Ginzburg, for 5 years, he has been a continual source of stimulation to me. He died in Leningrad in 1981, and this book is dedicated to him as my most influential teacher.

Lev R. Ginzburg
Stony Brook, New York

Contents

Chapter 1 Introduction 1

Main Assumptions and Goals 1
Basic Scheme of Natural-Selection Modeling 2
Basic Scheme of Population Growth Models 6
Methodological Notes 8

Chapter 2 Species Interactions in Ecosystem Modeling 12

Lotka-Volterra and Kolmogorov Models 12
Equations of Ecosystem Dynamics 15
Classification of the Interaction Types 18
Hypotheses of Pair Interactions and Homogeneous Density-Dependence 24
The Parametric Form of General Equations 28
Neutral and Limited Ecosystems 31
Two-Species Ecosystems 41
Problems and Discussion 47

Chapter 3 Models of Natural Selection 49

Equilibria and Stability 49
Conservation of Allelic Fitnesses 52

xiii

Fisher's Theorem and Wright's Principles 53
Recombination 55
Linear and Quadratic Functions on the Standard Simplex of Growing Dimension 60
Relative Importance of Selection and Recombination 64
Evolutionary Interpretations 69
Problems and Discussion 71

Chapter 4 Polymorphism and Natural Selection 74

The Triangle Inequalities 74
Why Should Heterozygotes Often Be Superior in Fitness? 79
Allowable Variability in Heterozygote Fitness 79
Chances for Coexistence of Multiple Alleles 85
Selection and Neutrality as Complementary Explanations of Genetic Polymorphism 88
Problems and Discussion 95

Chapter 5 "Exponential" Growth with Selection 99

Selective Delay 99
Entropy Distance 101
Rate of Adaptation 105
Experimental Confirmation 106
Problems and Discussion 109

Chapter 6 Growth with Density- and Frequency-Dependent Selection 112

Linear Density-Dependence 113
General Density-Dependence 118
Density-Dependent Coevolution 121
Frequency-Dependence 129
Problems and Discussion 133

Chapter 7 Ecological Implications of Natural Selection 135

Malthus' Law 136
Evolutionary Adaptation in Models of Population Dynamics 137

Examples 140
  Density-Independent Growth in a Stationary
    Environment 140
  Density-Independent Growth in a Time-Dependent
    Environment 142
  Density-Dependent Growth 142
Bimodality of Evolutionary Rate 143
Summation 149

Literature Cited 151

Index 157

1 Introduction

1.1 Main Assumptions and Goals

First I would like to clarify the title of this book, *Natural Selection and Population Growth*, by which I mean *only* natural selection and population growth. Although natural selection is clearly not the only factor that affects evolution, the book is devoted to this single factor and its interaction with population growth. Thus I have focused my attention on a very specific and reasonably well-developed part of theoretical population genetics and have not discussed the multiplicity of other evolutionary models that may involve selection, but where the action of selection is obscured by other mechanisms of evolution. My focus is not intended as a value judgment; these other mechanisms may well be as important, or sometimes more important, than selection. The choice of subject is dictated by the development of current theory and, to a large extent, by my personal preferences.

The subject of this book is presently undergoing such rapid development that no book can be considered the "final word." This book is simply a description of the picture as I see it at present; it is hard to predict how much of the theory will survive the next dozen years of scientific evolution. I am trying, therefore, to concentrate on the existing problems and their possible solutions. The problems I suggest at the end of the chapters are not typical homework problems to be solved in one afternoon. Instead, they are suggested directions of thought, or my attempts to foresee future developments. These usually prove to be ineffective, but it is nevertheless a natural temptation, and I will be happy if some of my guesses turn out to be correct.

An important factor in classifying models in theoretical population biology is the time scale for which a particular model is constructed. Demographic models, for instance, deal with time intervals on the order of the length of a generation for the species or less. Evolutionary models typically consider one generation as a unit of time and describe processes which occur over many generations. Lotka-Volterra–type models of population growth and interaction, where each population is represented by a single variable, also deal with time intervals greatly exceeding one generation. The separation of time scales is therefore an important means of simplifying models; one ignores fast processes for large-scale phenomena and slow processes for shorter-scale events. This distinction has often been used to separate evolutionary models from the models of population growth. Whether this separation is acceptable or not depends, of course, on selection intensities and the particular type of ecological situation controlling population growth. One thing is certain: Both processes take place on the scale of many generations. A number of people have analyzed mixed models that involve the interrelation of evolutionary mechanisms and population dynamics by assuming that both phenomena are happening on the same time scale. The best recent summaries of this kind of work are contained in Chapter 5 of Roughgarden's book (1979) and in the review paper by Slatkin and Maynard Smith (1979). This book partially overlaps both of these summaries; however, it contains much additional material, primarily due to its focus on natural selection at the expense of other evolutionary mechanisms.

1.2 Basic Scheme of Natural-Selection Modeling

The core model describing the process of natural selection in diploid species is the model of selection for one locus with an arbitrary number of alleles. I first discuss a number of fundamental assumptions on which this model is based and then develop the model itself.

The first assumption is *nonoverlapping generations*. This assumption allows us to ignore the demographic problems and is probably not very restrictive if the time intervals under consideration are considerably larger than the mean generation time for the species in question. Models that combine demography and natural selection have been the subject of a number of recent studies, particularly in relation to the problems of optimal life-history strategies. This subject has been summarized by Charlesworth (1980), who is one of the major contributors to this area of theoretical population biology.

The second assumption is *panmixia*. Preferential mating, spatial structure, sexual structure, different forms of inbreeding, and other deviations from panmixia are all subjects of intensive studies in population biology as important evolutionary forces. All of these mechanisms contribute significantly to the way a natural population looks and behaves; however, these deviations lie outside my primary focus and will not be discussed here. (The interested reader will find chapters discussing these mechanisms in any text on population genetics.) For our model, we assume that populations have no structure other than consisting of different genotypes on which natural selection may act.

Third is the assumption of *large population size*. This means that we are dealing with deterministic models and disregarding random effects caused by genetic drift. Evolutionary models accounting for drift have existed since they were introduced by Wright in the 1920s. Since the development of the neutral theory of evolution, analysis of genetic drift has become one of the most important parts of modern evolutionary theory. Ewens' book (1979) is the most recent and beautiful account of this theory.

Although mutations are the basic cause of genetic variability, I will not deal explicitly with mutations in this book. Our models of natural selection operate on an arbitrary—but fixed—set of genotypes. We understand that the set can always be extended if we wish to incorporate additional genotypes which may appear as a result of mutation.

The question might now arise: are there any interesting problems left after this severe narrowing of the subject? I hope to show that the theory of natural selection involves such a rich set of phenomena that even without the inclusion of additional evolutionary mechanisms, it presents and solves a number of interesting problems.

Let us now formulate the basic system of dynamic equations. Assume that there are n alleles at one locus and use the following notation:

p_i is the frequency of the ith allele, $i = 1, \ldots, n$
N is the overall population size
W_{ij} is the fitness of the genotype (i, j), $i, j = 1, \ldots, n$

Chapter 1: Introduction

We define fitness in an absolute sense, where W_{ij} equals the average number of surviving offspring produced by the genotype (i,j) at the end of one generation. Since genotypes (i,j) and (j,i) are indistinguishable, the matrix of fitnesses $\|W_{ij}\|$ is symmetric, $W_{ij} = W_{ji}$, $i, j = 1, \ldots, n$.

If Δp_i and ΔN denote changes in the frequency of the ith allele and in the population size in one generation, the basic system takes the familiar form

$$\Delta p_i = p_i \frac{W_i - \overline{W}}{\overline{W}}, \qquad i = 1, \ldots, n$$

$$\Delta N = (\overline{W} - 1)N \tag{1.1}$$

where

$$W_i = \sum_{j=1}^{n} W_{ij} p_j, \qquad i = 1, \ldots, n$$

and

$$\overline{W} = \sum_{i=1}^{n} p_i W_i = \sum_{i,j=1}^{n} p_i p_j W_{ij}$$

The quantity W_i is sometimes called an *allelic fitness* and $\overline{W}$ is the *average fitness* of the population, which is at the same time a Malthusian parameter describing the rate of population growth. In classical population genetics, fitnesses W_{ij} were usually assumed to be constant. There was therefore no need for the last equation (describing the population growth), which is then separated from the main system describing evolution. The last equation cannot be avoided in the case of density-dependent selection, when

$$W_{ij} = W_{ij}(N), \qquad i, j = 1, \ldots, n$$

In this case, all equations in (1.1) are interrelated and must be considered together. The same statement is correct for the models of coevolution when the fitnesses of genotypes in one population can depend on parameters related to other populations. Since the relation of natural selection to population growth is our main subject, we will always deal with the full system of (1.1) as the basic model for evolution of one population.

Since we plan to connect the basic model of selection (1.1) to the equations of population dynamics, there is one additional problem which relates again to time scales. Consider, for instance, two interacting and coevolving populations, prey and predator. If the generation times for the two populations are different, it will be difficult to connect models describing selection in the two different species. In reality, this difficulty has existed from the very early stages of theoretical ecology when species interactions were first

1.2 Basic Scheme of Natural-Selection Modeling

considered. The traditional and often unconscious way of dealing with the problem is to write the models in continuous time instead of in generations. Lotka-Volterra models were first written in continuous time, and this approach is more customary in population dynamics theory. In population genetics, both discrete and continuous-time models have been used, mostly depending on personal preferences. Although discrete models are not really equivalent to their continuous analogs, most of the results obtained first for continuous-time models were later re-proved for the "exact" discrete originals. Proofs are always much more difficult for discrete models and each one of these "re-proofs" is an accomplishment by itself. In the context of this book the transition to the unified, generation-independent time scale is a necessity, not a question of preferences. Continuous-time models will be used throughout this book as a way to combine models of selection and population growth without worrying about differences in generation time of the species. The work of Nagylaki and Crow (1974) should be consulted for a discussion of the accuracy of continuous approximation for the basically discrete selection models.

The basic argument for the continuous-time transition is sketched below in order to clarify the character of the approximations we are making. Assume that selection is weak; that is,

$$W_{ij} = (1 + \varepsilon_{ij}\Delta t), \qquad i, j = 1, \ldots, n$$
$$\max_{i,j} |\varepsilon_{ij}| \ll 1$$
(1.2)

where Δt denotes the generation time. Substituting this into system (1.1), we obtain

$$\frac{\Delta p_i}{\Delta t} = p_i \frac{\varepsilon_i - \bar{\varepsilon}}{1 + \bar{\varepsilon}\Delta t} \approx p_i(\varepsilon_i - \bar{\varepsilon}), \qquad i = 1, \ldots, n$$

$$\frac{\Delta N}{\Delta t} = \bar{\varepsilon} N$$

where

$$\varepsilon_i = \sum_{j=1}^{n} \varepsilon_{ij} p_j, \qquad i = 1, \ldots, n$$

and

$$\bar{\varepsilon} = \sum_{i,j=1}^{n} \varepsilon_{ij} p_i p_j$$

Here ε_{ij}, ε_i, and $\bar{\varepsilon}$ are the continuous-time analogs for genotypic, allelic, and average fitnesses, W_{ij}, W_i, and $\bar{W}$, respectively. In the case of weak selection, changes in p_i will be very slow, so the original system (1.1) can be replaced by the approximate

Chapter 1: Introduction

continuous-time system

$$\frac{dp_i}{dt} = p_i(\varepsilon_i - \bar{\varepsilon}), \qquad i = 1, \ldots, n$$

$$\frac{dN}{dt} = \bar{\varepsilon} N \qquad (1.3)$$

This is only an approximate method. We cannot let Δt approach 0 as is customarily done; Δt is a fixed time interval. Instead, we have argued from the viewpoint of weak selection.

In summary, the simplicity of analyses and the necessity to coordinate time scales are two factors influencing the decision to use continuous time models in cases involving the interaction of evolutionary and ecological mechanisms.* To keep the customary notations for fitnesses, W_{ij}, for the continuous models, equations (1.3) are rewritten once again in the form in which they will be used in subsequent chapters.

$$\frac{dp_i}{dt} = p_i(W_i - \bar{W}), \qquad i = 1, \ldots, n$$

$$\frac{dN}{dt} = \bar{W} N \qquad (1.4)$$

This system only is valid, of course, for the case of one locus. The equations are much more complicated for the case of multiple loci, since recombination brings a large number of additional terms into the evolutionary part of the system. The roles of recombination and multiple-locus models will be discussed in Chapter 3.

1.3 Basic Scheme of Population Growth Models

Mathematical ecology has advanced since its early days, and Lotka-Volterra models are no longer the only approach to the description of species interactions. It remains the case, however, that the majority of ecological models are still constructed as systems of ordinary differential equations of the form

$$\frac{dN_i}{dt} = N_i f_i(N_1, \ldots, N_n, \mathbf{E}(t)), \qquad i = 1, \ldots, n \qquad (1.5)$$

Here N_i is the size of the ith population, n is the number of

---

* One other argument is often used to justify the continuous time approach: avoidance of the restriction of nonoverlapping generations. I do not think it is a serious argument; it is still disregarding rather than avoiding the problem.

1.3 Basic Scheme of Population Growth Models

populations in the ecosystem, $\mathbf{E}(t)$ is a formal parameter (possibly a vector) representing the environment at time t, and f_i is the difference between the birth and death rates for the ith population.

Any differences among various models involve the forms of the right-hand sides of the equations or, in other words, the basic assumptions about the character of interpopulation and intrapopulation interactions. By accepting the ecosystem model in the form of equations (1.5), one accepts the population sizes $N_i, \ldots, N_n$ as the full description of the state of the dynamical system. The state of the ecosystem at the moment $t + \Delta t$ is assumed to be completely defined by its state at time t and by the dynamics of the environment, $\mathbf{E}(t)$, in the interval $(t, t + \Delta t)$. The dynamical system (1.5) is simply the analytical form of this assumption.

The use of the model (1.1) implies a number of natural restrictions. The time intervals considered are assumed small enough that evolution may be neglected, yet large enough that age structure need not be explicitly considered. (The former assumption is specifically the one which will be relaxed when we consider the interaction of natural selection and population growth.) Furthermore, population sizes N_i are assumed large enough for deterministic consideration and for each N_i to be treated as a continuous variable.

Another implicit assumption in system (1.5) is that we can ignore the influence of the biological community on the environmental parameters. More generally, we might append to system (1.1) the associated system

$$\frac{d\mathbf{E}}{dt} = f_{\mathbf{E}}(N_1, \ldots, N_n, \mathbf{E})$$

This addition is necessary in many microbiological models, where environmental parameters are substrate concentrations for example. Neglecting the biolgical feedback through the environmental terms implies the assumption that environmental changes are slow compared to changes in the state variables (or fast enough to permit the averaging of environmental fluctuations).

Ecological theory within the framework of the system of differential equations (1.5) has been developed along two basic lines. One line is concerned with Lotka-Volterra models and other specific modifications of the functions f_i. The other line, originated by Kolmogorov, deals with the qualitative analysis of the system (1.5) under very general assumptions about the functions f_i. The idea behind this latter approach is very attractive, but unfortunately such qualitative analysis is often difficult to achieve in practice. The mathematical difficulties grow dramatically with the number of species.

For two-species systems, the qualitative approach is very fruitful. However, the absence of a parametric form for the functions f_i is a disadvantage. With very limited data, reliable estimates of the functions are impossible. The alternative Lotka-Volterra models, though simple and parametric, are now recognized universally as being oversimplified. They describe only a few experimental observations and thus have few applications, despite the fact that when variations in population sizes are small, one can normally use Lotka-Volterra models as lower-order approximations to the more complicated cases. There is no distinct boundary between the two approaches, and both have advantages and disadvantages. The next chapter proposes a compromise model lying between the oversimplified Lotka-Volterra models and the overgeneralized qualitative models of the Kolmogorov type. The goal of this consideration is twofold. First, I hope that "hybrid vigor" will allow a retention of some of the benefits of each of the polar approaches. Second, and probably more important, the equations of intermediate complexity developed and analyzed in Chapter 2 will be strikingly similar to the model of natural selection described in the previous section. Inspection of the models of population growth from the proper perspective shows that the historical separation of the two fields of population dynamics and population genetics has been, to a large extent, accidental. There are more similarities than differences.

1.4 Methodological Notes

This book is written on the "physical" level of rigor. This means, for instance, that we assume without proof the existence, uniqueness, and smoothness of the solutions to the differential equations under consideration. All functions are assumed to have as many derivatives as necessary for the required calculations.

We will restrict our attention to deterministic dynamical systems of finite dimension; however, the question of whether or not the addition of stochastic effect will cause important changes in the behavior of the models remains open. Because the models are generally nonlinear, an agreement between the deterministic models and the means of the corresponding random processes is not expected. It is hoped that if population sizes are sufficiently large, then the expectation of the random processes will be sufficiently close to the deterministic behavior, although not necessarily in exact agreement.

All parameters of the models have specific biological meanings and in principle can be estimated experimentally or from the observation of trajectories in real systems; however, the accuracy of such estimates made from biological experiments usually is not very good. It therefore does not make much sense to study the effects of small variations of parameters except to confirm that such variations do not cause qualitative shifts in the behavior of the system. To this end, when given a general polynomial we will always suppose that its roots are distinct, because they can always be made so by a slight change of the coefficients. Similarly, we will not analyze critical cases of stability, but will instead consider the asymptotic stability of the first approximation system as both necessary and sufficient for stability. Clearly, these limitations make the analysis of the models easier, yet they do not restrict the models' applicability in any substantial way. One must not forget, however, that there are certain natural constraints that are exact. For example, differential equations for frequencies, p_i, always have the first integral $\sum_{i=1}^{n} p_i = 1$, and this leads to a zero eigenvalue for the matrix of the first approximation system. It is impossible to avoid this eigenvalue by varying the parameters of the system unless a model of reduced dimension is derived. Therefore, arguments based on ignoring critical cases should be used very carefully and may need to be justified in some cases.

A variety of meanings, each pertinent to a particular frame of reference, may legitimately be attached to the word *fitness* in population theory. For our purposes, it is sufficient to define the *fitness* of a population as the relative growth rate:

$$f(t) = \frac{1}{N(t)} \frac{dN}{dt} \tag{1.6}$$

This is the only meaning of fitness in this book. The basic population growth model (1.5) is then the system of equations describing the dependence of the fitnesses of all the populations in the ecosystem on the external environment, both physical and biological, and on the other species in the system.

The definition (1.6) is in complete agreement with the meaning of an absolute fitness of a genotype (Section 1.2). The use of absolute rather than relative fitnesses is forced by the goal of bridging evolution and population growth. Relative fitnesses can, of course, be defined, but the concept would not be helpful in the context of population dynamics. Equation (1.6) was selected as the most reasonable definition of fitness for use here because it fully satisfies all the following requirements:

1. Fitness is a local concept in time; that is, fitness at time t depends only on the local character of the curve $N(t)$.

Chapter 1: Introduction

2. The fitness trajectory is completely defined by the population growth curve. In other words, to define fitness means to define the mapping from the set of all possible growth curves $\{N(t)\}$ to the set of all possible fitness trajectories.
3. Fitness is a stationary concept in the sense that it depends only on the shape of the curve $N(t)$. More precisely, if $\{f(t)\} = \Gamma\{N(t)\}$, then

$$\{f(t+\tau)\} = \Gamma\{N(t+\tau)\}$$

4. Fitness is also a continuous concept; roughly speaking, for similar growth curves $N_1(t)$ and $N_2(t)$, the fitness values $f_1(t)$ and $f_2(t)$ will also be similar.
5. Fitness equals zero if and only if $N(t)$ is constant.
6. The fitness of a mixed population is the arithmetic mean of the fitness of its components. That is, let the population be decomposed into k components of density $N_1, \ldots, N_k$ with associate fitnesses $f_1, \ldots, f_k$. Then for the population as a whole,

$$f = \frac{\sum_{i=1}^{k} f_i N_i}{\sum_{i=1}^{k} N_i} \tag{1.7}$$

It is easy to see that if fitness is to be defined as in (1.6), it satisfies Properties 1–6. Less obvious, however, is that—except for a scaling constant—the converse is also true; it was shown (Ginzburg, 1975) that all mappings, Γ, satisfying these properties have the form

$$f(t) = c \frac{1}{N} \frac{dN}{dt}$$

One might criticize the sixth property because of the use of the arithmetic average; however, this is not an important consideration. Any kind of average is isomorphic to the arithmetic average (Hardy, Littlewood, Polya, 1934), so if the last hypothesis is weakened, one arrives at the more general relation

$$f(t) = \Psi\left(\frac{1}{N} \frac{dN}{dt}\right)$$

where Ψ is a monotonic function dependent on the sort of averaging

1.4 Methodological Notes

employed. Thus for all cases, the expression

$$\frac{1}{N}\frac{dN}{dt}$$

will characterize fitness completely, with appropriate scaling if necessary.

Finally, a few words on the structure of the book. The next chapter is devoted to the deduction and analysis of population dynamics models, with the goal of stressing similarities between them and models of natural selection within one population. Chapters 3 and 4 deal with models of natural selection within one population. The last three chapters are devoted to the interaction between natural selection within populations and population dynamics.

It is accepted wisdom that one cannot understand ecology without studying evolution, and vice versa. If I am able to create the same feeling with respect to the theoretical (mathematical) parts of these two fields, I will have fulfilled my goal.

2 Species Interactions in Ecosystem Modeling

In this chapter a new approach to the description of species interactions in ecosystem modeling is suggested. The equations developed in this chapter comprise a model of intermediate complexity between the "oversimplified" Lotka-Volterra type equations and "overgeneralized" models of the Kolmogorov type. The second goal of this chapter is to stress formal similarities between population-dynamics and population-genetics models.

This is the most technical chapter in the book and can be omitted without serious damage to the understanding of the rest of the book. I would recommend, however, reading the first three sections, which are sufficiently descriptive to give an idea of the material in the rest of the chapter.

2.1 Lotka-Volterra and Kolmogorov Models

Ecosystem dynamics were first described with differential equations by Lotka (1925) and Volterra (1931). Their models were the first serious attempts to apply mathematical methods to ecology. The simplicity of these models combined with their elegant analyses has made them widely known in biological circles. Research continues on the development and generalization of Lotka-Volterra models

2.1 Lotka-Volterra and Kolmogorov Models

despite recent criticism of their basic validity. (These criticisms will be discussed later in the chapter.) Though certainly oversimplified from the modern point of view, these models do have a field of limited application, and newer theories usually include them as a special case.

In Lotka-Volterra models, functions f_i for the system of (1.5) are assumed to be linear with respect to population sizes:

$$f_i = \varepsilon_i(\mathbf{E}) + \sum_{j=1}^{n} \gamma_{ij}(\mathbf{E}) N_j, \qquad i = 1, \ldots, n \tag{2.1}$$

Here ε_i is the growth rate of the ith population in the absence of all the other populations when the size of ith population is small. The diagonal elements γ_{ii} of the matrix $||\gamma_{ij}||$ characterize the influence of the size of the ith population on its own growth; the nondiagonal elements $\gamma_{ij}\,(i \neq j)$ reflect the structure of interpopulation interactions. Lotka and Volterra actually considered only some special cases of matrices $||\gamma_{ij}||$, but I will apply the term Lotka-Volterra to all models in which f_i is linear in $N_1, \ldots, N_n$. Thus I include, for example, the models studied by Kostitzin (1938) and others.

One of the first attempts to generalize Lotka-Volterra models is found in a paper by Kolmogorov (1936), which was republished in somewhat altered form in Kolmogorov (1972). He considered the general system

$$\begin{aligned}\dot{N}_1 &= N_1 f_1(N_1, N_2) \\ \dot{N}_2 &= N_2 f_2(N_1, N_2)\end{aligned} \tag{2.2}$$

describing a prey-predator interaction, where $(\cdot) = d/dt$. Functions f_1 and f_2 were not given any parametric form and had only some qualitative restrictions on the signs of partial derivatives $\partial f_i / \partial n_j$. The idea was to obtain qualitative results from qualitative suppositions. This idea is very attractive, since in many cases we know very little about the exact nature of these functions but qualitative properties are much easier to establish. Since qualitative theory of differential equations has been developed for two-dimensional systems, most of these models deal with two-population ecosystems. We will call such qualitative models *Kolmogorov models*. They can be considered to be the second step in the development of mathematical ecology.

We will briefly illustrate the advantages and disadvantages of these two approaches. This section will also introduce the new approach suggested in this chapter. A very good review of the Lotka-Volterra type of models can be found in Wangersky (1978).

In the ecological literature, the Lotka-Volterra equations have been criticized from a variety of different points of view. Most of the criticism is concerned with the oscillatory behavior of the most simplistic predator-prey version. It is very hard to obtain oscillation in experimental predator-prey systems without great ingenuity and artifice. In the classical experiments of Gause (1934), periodic behavior was obtained only by artificially imposing migration on one or both of the populations. Because of the difficulties with such experimental systems, we certainly do not have direct experimental verification of such simplistic models. Indeed, the situation is quite the contrary. For cyclic dynamics in natural populations, first attributed to the Volterra mechanism, there now exist a number of competing explanations, including age-structure dynamics, time-delay mechanisms, and epidemiological processes.

One reason why the predator-prey model is so unsatisfactory is the assumption of linearity of the predator growth rate versus prey population size. The equation for the predator may be written as

$$\frac{1}{N_2} \dot{N}_2 = -\varepsilon_2 + \gamma_{21} N_1 - \gamma_{22} N_2$$

where all parameters are assumed to be positive; no predator saturation effects are considered. Thus, as N_1 becomes large, the predator's relative growth rate becomes arbitrarily large. This clearly contradicts common sense, since the average number of offspring per parent per unit time should be bounded. In place of the term $\gamma_{21} N_1$, it would be much more natural to have some sort of nonlinear function, tending to a finite limit as $N_1 \to \infty$, such as a Michaelis-type function, $\gamma_{12} N_1 (\alpha + N_1)^{-1}$.

A somewhat less-serious objection to the assumption of linearity in this function is that it ignores the population size of the predator, which is important because of competition for food. The same is true for the corresponding term in the prey equation. Thus, despite having six different parameters, the prey-predator model exhibits a very poor range of possible qualitative behavior. For example, the model can neither describe prey extinction followed by predator extinction, nor can it describe limit-cycle behavior.

The situation is not much better for competition equations. The notion of resources has been replaced by the more general notion of limiting factors (Levin, 1970), and Armstrong and McGehee (1980) show that for these more general systems the competitive exclusion principle is invalid. Thus the Lotka-Volterra competition model is exposed as a very special case, which cannot serve as a basis for competition theory (see further discussion in Whittaker and Levin (1976)). Only two types of behavior are possible within the framework of the Lotka-Volterra competition models: exclusion of one of the populations and stable coexistence

The inadequacy of these models was understood a long time ago and it stimulated development of new models, beginning with Kolmogorov (1936).

The most interesting result obtained in Kolmogorov's first paper was the possibility of stable limit-cycle dynamics for predator-prey models. A number of authors have since published works in this connection (Rescigno, Aldo, and Richardson 1967, 1968; Strebel and Goel 1973, May 1974). The latter book (May 1974) has an interesting discussion of these recent models.

One of the most important restrictions on the functions f_1 and f_2 in all of the above models is their behavior with respect to simultaneous proportional changes in both populations:

$$f_1(cN_1, cN_2) < f_1(N_1, N_2)$$
$$f_2(cN_1, cN_2) > f_2(N_1, N_2)$$

for any $c > 1$. These conditions mean the proportional increases of both populations invariably benefit the predator and hurt the prey.

The marginal case of neutral ecosystems where a proportional increase does not make any difference,

$$f_1(cN_1, cN_2) \equiv f_1(N_1, N_2)$$
$$f_2(cN_1, cN_2) \equiv f_2(N_1, N_2)$$

was considered in Ginzburg, Goldman, and Railkin (1971, 1972). Oscillations are clearly impossible in such a case because the system can be reduced to a one-dimensional equation with respect to the ratio N_1/N_2, but we can obtain a neutrally stable coexistence, disappearance of both populations (first prey, then predator), and many other possibilities that agree with biological intuition. Unfortunately, the qualitative models of the Kolmogorov type tend to be so broadly generalized that their applications are hindered by a plethora of extraneous, biologically unreasonable possibilities.

What we need is a less-general model that can accommodate all of the realistic biological dynamics in terms of easily interpretable parametric functions and can also be flexible with respect to the number of populations that can be treated as part of a single ecosystem.

2.2 Equations of Ecosystem Dynamics

A comment about terminology is in order at this point. The word *ecosystem* is loaded with a variety of meanings, depending on the context. What we are discussing in this and the next chapter is a group of interacting populations from the point of view of equations describing their joint dynamics. The concept of ecosystem usually includes the physical environment as well.

We assume that the environment is incorporated through its influence upon the parameters of the dynamic system. The simplest models usually ignore the possible dynamic feedback through nonbiological environment, which would increase the differential order of the system (see Section 1.3). With this clarification we will use *ecosystem* in the sense of a set of interacting populations in an otherwise stationary environment. This is the usual sense in which this term was often used in the modeling literature.

Before we develop a new model, let us briefly summarize the strong and weak points of the Lotka-Volterra and Kolmogorov approaches. The Lotka-Volterra models are simple, their parameters are easy to interpret, and they describe some situations well. In most cases, however, they are clearly oversimplified and their conclusions are unrealistic. The Kolmogorov models are complicated with no easily interpretable parameters. Due to their generality, they are more realistic than Lotka-Volterra models, but this generality is an obstacle to future development. These models can be characterized as overgeneralized. Both types of models play an important role in mathematical ecology and continue to receive considerable attention. My goal, however, is to develop a compromise model that will combine the advantages and minimize the disadvantages of the two.

Consider an ecosystem consisting of n populations with sizes $N_1, \ldots, N_n$. Population sizes in the usual sense may not be the appropriate descriptions; biomasses, for example, may be more meaningful. In the simplest case this requires only a change in scale and lets us retain the more usual terms *population number* or *population size*. The measurement problem will reappear, however, when we try to evaluate the parameters of the model from the biomass data. An example of this sort will be considered in Section 2.7.

Let us call column vector $\mathbf{N} = (N_1, \ldots, N_m)^T$ the *state vector* of the ecosystem. The total size of the ecosystem is the sum

$$\bar{N} = \sum_{i=1}^{n} N_i$$

or in vector notation, $\bar{N} = (\mathbf{e}, \mathbf{N})$ where $\mathbf{e} = (1, 1, \ldots, 1)^T$.

From the basic equations of (1.5), we define the dependence of the fitnesses on population sizes and environment by

$$\frac{1}{N_i}\dot{N}_i = f_i(\mathbf{N}, \mathbf{E}), \qquad i = 1, \ldots, n \tag{2.3}$$

2.2 Equations of Ecosystem Dynamics

We assume the ecosystem under consideration is isolated in the sense that it cannot exchange individuals with other systems. For a very general and abstract consideration this is not a very restrictive assumption; by extending our concept of ecosystem we can always include all connected populations and will simply increase the dimension n. In applying models to concrete systems, however, this is not a trivial issue. It can be resolved only on a case-by-case basis. There are no general recipes for determining where one ecosystem ends and another begins.

All fitnesses f_i in formula (2.3) are assumed to be defined, continuously differentiable, and bounded for all $(\mathbf{N}, \mathbf{E})$ where $\mathbf{N}_i \geqslant 0$; f_i may be interpreted as the average number of offspring per parent of species i per unit of time. It follows that any trajectory initiated in the nonnegative orthant $N_i \geqslant 0$, $i = 1, \ldots, n$ will remain there forever, and further that the hyperplane $N_i = 0$ is invariant. This means that a population not present cannot enter the system (i.e. there is no flow from the outside of the ecosystem).

Let us define mean fitness of the ecosystem by

$$F = \frac{1}{\bar{N}} \dot{\bar{N}}$$

Clearly

$$F = \frac{1}{\bar{N}} \dot{\bar{N}} = \sum_{i=1}^{n} \frac{N_i}{\bar{N}} f_i = \frac{1}{\bar{N}} (\mathbf{N}, \mathbf{f})$$

where $\mathbf{f}$ is the column vector $\mathbf{f} = (f_1, \ldots, f_n)^T$. Further, define the *structure* of the ecosystem by

$$\mathbf{p} = (p_1, \ldots, p_n)^T = \mathbf{N}/\bar{N}$$

where p_i is the frequency of the ith population in the ecosystem. The set of all possible structures is called the *standard simplex*, or simply the *simplex* δ_n:

$$\delta_n = \{\mathbf{p} \mid \mathbf{p} \geqslant 0, (\mathbf{e}, \mathbf{p}) = 1\}$$

By this change of variables, a full description of the state of the ecosystem may be achieved in terms of the $(n + 1)$-tuple $(p_1, \ldots, p_n; \bar{N})$, but of these components only n are independent since

$$(\mathbf{e}, \mathbf{p}) = 1$$

Given these new variables, the fitnesses f_i may be expressed in terms of new functional forms f_i^* by

$$f_i(\mathbf{N}, \mathbf{E}) = f_i(\bar{N}\mathbf{p}, \mathbf{E}) = f_i^*(\mathbf{p}, \bar{N}, \mathbf{E}), \qquad i = 1, \ldots, n$$

The asterisk will be removed in all subsequent equations, since no ambiguities will result. Thus for the mean fitness we write

$$F(\mathbf{p}, \bar{\mathbf{N}}, \mathbf{E}) = \sum_{i=1}^{n} p_i f_i(\mathbf{p}, \bar{\mathbf{N}}, \mathbf{E}) = (\mathbf{p}, \mathbf{f})$$

It is trivial to show that (2.3) is equivalent to

$$\dot{p}_i = p_i(f_i - F), \qquad i = 1, \ldots, n$$

Adding the equation for the ecosystem size $\dot{\bar{N}} = \bar{N}F$ yields the system of $n + 1$ equations

$$\dot{p}_i = p_i[f_i(\mathbf{p}, \bar{\mathbf{N}}, \mathbf{E}) - F(\mathbf{p}, \bar{\mathbf{N}}, \mathbf{E})], \qquad i = 1, \ldots, n$$
$$\dot{\bar{N}} = \bar{N}F(\mathbf{p}, \bar{\mathbf{N}}, \mathbf{E}) \tag{2.4}$$

with the constraint $(\mathbf{e}, \mathbf{p}) = 1$. The first n equations describe the dynamics of the ecosystem structure; the last describes the total ecosystem size. Note the similarity between (2.4) and (1.4). Except for notation and the specific form of the fitness functions in the genetic model of (1.4), they are identical.

2.3 Classification of the Interaction Types

There are, certainly, a variety of ways to classify interactions in the system. A typical approach is a pairwise interaction classification where, for every pair of populations in the ecosystem, a particular term is assigned. This classification subdivides all possible interactions into classes according to the direction of the influence of one population upon another. Mathematically, it is symbolized in the signs of the partial derivatives $\partial f_i/\partial N_j$. The typical system looks as follows

Influence of the species i on j	Influence of the species j on j	Category
+	+	Symbiosis
+	0	Commensalism
+	−	Prey-predator (host parasite)
0	−	Amensalism
−	−	Competition
0	0	Neutrality

This classification is useful in cases of two-dimensional systems when the suggested subdivision fully defines the system under

2.3 Classification of the Interaction Types

consideration. The value of this classification declines with the growing dimension.

I would like to suggest another dimension-independent way of classifying interactions in the system. The value of any classification, as always, lies in the number of useful statements one can make using its terms. I will attempt to show in this chapter that there are useful statements formulated in terms of the suggested classes of interactions. My second goal here is to support the choice of the specific expressions for the fitness functions f_i, which will be made in the next section.

The first step in the classification considers the influence of the ecosystem size on the ecosystem at the state $(\mathbf{p}, \bar{\mathbf{N}})$ to be locally inhibiting, neutral, or stimulating if, correspondingly,

$$\frac{\partial F}{\partial \bar{\mathbf{N}}} < 0, \qquad \frac{\partial F}{\partial \bar{\mathbf{N}}} = 0, \qquad \frac{\partial F}{\partial \bar{\mathbf{N}}} > 0 \qquad (2.5)$$

In such cases, the states are referred to as *inhibited*, *neutral*, or *stimulated*, respectively.

The geometrical meaning of this classification will be clear if we consider the level surfaces of F in the space of the old variables $N_1, \ldots, N_n$, for which inequality (2.5) has the form

$$(\operatorname{grad}_{\mathbf{N}} F, \mathbf{N}) < 0, \qquad (\operatorname{grad}_{\mathbf{N}} F, \mathbf{N}) = 0, \quad \text{or} \quad (\operatorname{grad}_{\mathbf{N}} F, \mathbf{N}) > 0$$

Grad$_{\mathbf{N}} F$ is orthogonal to the surface, and $(\operatorname{grad}_{\mathbf{N}} F, \mathbf{N})$ is the component in the direction of vector $\mathbf{N}$. The inhibiting type corresponds to a negative projection, the neutral type to the case of orthogonality, and the stimulating type to a positive projection.

One can introduce the same concepts for any population in the ecosystem. The type of influence will be defined by the sign of the partial derivative, $\partial f_i / \partial \bar{\mathbf{N}}$, which indicates the influence of the overall size of the ecosystem on the fitness of the ith population.

A second step in classification concerns the influence of the structure of the ecosystem, $\mathbf{p}$, upon the fitnesses of the populations and upon the average fitness of the ecosystem. We will start with the latter, but first we will need one simple calculation.

Consider two ecosystems with the same basic state description and fitness functions but with different sizes $\bar{\mathbf{N}}^{(1)}$ and $\bar{\mathbf{N}}^{(2)}$ and structures $\mathbf{p}^{(1)}$ and $\mathbf{p}^{(2)}$. If these are added and treated as a single system, then the values of $\bar{\mathbf{N}}$ and $\mathbf{p}$ for the sum are given by

$$\bar{\mathbf{N}} = \bar{\mathbf{N}}^{(1)} + \bar{\mathbf{N}}^{(2)}$$

$$\mathbf{p} = \lambda \mathbf{p}^{(1)} + (1 - \lambda) \mathbf{p}^{(2)}$$

where $\lambda = \bar{N}_1/(\bar{N}_1 + \bar{N}_2)$. When the ecosystems are mixed in this manner, their sizes are added and their structures are averaged with weights that correspond to their relative sizes.

Now imagine the following experiment. Mix two ecosystems of the same size but different structures, $\{\mathbf{p}^{(1)}, \bar{\mathbf{N}}\}$ and $\{\mathbf{p}^{(2)}, \bar{\mathbf{N}}\}$. After mixing, decrease the size of the mixed ecosystem by half without changing the structure. Let us list all possible effects of mixing that may appear.

If the populations within the ecosystem are noninteracting, the mean fitness of the mixture will be just the arithmetic average

$$\tfrac{1}{2} F(\mathbf{p}^{(1)}, \bar{\mathbf{N}}) + \tfrac{1}{2} F(\mathbf{p}^{(2)}, \bar{\mathbf{N}})$$

More generally, the mean fitness of the mixture will differ from this value depending on whether the mixing has stimulated or inhibited the average growth rate. The overall result of mixing can therefore be categorized according to one of three cases:

1. $F(\tfrac{1}{2}\mathbf{p}^{(1)} + \tfrac{1}{2}\mathbf{p}^{(2)}, \bar{\mathbf{N}}) < \tfrac{1}{2} F(\mathbf{p}^{(1)}, \bar{\mathbf{N}}) + \tfrac{1}{2} F(\mathbf{p}^{(2)}, \bar{\mathbf{N}})$
2. $F(\tfrac{1}{2}\mathbf{p}^{(1)} + \tfrac{1}{2}\mathbf{p}^{(2)}, \bar{\mathbf{N}}) = \tfrac{1}{2} F(\mathbf{p}^{(2)}, \bar{\mathbf{N}})$ (2.6)
3. $F(\tfrac{1}{2}\mathbf{p}^{(1)} + \tfrac{1}{2}\mathbf{p}^{(2)}, \bar{\mathbf{N}}) > \tfrac{1}{2} F(\mathbf{p}^{(1)}, \bar{\mathbf{N}}) + \tfrac{1}{2} F(\mathbf{p}^{(2)}, \bar{\mathbf{N}})$

Let us consider the ecosystem at the state $\{\mathbf{p}, \bar{\mathbf{N}}\}$. Consider any two structures $\mathbf{p}^{(1)}$ and $\mathbf{p}^{(2)}$ that are sufficiently close to the vector $\mathbf{p}$: If (1) is true, we will call the ecosystem *competitive* at the state $\{\mathbf{p}, \bar{\mathbf{N}}\}$; if (2) applies, we will call it *conservative*; if (3) is true, we will call it *mutualistic*. We therefore classify interactions according to the inhibiting or stimulating effect of mixing on the average fitness of the ecosystem. This classification reflects the influence of the structure of the ecosystem upon its fitness at a point $\{\mathbf{p}, \bar{\mathbf{N}}\}$. The classification is clearly not complete; there are functions that do not satisfy any of the inequalities (2.6) — a function with a saddle point, for example. We will consider the question of completeness later.

To understand this classification analytically, consider the Taylor series for the function F in the neighborhood of the point $\{\mathbf{p}^{(+o)}, \bar{\mathbf{N}}_0\}$ with respect to the variables of $\mathbf{p}$:

$$F(\mathbf{p}, \mathbf{N}) = F(\mathbf{p}^{(0)}, \bar{\mathbf{N}}_0) + (\operatorname*{grad}_{\mathbf{p}^{(0)}} F(p, \bar{N}), \mathbf{p} - \mathbf{p}_0)$$
$$+ \frac{1}{2} \sum_{i,j=1}^{n} \left[\frac{\partial^2 F}{\partial p_i \partial p_j}(\mathbf{p}^{(0)}, \bar{\mathbf{N}}) \cdot (p_i - p_i^{(0)})(p_j - p_j^{(0)}) \right] + 0(|\mathbf{p} - \mathbf{p}^{(0)}|^2)$$

If F is linear, the system is always conservative (and the quadratic terms vanish). More often, the quadratic form will be the critical term. If the quadratic form is positive, the system is competitive; if the form is negative, it is mutualistic. Alternatively the quadratic

2.3 Classification of the Interaction Types

form could be taken as the basis for the classification, in which case inequalities (2.6) would emerge as a theorem.

The geometrical meaning of the inequalities relates to the convexity-concavity of the function F in the neighborhood of a point $\{\mathbf{p}, \bar{\mathbf{N}}\}$ with respect to the structural variables. The easiest case for geometrical interpretation is the neutral case, when F is independent of $\mathbf{N}$. The different types of the interactions are illustrated in Figure 2.1; (a) corresponds to the competitive ecosystem, (b) corresponds to the conservative case, and (c) corresponds to the mutualistic case.

We can use the same terminology to characterize a particular state of the ecosystem or the set of its states. If one of the

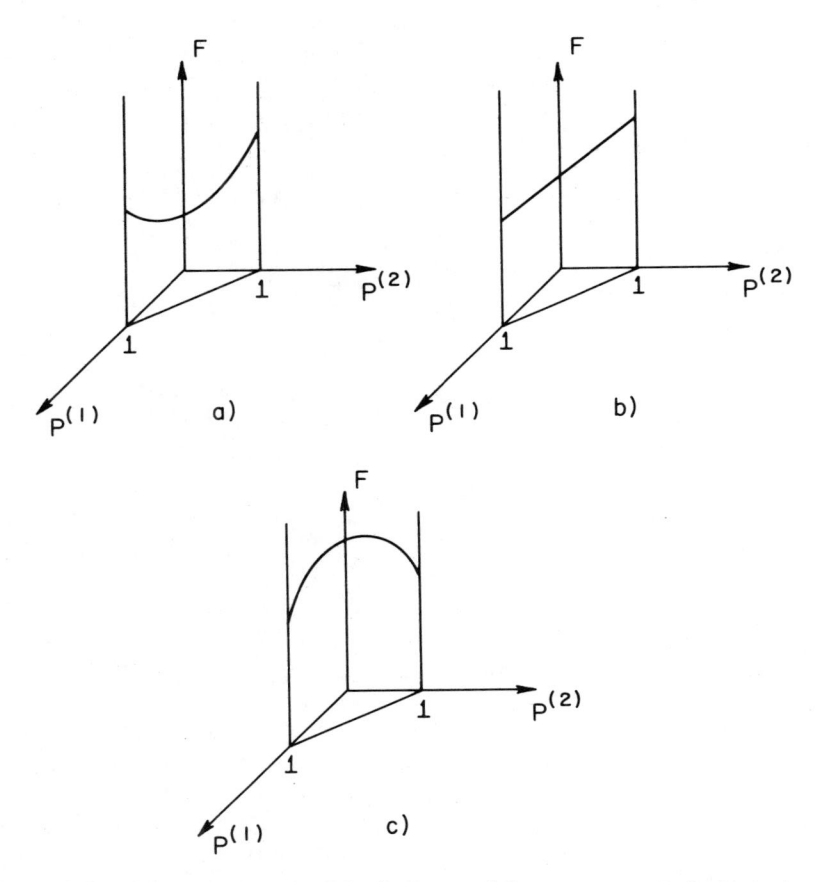

Figure 2.1 Average fitness as the function of the component's frequencies. (a) Competitive case. (b) Conservative case. (c) Mutualistic case.

relationships in (2.6) is true globally, we will refer to the ecosystem itself as *competitive*, or *mutualistic*.

The classification relates to the ecosystem as a whole. If we want to repeat it for the populations, we would use the functions

$$p_i f_i(\mathbf{p}, \bar{\mathbf{N}}), \quad i = 1, \ldots, n$$

and repeat the procedures already done for the ecosystem fitness. The mixing thought experiment is still the same but we are now looking only at the *i*th-population fitness.

We now come to the question of completeness of the classifications. The first, size-dependence classification is locally complete in the sense that it covers all possible behavior of the function F. Globally it is not complete, since the function is not necessarily monotonic. The second classification is not complete even locally; for $n \geq 3$, a saddle point is a natural possibility, and this case is not included. Both classifications are complete, though, in the sense that for any function F (given the supposition of reasonable smoothness), it is true that

$$F = F_- + F_0 + F_+$$

where F_-, F_0, and F_+ are the functions satisfying the first, second, and third inequalities of (2.6). The proof is a well-known theorem about the representation of any function as a sum of convex and concave functions.

The classifications we have chosen are basic, since more complicated functions involve the superposition of the basic cases. Although the selection of the "basic terms" for any given function is not unique, it can be made unique by some restrictions that we will discuss later.

Everything so far has been done under the assumption of a constant environment. In a changing environment the ecosystem might change its type. In principle, if we know how the environment changes then we can relate all of the concepts that we have so far introduced not only to the state of the ecosystem, $\{\mathbf{p}, \bar{\mathbf{N}}\}$, but also to the time ($t$), or more generally, to the state of the environment at any specified time, $\{\mathbf{p}, \bar{\mathbf{N}}, \mathbf{E}(t)\}$.

The classifications we have obtained will serve as a guide for choosing the explicit parametric form of the fitness functions f_i. We are going to choose the "simplest" possible parametric class of the functions such that by changing only the parameters within this class, we can obtain functions of all the types listed in our classification. In other words, we want to find a family of functions containing at least those properties reflected in our classification. Unfortunately, the concept of simplest is hard to formalize. Any choice

2.3 Classification of the Interaction Types

inevitably will be subjective. We make our choice based on the following idea: A monotonic increase or decrease can be modeled in the simplest way with a linear function, and the property of being convex-concave can be modeled by the quadratic function. Let us then choose the function $F(\mathbf{p}, \bar{\mathbf{N}})$ to be linear in $\bar{\mathbf{N}}$ and quadratic in $\mathbf{p}$:

$$F = \sum_{i,j=1}^{n} f_{ij}(\bar{\mathbf{N}}) p_i p_j$$
$$f_{ij} = \varepsilon_{ij}(\mathbf{E}) - \bar{\mathbf{N}} \gamma_{ij}(\mathbf{E}), \qquad i, j = 1, \ldots, n \tag{2.7}$$

In this form, all environmental dependence is expressed by the parameters ε_{ij} and γ_{ij}. The same idea of simplicity leads to the following form for the population fitness functions.

$$p_i f_i = \sum_{k,j=1}^{n} (\varepsilon_{kji} - \bar{\mathbf{N}} \beta_{kji}) p_k p_j, \qquad i = 1, \ldots, n$$

Because all of the functions f_i should be uniformly bounded for all $\{\mathbf{p}, \bar{\mathbf{N}}\}$, this gives

$$f_i = \sum_{j=1}^{n} (\varepsilon_{ij} - \bar{\mathbf{N}} \gamma_{ij}) p_j, \qquad i = 1, \ldots, n \tag{2.8}$$

Otherwise, p_i's will not cancel out and f_i can become infinitely large. This clearly contradicts the biological meaning of fitness. Here we use the same notation for parameters so that (2.8) is in agreement with the formula for the average fitness of the ecosystem. Expressed in the old variables, this formula is

$$f_i = \sum_{j=1}^{n} \left(\varepsilon_{ij} \frac{N_j}{\sum_{k=1}^{n} N_k} - \gamma_{ij} N_j \right), \qquad i = 1, \ldots, n$$

There are two ways of heuristically obtaining the parametric form of unknown functions: the "honest" and the "axiomatic" ways. The honest way was just shown; we based our choice on the intuitive notion that the simplest functions should reflect all the properties required within the parametric class. The axiomatic way is to obtain the class of functions by using exact quantitative axioms describing the character of the interaction. To satisfy everyone, in the next section we will suggest two exact axioms that lead to the same parametric representation of the fitness functions. The exact axioms in most cases create the illusion of objectivity, so we will not need any kind of simplicity arguments. As far as the axioms are accepted, the functions f_i will have the form of (2.8). The axiomatic approach clarifies the limitations of the theory: We know that the

Chapter 2: Species Interactions in Ecosystem Modeling

theory does not hold when the axioms are not true. In this sense, the material of the next section is more than just a formal exercise.

2.4 Hypotheses of Pair Interactions and Homogeneous Density-Dependence

Consider the influence of the ecosystem structure **p** on the average fitness F. For simplicity, assume that we are dealing with the neutral ecosystem; that is, $\partial F/\partial \bar{\mathbf{N}} = 0$ and F depends only on the frequencies p_i.

We postulate that the average fitness of the ecosystem is the result of simple pair interactions between individuals. Although there are cases of triple interaction (as when interaction between populations i and j occurs only in the presence of population k), we will limit our consideration to pair effects.

Consider the same mixing experiment as in the previous section. If λ is the portion corresponding to the first ecosystem in a mixture of two systems, then the percentage of pairs randomly chosen from the first ecosystem is λ^2, for the second it is $(1-\lambda)^2$, and for the pair consisting of individuals of two distinct systems, it is $2\lambda(1-\lambda)$. Certainly $\lambda^2 + (1-\lambda)^2 + 2\lambda(1-\lambda) = 1$. We now postulate the identity

$$F(\lambda \mathbf{p}^{(1)}) + (1-\lambda)(\mathbf{p}^{(2)}) = \lambda^2 F(\mathbf{p}^{(1)}) + (1-\lambda)^2 F(\mathbf{p}^{(2)}) \\ + 2\lambda(1-\lambda)\Phi(\mathbf{p}^{(1)}, \mathbf{p}^{(2)}, \bar{\mathbf{N}}^{(1)}, \bar{\mathbf{N}}^{(2)}) \quad (2.9)$$

where Φ is a function characterizing interactions between the two subecosystems in the mixture. The axiom means that the fitness of a mixed ecosystem is the weighted average of the fitnesses of the two ecosystems plus a term describing the interaction. We suppose (2.9) to be identically true for all $0 \leq \lambda \leq 1$ and for all $\mathbf{p}^{(1)}$ and $\mathbf{p}^{(2)}$. We do not assume anything about the function Φ, but we do suppose that the unknown function F is twice continuously differentiable on the whole simplex δ_n.

We now go over some calculations arising from (2.9). We will call this formula *the hypothesis of pair interactions*. Calculating the second derivative of both sides in (2.9) with respect to $p_i^{(1)}$ and $p_j^{(1)}$, we obtain

$$\lambda^2 \frac{\partial^2 F(\lambda \mathbf{p}^{(1)} + (1-\lambda)\mathbf{p}^{(2)})}{\partial p_i^{(1)} \partial p_j^{(1)}} = \lambda^2 \frac{\partial^2 F(\mathbf{p}^{(1)})}{\partial p_i^{(1)} \partial p_j^{(1)}} + 2\lambda(1-\lambda) \frac{\partial^2 \Phi}{\partial p_i^{(1)} \partial p_j^{(1)}}$$

Dividing by λ^2 ($\lambda \neq 0$), we have

$$\frac{\partial^2 F(\lambda \mathbf{p}^{(1)} + (1-\lambda)\mathbf{p}^{(2)})}{\partial p_i \partial p_j} - \frac{\partial^2 F(\mathbf{p}^{(1)})}{\partial p_i \partial p_j} = \frac{2(1-\lambda)}{\lambda} \frac{\partial^2 \Phi}{\partial p_i^{(1)} \partial p_j^{(1)}}$$

2.4 Hypotheses of Pair Interactions and Homogeneous Density-Dependence

Because the left side of the equation is continuous on the closed set δ_n, it is globally bounded. At the same time, the right side of the equation can be made arbitrarily large when $\lambda \to 0$ if $\partial^2 \Phi / \partial p_i^{(1)} \partial p_j^{(1)} \neq 0$. Therefore,

$$\frac{\partial^2 \Phi}{\partial p_i^{(1)} \partial p_j^{(1)}} = 0$$

Then, considering the limit when $\lambda \to 0$, we obtain

$$\frac{\partial^2 F(\mathbf{p}^{(1)})}{\partial p_i \partial p_j} = \frac{\partial^2 F(\mathbf{p}^{(2)})}{\partial p_i \partial p_j}$$

Because $\mathbf{p}^{(1)}$ and $\mathbf{p}^{(2)}$ are the independent variables, it immediately follows that

$$\frac{\partial^2 F}{\partial p_i \partial p_j} = f_{ij} = \text{constant}$$

Thus

$$F = a_0 + \sum_{i=1}^{n} a_i p_i + \sum_{i,j=1}^{n} f_{ij} p_i p_j$$

Now, remembering the identity $\sum_{i=1}^{n} p_i = 1$, we can multiply a_0 by $\left(\sum_{i=1}^{n} p_i\right)^2$ and the linear term by $\sum_{i=1}^{n} p_i$ and reduce the whole function to the quadratic form. So, without loss of generality, we can write

$$F = \sum_{i,j=1}^{n} f_{ij} p_i p_j \qquad (2.10)$$

Note that the result was obtained without any explicit assumptions about the interaction term, Φ. This function should automatically be bilinear, as follows from the hypothesis of pair interactions. Formula (2.10) is the final form of how the average fitness, F, depends on the ecosystem structure, if we assume the hypothesis of pair-interactions.

We can show that for the size-dependent case (for either stimulated or inhibited ecosystems), the result will be similar:

$$f = \sum_{i,j=1}^{n} f_{ij}(\mathbf{N}, \mathbf{E}) p_i p_j \qquad (2.11)$$

In other words, all the size-dependence is expressed in the coefficients of the quadratic form.

Consider now the hypothesis of homogeneous density-dependence (or size-dependence). We will formulate this for the simple one-dimensional case.

The growth of a limited population is usually described by the equation

$$\dot{N} = [\varepsilon - \gamma\Phi(N)]N = \psi(\gamma, N) \tag{2.12}$$

where γ is the intensity of the limiting factor. When $\Phi(N) = N$, equation (2.12) is the logistic equation. Consider the family of growth curves produced by the equation (2.12) with γ fixed:

$$N = N(t, \gamma, N_0)$$

Suppose that the intensity of the limiting factor has been increased by a factor k, becoming $k\gamma$. This means that the availability of some necessary environmental component has become k times smaller. If on the average this component influences each individual equally, then such a reduction can be thought of as equivalent to an increase of the population number by the same factor k. In other words, from the fitness point of view, a population of size kN_0 in an environment limited by intensity γ should be identical to a population of size N_0 in an environment limited by intensity $k\gamma$. The formal identity is

$$N(t, k\gamma, N_0) \equiv \frac{1}{k} N(t, \gamma, kN_0)$$

for any $k > 0$. We will call this identity *the hypothesis of homogeneous density-dependence*.

If we differentiate this density with respect to time and consider it at $t = 0$, we will get the relationship for the right-hand side of the equation $\psi(\gamma, N)$:

$$\psi(k\gamma, N) = \frac{1}{k}\psi(\gamma, kN)$$

Separating the factor N in the function $\psi_1 = \psi/N$, we have

$$\psi_1(k\gamma, N) = \psi_1(\gamma, kN)$$

It follows that

$$\dot{N} = N \cdot \psi_1(\gamma, N) \tag{2.13}$$

Comparing (2.13) with equation (2.9), we see that $\Phi(N)$ should be proportional to N, which is the same as $\Phi(N) = N$ if one allows for arbitrary scaling. Thus we obtain

$$\dot{N} = N(\varepsilon - \gamma N)$$

as a result of the hypothesis. In the multispecies context, this hypothesis is true for all Lotka-Volterra models; thus we might call it the *Lotka-Volterra hypothesis* as well. If we make the statement a bit more complex, we can include consideration of the structural

2.4 Hypotheses of Pair Interactions and Homogeneous Density-Dependence

variables and arrive at the form

$$F(\mathbf{p}, \bar{\mathbf{N}}, \mathbf{E}) = \varepsilon(\mathbf{p}, \mathbf{E}) - \gamma(\mathbf{p}, \mathbf{E}) \cdot \bar{\mathbf{N}} \qquad (2.14)$$

Note the minus sign in front of the size-dependent term; within the framework of linearity we cannot consider positive size influence. The fitness, again, should be globally bounded since it is the average offspring per parent per unit of time. So, within the form of (2.14), it is impossible to consider the stimulating influence of the ecosystem's size on its fitness. As a first approximation, however, the linear form can serve quite well for the case of large sizes when a stimulating influence is not expected. It is important to remember that when the function F, in the form of (2.14), is considered globally

$$\gamma(\mathbf{p}, \mathbf{E}) \geq 0$$

Comparing (2.14) and (2.11), we obtain the same expression as in the previous section:

$$F = \sum_{i,j=1}^{n} (\varepsilon_{ij} - \bar{\mathbf{N}} \gamma_{ij}) p_i p_j \qquad (2.15)$$

There is no reason to treat in detail the analogous axiomatic deduction for the single population fitnesses, f_i. Remember only that one should deal with the behavior of the product $p_i f_j$ and then take into account the boundedness of the fitness functions for all $\mathbf{p}$ and $\bar{\mathbf{N}}$. Finally, one can arrive at the same result:

$$f_i = \sum_{j=1}^{n} (\varepsilon_{ij} - \bar{\mathbf{N}} \gamma_{ij}) p_j, \qquad i = 1, \ldots, n$$

Let us now discuss the classification of the interaction types as it reflects the chosen parametric class of the fitness functions. It is interesting to note that the local properties of the functions, which were the basis of our classification, become global within the chosen class. The sign of $\partial F / \partial \bar{\mathbf{N}}$ will be the same for all points $\{\mathbf{p}^{(+o)}, \bar{\mathbf{N}}\}$, $\bar{\mathbf{N}} \geq 0$. Furthermore, the convexity-concavity character of the quadratic form (2.15) at the point $(\mathbf{p}_0, \bar{\mathbf{N}}_0)$, will be maintained for all $\{\mathbf{p}, \bar{\mathbf{N}}_0\}$, $\mathbf{p} \in \delta_n$. With a fixed ecosystem size, the influence of the structure is globally fixed, and with a fixed structure, the type of size-dependence is fixed.

Every quadratic form can be represented as the sum of the convex and concave forms. To obtain these "projections," it is enough to diagonalize the matrix associated with the quadratic form and then separate all positive and negative squares in the diagonal form. Then we could transform back into the original variables. This procedure shows the uniqueness of the representation of any fitness function as a sum of the "pure types" within the chosen class. To exclude the possibility of other representations, one might accept the additional rule: If the function $F(\mathbf{p}, \bar{\mathbf{N}})$ belongs to a pure type (that is, it is concave, convex, or flat), then the other two components should be zero. In other words, for the pure cases F itself is its own projection to the corresponding interaction type. The suggested rule excludes the possibility of adding the same terms with opposite signs to the mutualistic and competitive components of the fitness.

There is clearly no universal parametric representation for the fitness functions that would cover all imaginable biological situations. The triple-interaction case and the cooperative-density effect are two counterexamples for the choice of parameters described here. We can only try to cover as much as is possible within the framework of the simplified model. One way of defending our choice is to work out interpretable results and compare them with experimental data, which is what we will try to do in Sections 2.5 and 2.6. First however, we must discuss some general properties of the basic system of differential equations (2.4) after having chosen the form of the functions f_i.

2.5 The Parametric Form of General Equations

In this section we will discuss several special cases of the general system (2.4) with the functions f_i defined as in the previous section. We will omit the argument **E** from the notation and assume that the growth process takes place in a stationary environment. This assumption needs to be qualified. Its significance depends on the difference between the typical time scale of environmental changes and the typical time scale of changes in the structure and size of the system under consideration. When looking at a microbial ecosystem for 1 month, we can neglect annual meteorological factors because they are variables that change slowly when compared to the ecosystem dynamics. That same annual environmental change can be neglected because it is too fast when compared to the generation time of a forest ecosystem. We might assume that the annual environment, on the average, is the same for different generations. The assumption of a stationary environment need not be as restrictive as it sounds; it simply implies that there are no environmental changes on the same time scale as the typical generation time within the ecosystem. If there are such changes, the parameters of the system should be considered to be time-dependent, and the environmental dynamics should be superimposed on the internal ecosystem dynamics. Concentrating on the internal processes, we will not consider the case of time-dependent parameters.

2.5 The Parametric Form of General Equations

The system under consideration has been

$$\dot{p}_i = p_i(f_i - F), \quad i = 1, \ldots, n$$
$$\dot{N} = \bar{N}F \qquad (2.16)$$

where

$$f_i = \sum_{j=1}^{n} (\varepsilon_{ij} - N\gamma_{ij})p_j, \quad i = 1, \ldots, n$$

$$F = \sum_{i=1}^{n} p_i f_i$$

Let us show how some of the well-known special models can be obtained from this system. If $n = 1$, we obviously get the logistic equation

$$\dot{N} = N(\varepsilon - \gamma N)$$

In general, ε and γ represent simple averages of the corresponding parameters from (2.16):

$$\varepsilon = \sum_{i,j}^{n} \varepsilon_{ij} p_i p_j, \quad \gamma = \sum_{i,j}^{n} \gamma_{ij} p_i p_j$$

If $\varepsilon_{ij} = \varepsilon_i$, the model in (2.16) resembles a Lotka-Volterra system,

$$f_i = \varepsilon_i - \sum_{j=1}^{n} \gamma_{ij} N p_j = \varepsilon_i - \sum_{j=1}^{n} \gamma_{ij} N_j$$

There is a major difference, however; we do not allow the parameters γ_{ij} to be negative. So, formally speaking, in our model the prey-predator interactions are reflected in the ε_{ij} parameters but not in the γ_{ij}, which are the interpopulation $(i \neq j)$ and intrapopulation $(i = j)$ competition intensities. We might say that in our model the prey-predator interactions are frequency-dependent, whereas the competition interactions are density-dependent. This distinction reflects in a crude way the major difference between our scheme and the Lotka-Volterra equations.

The other important point is that equations (2.16) also generalize our model of natural selection (1.4). If we interpret p_i as allelic frequencies and ε_{ij} as genotypic fitnesses ($\varepsilon_{ij} = W_{ij}$) and if we set $\gamma_{ij} = 0$, then we will obtain the model of natural selection in (1.4).

$$\dot{p}_i = p_i \left(\sum_{j=1}^{n} \varepsilon_{ij} p_j - \sum_{i,j}^{n} \varepsilon_{ij} p_i p_j \right) \qquad (2.17)$$

$$\dot{N} = N \sum_{i,j=1}^{n} \varepsilon_{ij} p_i p_j$$

Chapter 2: Species Interactions in Ecosystem Modeling

The case of $\gamma_{ij} \neq 0$ corresponds to the case of density-dependent selection, which will be considered in Chapter 6. System (2.16) therefore covers the logistic equation, the Lotka-Volterra ecosystem equations, and one-locus models of natural selection. This is not surprising since our choice in (2.8) basically assumes pair interactions between components of the system, which is exactly what the traditional genetic and ecological models have in common. In the ecological models, it is pair interactions between species, and in genetic models selection operates on pairs of gametes. This similarity is important because it implies that many results obtained in one field can be interpreted relative to the other. It also opens the possibility of formulating mixed coevolutionary models in standardized mathematical form (see Section 2.8, Problems and Discussions). We will use the population-dynamics language in this chapter, but we will keep in mind the possibility of reinterpretation, which will be needed in the next chapter.

If we do not impose the restriction of symmetry on the parameters, then the system in (2.17) will represent the general case of a neutral ecosystem. Equations that describe the dynamics of the structure can be considered separately from equation (2.17). The substitution of the solution of system (2.16) into the last equation gives the dynamics of the ecosystem size:

$$\bar{N}(t) = \bar{N}_0 e^{\int_0^t F(\mathbf{p}(t)) \, dt}$$

This is a natural generalization of Malthusian growth with the Malthusian parameters averaged over the ecosystem structure.

The equations of the ecosystem structure can be separated from the system for other than the neutral case. In fact, it is necessary and sufficient for separation that $\gamma_{ij} = \gamma \, (i,j = 1, \ldots, n)$. This leads to the same equations for the frequencies as in (2.17) and a different equation for the size:

$$\bar{N} = \bar{N} \left(\sum_{i,j=1}^{n} \varepsilon_{ij} p_i p_j - \gamma \bar{N} \right)$$

The proof of this statement is trivial. Note that the supposition that all γ_{ij} are equal can be reasonable in models of competition between similar species and in some models of genetical ecology.

Balanced growth can be defined as the trajectory of the ecosystem's development when it has the form

$$\mathbf{p} = \hat{\mathbf{p}} = \text{constant}, \qquad \bar{N} = \bar{N}(t) \neq \text{constant}$$

This concept has sometimes been used in economic models in a narrower sense—that is, when $\bar{N}$ changes exponentially. It makes sense to speak about balanced growth either for neutral ecosystems or for limited ecosystems with standard density-dependence $\gamma_{ij} = \gamma(i, j = 1, \ldots, n)$. In the latter case,

$$\frac{\partial f_1}{\partial \bar{N}} = \cdots = \frac{\partial f_n}{\partial \bar{N}} = \frac{\partial F}{\partial \bar{N}}$$

so that the equations for frequencies are independent of the variable $\bar{N}$. It is clear that this is the only nonneutral case where balanced growth exists.

Therefore, considering the neutral ecosystems, we should keep in mind that all results can be reinterpreted for the case of equal limiting intensities. The only difference in the latter case is that the ecosystem size $\bar{N}(t)$ will grow according to the logistic equation, rather than exponentially.

2.6 Neutral and Limited Ecosystems

The hypothesis of neutrality is sensible only for the initial period of ecosystem development, when it is reasonable to neglect the influence of density-dependent factors. With density-dependence, the case becomes that of a limited ecosystem. Most of this section deals with the balanced growth regimes and with the location and stability of equilibrium states. It is often assumed that ecosystems spend most of their time in the neighborhood of the equilibrium states, switching relatively fast from one state to another under external perturbations. That is why the problems of equilibrium and stability have always been central to the analysis of population growth models.

Let us consider the equations for the frequencies,

$$p_i = p_i \left(\sum_{j=1}^{n} \varepsilon_{ij} p_j - \sum_{i,j=1}^{n} \varepsilon_{ij} p_i p_j \right), \quad i = 1, \ldots, n \quad (2.18)$$

Balanced growth corresponds to the equilibrium states of the system. These states can be found from the algebraic equations, which we can rewrite in vector-matrix notation:

$$p_i[(\sigma_{i.}, \mathbf{p}) - (\mathbf{p}, \Sigma \mathbf{p})] = 0, \quad i = 1, \ldots, n$$

Here Σ denotes the matrix of all the coefficients, $\|\varepsilon_{ij}\|$, and $\Sigma_{i.}$ is the ith row of the matrix.

We start from the equilibrium state, where all populations coexist—that is, $\mathbf{p}^* > 0$ ($p_i^* > 0, i = 1, \ldots, n$). For this state we have

$$(\sigma_{i.}, \mathbf{p}^*) = (\mathbf{p}, \Sigma \mathbf{p}^*), \quad i = 1, \ldots, n \quad (2.19)$$

Let us denote the quadratic form $(\mathbf{p}, \Sigma \mathbf{p})$ as $\bar{\varepsilon}$ and introduce the vector containing all elements equal to 1, $\mathbf{e} = \{1, \ldots, 1\}$. Then equation

(2.19) can be rewritten in the form

$$\Sigma \mathbf{p}^* = \bar{\varepsilon}^* \mathbf{e} \tag{2.20}$$

Conditions (2.19) imply that for balanced growth, when populations coexist their fitnesses should be equal to the average fitness, and therefore equal to each other. If we remember the definition (Chapter 1) of the fitness $f_i = (1/N_i)\dot{N}_i$, it is obvious that the sizes of all populations with balanced growth change exponentially with exponent $\bar{\varepsilon}$.

Now suppose that $\det|\Sigma| \neq 0$. Then it is easy to find the solution of equations (2.19). Multiplying by Σ^{-1}, we obtain

$$\mathbf{p}^* = \bar{\varepsilon} \Sigma^{-1} \mathbf{e} \tag{2.21}$$

If we use the normalizing conditions for the frequencies $(\mathbf{e}, \mathbf{p}) = 1$, we get

$$1 = (\mathbf{e}, \mathbf{p}^*) = \bar{\varepsilon}(\mathbf{e}, \Sigma^{-1}\mathbf{e})$$

Then

$$\bar{\varepsilon} = \frac{1}{(\mathbf{e}, \Sigma^{-1}\mathbf{e})}$$

Substituting $\bar{\varepsilon}$ into (2.20), we obtain

$$\mathbf{p}^* = \frac{\Sigma^{-1}\mathbf{e}}{(\mathbf{e}, \Sigma^{-1}\mathbf{e})} \tag{2.22}$$

This solution is biologically meaningful only if the $\mathbf{p}^*$ in (2.21) is positive. This implies that all components of the vector $\Sigma^{-1}\mathbf{e}$ should have the same sign.

Let us clarify the geometrical meaning of the solution's positiveness, that is, the possibility of complete coexistence. Imagine that we have placed all the vector columns $\Sigma_{\cdot j}$ of the matrix Σ in an n-dimensional Euclidian space. The existence of a positive solution for system (2.2) means that the vector $\mathbf{e}$ is in the interior of the cone formed by these vectors. The absence of a positive solution corresponds to the vector $\mathbf{e}$ being outside of this cone. Therefore, the conditions of coexistence are that the vector columns $\Sigma_{\cdot j}$ surround the e-vector (Figure 2.2).

We will not consider the set of equilibrium points for the degenerate matrices $\Sigma(\det \Sigma = 0)$. For these cases it may be useful to refer to the introduction (Section 1.4).

Consider now the equilibrium states where some of the frequencies are zero. Formally speaking, $p_i = 0$ does not mean that the ith population is absent. The value $\lim_{t \to \infty} N_i(t)/\overline{N}(t)$ might be zero for a

2.6 Neutral and Limited Ecosystems

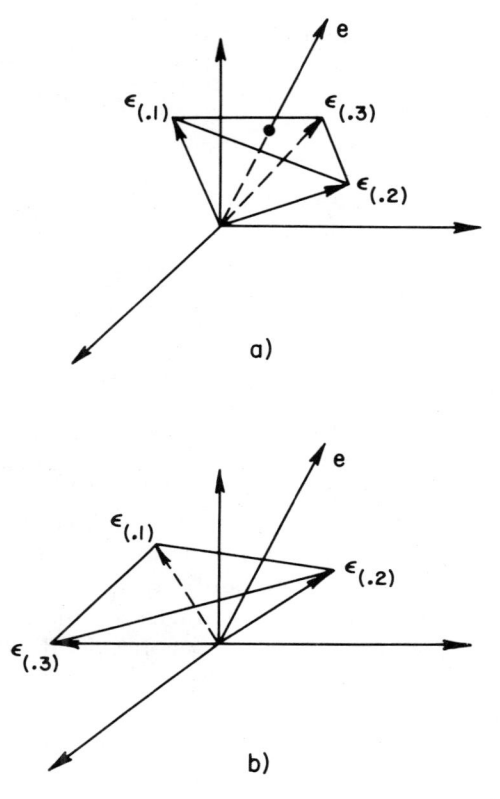

Figure 2.2 Geometric meaning of the coexistence
(a) Vector **e** is inside the cone; equilibrium exists. (b) Vector **e** is outside the cone; equilibrium does not exist.

case when $N_i(t)$ does not tend to zero. In the case of a limited ecosystem, however, $p_i = 0$ is equivalent to $N_i = 0$, since the size of the ecosystem $\bar{N}$ is limited.

Let us introduce a new notation. Let $\bar{L}$ be the set of all integers l for which $p_l{}^* = 0$ at the equilibrium point under consideration. The complement of $\bar{L}$ in the set of all numbers $1, 2, \ldots, n$ will be denoted by L. The normalizing condition now has the form

$$\sum_{i \in L} p_i{}^* = 1$$

We denote $\mathbf{p}^L$, the vector obtained from p, by omitting the components with numbers from L. Similarly, Σ^L is the matrix that is obtained from Σ by omitting the rows and columns with numbers from L. Then system (2.18) will have the form

$$\Sigma^L \mathbf{p}^L = (\mathbf{p}^L, \Sigma^L \mathbf{p}^L) \mathbf{e}^L$$
$$p_i = 0, \quad i \in L$$

Without repeating all calculations, we can write the solution for the nonzero components as

$$\hat{\mathbf{p}}^L = \frac{(\Sigma^L)^{-1} \mathbf{e}^L}{(\mathbf{e}^L, (\Sigma^L)^{-1} \mathbf{e}^L)} \quad (2.23)$$

This solution makes sense under the assumptions that $\det|\Sigma^L| \neq 0$ and all p_i^* ($i \in L$) are positive.

In general there are $2^n - 1$ ways to choose a subset from the set of n populations. This number includes all possible cases when one or more of the populations is excluded from the ecosystem. If we suppose that the essential minors of the matrix are not degenerate, there can be only one equilibrium for each subecosystem. Therefore the overall number of the equilibrium states cannot exceed $2^n - 1$. Of these subecosystems, n will correspond to cases when only one population is present and they correspond to the trivial solutions $p_i^* = 1$, $\bar{\varepsilon} = \varepsilon_{ii}$ (these "equilibria" always exist); $\binom{n}{2}$ of the systems will correspond to the cases when only two populations are present, and so on. Summing, we obtain

$$\binom{n}{1} + \binom{n}{2} + \cdots + \binom{n}{n} = 2^n - 1$$

In practice, the number of equilibrium states is much less. Mathematically, this happens because formula (2.23) does not often give a positive solution. Biologically, it means that not all combinations of the populations in an ecosystem can coexist. Hierarchic structure of an ecosystem is only one example which shows that the majority of formal "possibilities" are impossible. The actual number of equilibria is closely related to the structure of all trophic, competitive, and mutualistic relationships between the populations. It is to be hoped that all these kinds of interrelations will be reflected by the matrix Σ for the case of neutral ecosystems.

The inverse problem might be very interesting. For a given list of possible subsets of the populations that can coexist (the list might be given by an expert), find the properties of the system. There is an enormous amount of information about the character of the interactions in such a list and it should drastically restrict the mathematical model. Unfortunately no one has looked at the problem in this way. Mathematicians always deduce the equilibrium states from their

2.6 Neutral and Limited Ecosystems

models. That is why we often end up with statements such as "an equilibrium exists if the p_i^* are positive," which essentially means an equilibrium exists when it exists.

The next logical step is to study the stability of the equilibrium. Unstable equilibria are hard to observe. When we said at the beginning of the section that ecosystems spend a lot of time near equilibrium states, we meant stable equilibrium states. We will consider in this section only the case of the neutral ecosystem (with the possibility of reinterpretation for the equilimited case). So when speaking of an equilibrium for frequencies, we really mean balanced growth.

Some results on stability can be obtained by the usual linearization method (Ginzburg 1975). The exact necessary and sufficient conditions for asymptotic stability can be formulated using the matrix of the first approximation. These conditions are not very useful, since they involve the equilibrium vector along with the system parameters. Their interpretation is therefore not simple. Instead we will formulate without proof some simple, but only sufficient, conditions of stability that are easily interpretable.

Consider, first, a fully positive equilibrium point, $\mathbf{p}^*$, which corresponds to coexistence of all n species. Define the quadratic form

$$A(\mathbf{p}) = \sum_{i,j=1}^{n} a_{ij} \Delta p_i \Delta p_j$$

where $\Delta p_i = p_i - p^*$ is the deviation of the ith frequency from its equilibrium value and

$$a_{ij} = \frac{\partial^2 F}{\partial p_i \partial p_j} = \frac{1}{2}(\varepsilon_{ij} + \varepsilon_{ji})$$

The quadratic form is the same as the one used in the classification of the interaction types. The equilibrium is stable if this quadratic form is negatively definite on the simplex $A(\mathbf{p}) \leq 0$. In terms of our classification, the equilibrium is stable if the system is mutualistic and unstable if it is competitive. Unfortunately, this sufficient condition does not work when the system has both mutualistic and competitive components. Still, it can give a definite answer about stability of the equilibrium in some cases.

Now consider equilibria where some of the populations are absent

$$p_l^* = 0, \quad l \in L, \quad \sum_{i \in L} p_i^* = 1$$

In addition to stability within a coexisting subset of species ($i \in L$), we need here the conditions of noninvasibility, which take the form

$$(\mathbf{p}^*, \sigma_l) < (\mathbf{p}^*, \Sigma\mathbf{p}^*), \qquad l \in L$$

This set of conditions is exact (necessary and sufficient).

The conditions of stability can in general be divided into two groups. One group guarantees stability within the set of populations present at the equilibrium. The other group provides for the impossibility of introducing new species. Instability means that either the system of populations present at the equilibrium is unstable, or one of the noninvasibility inequalities does not hold. The latter means that there is a population that is absent at the equilibrium but which could survive within the system. It should be obvious, therefore, that the stability or instability of any particular equilibrium point depends on the species list chosen to represent the ecosystem.

Consider now the dynamic equations for a limited ecosystem, that is, the model that considers size-dependent effects. Let us rewrite the system:

$$\begin{aligned} \dot{p}_i &= p_i(f_i - F), \qquad i = 1, \ldots, n \\ \dot{\bar{N}} &= \bar{N} F \end{aligned} \qquad (2.24)$$

where

$$\begin{aligned} f_i &= \sum_{j=1}^{n} (\varepsilon_{ij} - \gamma_{ij}\bar{N}) p_j, \qquad i = 1, \ldots, n \\ F &= \sum_{i=1}^{n} p_i f_i \end{aligned} \qquad (2.25)$$

The equilibrium state is a trajectory of the form

$$\bar{N}^* = \text{constant}, \qquad \mathbf{p}^* = \text{constant}$$

To find all the equilibrium states, we set up the algebraic system

$$\begin{aligned} p_i(f_i - F) &= 0, \qquad i = 1, \ldots, n \\ \bar{N} F &= 0 \end{aligned} \qquad (2.26)$$

Consider the equilibrium state with $\bar{N}^* \neq 0$. From the last equation, we have $F = 0$. Therefore,

$$p_i f_i = 0, \qquad i = 1, \ldots, n$$

Suppose we are interested in a nontrivial equilibrium state $p_i^* > 0$ (complete coexistence). We have

$$f_i = 0, \qquad i = 1, \ldots, n$$

2.6 Neutral and Limited Ecosystems

or in vector-matrix notation (see (2.25)),

$$(\Sigma - \bar{N}\Gamma)\mathbf{p} = 0 \qquad (2.27)$$

Here Γ is the nonnegative matrix of the competition coefficients $||\gamma_{ij}||$. The condition of solvability of system (2.27) is that

$$\det(\Sigma - \bar{N}\Gamma) = 0$$

So, if $\det \Gamma \neq 0$, the equilibrium values of the ecosystem size are the eigenvalues of the matrix $\Gamma^{-1}\Sigma$:

$$\det(\Gamma^{-1}\Sigma - \bar{N} \cdot I) = 0 \qquad (2.28)$$

This is the natural generalization of the formula for the equilibrium population size of the logistic equation $\mathbf{N}^* = \varepsilon/\gamma$. Equilibrium structure $\mathbf{p}^*$ is the eigenvector of the matrix $\Gamma^{-1}\Sigma$ corresponding to the eigenvalue $\bar{N}^*$. The equilibrium ecosystem sizes and structures are the eigenvalues and eigenvectors of the matrix $\Sigma - \bar{N}\Gamma$. Since (2.27) is a homogeneous equation with respect to $\mathbf{p}$, the normalizing condition is satisfied automatically. We are of course only interested in the real and positive eigenvalues, $\bar{N}^*$, with positive eigenvectors, $\mathbf{p}^*$. Generally, the problem of finding all such pairs $\{\bar{N}^* > 0, \mathbf{p}^* > 0\}$ is complicated. Here we will discuss some necessary and some sufficient conditions for the existence and uniqueness of the solution to this problem. The same problem for symmetric matrices, which have a natural genetic interpretation, will be considered in Chapter 6.

Let matrix $\Gamma^{-1}\Sigma$ be nonnegative and nondecomposable. The exact definition of the concept of nondecomposition can be found in Bellman (1960). The meaning of the concept here is that an ecosystem cannot be divided into noninteracting parts. The Frobenius theorem (Bellman, 1960) guarantees the existence and uniqueness of the nonnegative eigenvalue $\bar{N}^*$ with corresponding eigenvector $\mathbf{p}^*$. The other sufficient condition for the existence and uniqueness is the nonnegativity of the matrix $\Sigma^{-1}\Gamma$. In this case we can consider equation (2.27) in the alternate form

$$\left(\Sigma^{-1}\Gamma - \frac{1}{\bar{N}}I\right)\mathbf{p} = 0$$

A simple necessary condition for equilibrium existence gives, at the same time, estimates of the interval for the equilibrium-size values. Let us introduce the matrix δ_{ij}, assuming that $\gamma_{ij} \neq 0$:

$$||\delta_{ij}|| = \left|\left|\frac{\varepsilon_{ij}}{\gamma_{ij}}\right|\right|$$

It follows from (2.27) that if $\mathbf{p}^* > 0$, then it is necessary that all elements in the row $(\varepsilon_{ij} - \bar{N}\gamma_{ij})$, $j = 1,\ldots,n$, either be zero or have different signs. Therefore $\bar{N}^*$ must belong to the interval

$$\min_j \delta_{ij} \leqslant \bar{N}^* \leqslant \max_j \delta_{ij}$$

These inequalities should be true for all $i = 1,\ldots,n$. Thus we obtain

$$\max_i \min_j \delta_{ij} \leqslant \bar{N}^* \leqslant \min_i \max_j \delta_{ij} \qquad (2.29)$$

Inequality (2.29) is easily checked as a necessary condition for the existence of the equilibrium. If

$$\max_i \min_j \delta_{ij} < \min_i \max_j \delta_{ij}$$

then the equilibrium does not exist. If the two expressions happen to be equal, we should determine whether or not $\bar{N}^*$ is the eigenvalue of the pencil of the matrices.

We have considered the case when all $p_i^* > 0$ $(i = 1,\ldots,n)$. Now let some $p_l^* = 0, l \in \bar{L}$. The substitution of these values into (2.26) results in the same problem, but in a smaller dimension—that is,

$$(\Sigma^L - \bar{N}\Gamma^L)\mathbf{p}^L = 0$$

All that was said before for $\mathbf{p}^* > 0$ remains true for these cases. As with the neutral case, we have $2^n - 1$ different subecosystems and thus $2^n - 1$ problems for the equilibrium state. The estimate in (2.29) can be used to preselect those cases where the equilibrium does not exist. The general estimate for the spectrum of all equilibrium sizes of the ecosystem is the union of intervals

$$\max_{i \in L} \min_{j \in L} \delta_{ij} \leqslant \bar{N}^* \leqslant \min_{i \in L} \max_{i \in L} \delta_{ij}$$

for all $L \in \{1,\ldots,n\}$. Note that the equilibrium states for a single population can be easily found:

$$p_i^* = 1, \qquad p_j^* = 0 \quad (j \neq i), \qquad \bar{N}^* = \frac{\varepsilon_{ii}}{\gamma_{ii}} > 0, \qquad i = 1,\ldots,n$$

We have already used the term *size spectrum* for the set of all equilibrium values for ecosystem size. The structure vector $\mathbf{p}^*$ corresponds to each of the points in the size spectrum. Usually it is a one-to-one correspondence, but there might be degenerate cases in which a subspace of the vectors $\mathbf{p}^*$ corresponds to the single point $\bar{N}^*$. On intersecting with the simplex δ_n, this subspace produces a linear set of the equilibrium structures. We will not treat these questions here, but we will consider one special point in the size

2.6 Neutral and Limited Ecosystems

spectrum that is always degenerate: $\bar{N}^* = 0$. For $\bar{N}^* = 0$, we have

$$p_i \left(\sum_{j=1}^{n} \varepsilon_{ij} p_j - \sum_{i,j=1}^{n} \varepsilon_{ij} p_i p_j \right) = 0, \quad i = 1, \ldots, n$$

The problem of equilibrium for the above system was discussed earlier in this section, so we know that this case can have quite a large number of equilibrium points. Though at first it may seem unrealistic to consider equilibria with $\bar{N}^* = 0$, there are two situations in which this does make sense. The first is in determining the conditions of extinction for the ecosystem. The second is in prehistoric studies, where trajectories traced in reverse time can tend to equilibria with $\bar{N}^* = 0$. These trajectories would certainly be unstable in forward time.

Let us consider now the question of stability. We calculate the matrix for the first approximation system, taken at an equilibrium point $\{\bar{N}^*, \mathbf{p}^*\}$.

$$\begin{vmatrix} \left[f_1 - F + p_1^* \frac{\partial(f_1 - F)}{\partial p_1} \right] & p_1^* \frac{\partial(f_1 - F)}{\partial p_2} & \cdots & p_1^* \frac{\partial(f_1 - F)}{\partial p_n} & p_1^* \frac{(f_1 - F)}{\partial \bar{N}} \\ \vdots & \vdots & & \vdots & \vdots \\ p_n^* \frac{\partial(f_n - F)}{\partial p_1} & p_n^* \frac{\partial(f_n - F)}{\partial p_2} & \cdots & \left[f_n - F + p_n^* \frac{\partial(f_n - F)}{\partial p_n} \right] & p_n^* \frac{\partial(f_n - F)}{\partial \bar{N}} \\ \bar{N}^* \frac{\partial F}{\partial p_1} & \bar{N}^* \frac{\partial F}{\partial p_2} & \cdots & \bar{N}^* \frac{\partial F}{\partial p_n} & \left[F + \bar{N}^* \frac{\partial F}{\partial \bar{N}} \right] \end{vmatrix}$$

(2.30)

It is necessary and sufficient for the asymptotic stability that all but one of the eigenvalues of this matrix have negative real parts. One eigenvalue is always zero since all trajectories belong to the hyperplane $\sum_{i=1}^{n} p_i = 1$. The sum of the first n rows of the matrix in (2.30) is equal to zero.

Consider some special cases. Let $\bar{N}^* = 0$. Then in the last row the first n elements are zero and the last element is F. Therefore, it is necessary for the stability of the equilibrium that $F < 0$. Remember that stability in this case means extinction. Now let $p_i^* = 0$. Then all elements of the ith row—except for the diagonal—vanish, and we obtain the other necessary condition for the case of the boundary equilibrium:

$$f_i < F$$

Chapter 2: Species Interactions in Ecosystem Modeling

This is similar to the condition of noninvasibility for the neutral case. Now let $\bar{N}^* \neq 0$; thus $F = 0$. We may assume without loss of generality that

$$p_i^* \neq 0, \quad i = 1, \ldots, k$$
$$p_l^* = 0, \quad l = k+1, \ldots, n$$

The necessary conditions of stability now have the form

$$f_l < 0, \quad l = k+1, \ldots, n \quad (2.31)$$

To obtain the sufficient conditions we write the matrix of (2.30), omitting all columns and rows with the numbers from $k+1$ to n. Note that $f_i = 0$, $i = 1, \ldots, k$.

$$\begin{bmatrix} p_1^* \dfrac{\partial(f_1 - F)}{\partial p_1} & p_1^* \dfrac{\partial(f_1 - F)}{\partial p_2} & \cdots & p_1^* \dfrac{\partial(f_1 - F)}{\partial p_k} & p_1^* \dfrac{\partial(f_1 - F)}{\partial \bar{N}} \\ \vdots & \vdots & & \vdots & \vdots \\ p_k^* \dfrac{\partial(f_k - F)}{\partial p_1} & p_k^* \dfrac{\partial(f_k - F)}{\partial p_2} & \cdots & p_k^* \dfrac{\partial(f_k - F)}{\partial p_k} & p_k^* \dfrac{\partial(f_k - F)}{\partial \bar{N}} \\ \bar{N}^* \dfrac{\partial F}{\partial p_1} & \bar{N}^* \dfrac{\partial F}{\partial p_2} & \cdots & \bar{N}^* \dfrac{\partial F}{\partial p_k} & \bar{N}^* \dfrac{\partial F}{\partial \bar{N}} \end{bmatrix} \quad (2.32)$$

It is necessary and sufficient for asymptotic stability that the conditions of (2.31) are satisfied and all but one of the eigenvalues of the matrix in (2.32) have negative real parts. Let us rewrite matrix (2.32) in block form:

$$\begin{vmatrix} p^L(\Sigma^L - N^L) & a^L \\ N^* \underset{L}{\operatorname{grad}} F & N^* \dfrac{\partial F}{\partial \bar{N}} \end{vmatrix}$$

We have introduced the following notation:

$$\underset{L}{\operatorname{grad}} F = \left(\dfrac{\partial F}{\partial p_1}, \ldots, \dfrac{\partial F}{\partial p_k} \right)$$

$$a^L = \left\| p_1 \dfrac{\partial(f_1 - F)}{\partial \bar{N}}, \ldots, p_k \dfrac{\partial(f_k - F)}{\partial \bar{N}} \right\|$$

Also, p^L is the diagonal matrix of elements $p_1^*, \ldots, p_k^*$. To obtain interpretable conditions of stability is a hard problem in the general case. We consider here only two special cases:

1. Suppose we have balanced growth,

$$\frac{\partial f_1}{\partial \bar{N}} = \cdots = \frac{\partial f_k}{\partial \bar{N}}$$

Here $a = 0$ and the conditions of stability are $\partial F/\partial \bar{N} < 0$, $f_i < 0$ ($i = k+1, \ldots, n$), and that the matrix $\mathbf{p}^L(\Sigma^L - \bar{\mathbf{N}}^*\Gamma^L)$ has all eigenvalues but one with negative real parts.

2. Suppose the equilibrium structure $\mathbf{p}^*$ is the extremum for the average fitness of the ecosystem. Then grad $F = 0$ at the equilibrium point, and it is possible to use the same reduction as in the previous case.

Note that $\partial F/\partial \bar{N} < 0$ is the condition of our classification. It means that the equilibrium state is the limited state. We see once again that classification of the interaction types is helpful for the stability analysis.

2.7 Two-Species Ecosystems

In this section we analyze the dynamics of the elementary two-species ecosystem for the cases of competition and prey-predator relationship. The purpose is to show the advantages of the new models over similar ones of the Lotka-Volterra and Kolmogorov types.

Let us start with the neutral case, $\gamma_{ij} = 0$. Functions f_1 and f_2 have the form

$$\left.\begin{aligned} f_1 &= \varepsilon_{11} p_1 + \varepsilon_{12} p_2 \\ f_2 &= \varepsilon_{21} p_1 + \varepsilon_{22} p_2 \end{aligned}\right\}$$

It will be helpful to introduce new parameters ε_1, ε_2 and α_1, α_2, which respectively characterize the growth rates of both populations in the absence of the other species, and the interpopulation interactions:

$$\varepsilon_1 = \varepsilon_{11} \qquad \alpha_1 = \varepsilon_{12} - \varepsilon_{11}$$
$$\varepsilon_2 = \varepsilon_{22} \qquad \alpha_2 = \varepsilon_{21} - \varepsilon_{22}$$

Then fitnesses f_1 and f_2 will have the form

$$\left.\begin{aligned} f_1 &= \varepsilon_1 + \alpha_1 p_2 \\ f_2 &= \varepsilon_2 + \alpha_2 p_1 \end{aligned}\right\}$$

Consider now the problem of competition for two similar species. In terms of our model, it means

$$\varepsilon_1 = \varepsilon_2 = \varepsilon > 0$$
$$\alpha_1 = \alpha_2 = \alpha < 0$$

The first assumption means that both populations have the same growth rates in the absence of the competitor. The second means that both populations have the same competitive ability. Both assumptions are accepted only for the sake of simplicity. The qualitative behavior of the system stays the same for unequal but positive $\varepsilon_1, \varepsilon_2$ and unequal but negative α_1, α_2.

One can find the solution of the system (Ginzburg, Konovalov, and Epelman, 1974). Without writing it explicitly, let us consider the properties of the solution: If $\varepsilon > \alpha$, both populations grow infinitely. If $\alpha > \varepsilon$, the population with the smaller initial size dies and the other population grows infinitely. The curve for the dying population will have a maximum point at some particular time. It does not make much sense to consider the case of exact equality $\varepsilon = \alpha$, because it is parametrically unstable (see Introduction).

The main disadvantage of the model is the infinite growth of the winning population. This is a consequence of the hypothesis of neutrality, which can be accepted only for the initial stages of growth when we neglect density-dependent effects.

For the prey-predator case the functions f_1 and f_2 will have the form

$$f_1 = \varepsilon_1 - \alpha p_2$$
$$f_2 = -\varepsilon_2 + \alpha p_1$$

where all constants are positive. The signs for ε_1 and ε_2 are chosen so that the predator dies without a prey and the prey grows exponentially without a predator. The system of differential equations can be solved analytically for this case (Ginzburg, Konovalov, and Epelman, 1974). The analysis of the solution from the point of view of the final result of the interaction gives the following types of behavior:

1. The predator eats all the prey population and then it too dies. Both curves have local maxima, and the maximum for the predator occurs later than the maximum for the prey.
2. The populations coexist. At the beginning of the process the predator population might decrease, but on reaching some minimum point, it will start to grow.

3. The minimum for the prey population occurs later and is also followed by growth. The populations coexist. At the beginning of the process both populations might decrease; the minimum point for predators occurs later than the minimum for prey.
4. The predators die and the prey grow, although there might have been a decrease in the prey population at the beginning of the process.
5. The predators die and the prey population grows monotonically. The relationship of the parameters ε_1, ε_2, and α completely defines the behavior of the process. The qualitative result is independent of the initial population sizes. Since we assume a neutral ecosystem, the surviving populations grow without bounds.

Consider now the density-dependent effects. We start with the competition model, with the fitness functions in the following form:

$$\left. \begin{array}{l} f_1 = \varepsilon - \alpha p_2 - \gamma \bar{N} \\ f_2 = \varepsilon - \alpha p_1 - \gamma \bar{N} \end{array} \right\}$$

The ecosystem has two stable steady states, which correspond to the elimination of one of the competitive populations

$$\left. \begin{array}{l} x_1 = 0 \\ x_2 = \dfrac{\varepsilon}{\gamma} \end{array} \right\} \quad \text{and} \quad \left. \begin{array}{l} x_1 = \dfrac{\varepsilon}{\gamma} \\ x_2 = 0 \end{array} \right\}$$

If $2\varepsilon > \alpha$ there is one more equilibrium state which is unstable,

$$x_1 = x_2 = \frac{2\varepsilon - \alpha}{4\gamma}$$

A qualitative analysis of the system yields the same results as those obtained in the previous neutral case. The winning population is the one that has the largest initial size. This is not an unexpected result, since the intensity of the density-dependence is assumed to be equal for both populations.

Considering a limited ecosystem of the predator-prey type, we assume first that the limiting factors act only for the prey population and that the ecosystem is neutral with respect to the predators. We have

$$\left. \begin{array}{l} f_1 = \varepsilon_1 - \alpha p_2 - \gamma \bar{N} \\ f_2 = -\varepsilon_2 + \alpha p_1 \end{array} \right\}$$

Chapter 2: Species Interactions in Ecosystem Modeling

We do not intend to go into detailed descriptions of all the possible cases. Let us list only the qualitatively distinct possibilities from the point of view of the final result of the predator-prey interaction.

1. There is the unique globally stable equilibrium state, where predators are eliminated and the prey population has the size ε/γ.

2. Both species coexist in the globally stable equilibrium

$$x_1 = \frac{\varepsilon_2(\varepsilon_1 + \varepsilon_2 - \alpha)}{\alpha\gamma}$$

$$x_2 = \frac{(\alpha - \varepsilon_2)(\varepsilon_1 + \varepsilon_2 - \alpha)}{\alpha\gamma}$$

3. Both populations die—first the prey, then the predator.

These cases match the descriptions for the neutral model except that all population sizes remain finite.

Let us compare our results with the classical experimental data of Gause (1934) for competition and predation. In Figure 2.3, we plot the dynamics of the infusorian populations *Paramecium aurelia* and *Paramecium caudatum* in percent of the equilibrium level. When growing separately, both populations follow the logistic curve quite well if we choose $\varepsilon = 2.0$ and $\gamma = 0.02$. The competition process between these populations is shown in Figure 2.4. The curves are calculated from our model with $\alpha = 0.6$. It is interesting to notice that the maximum for the eliminated population is simulated quite well by the model. Notice also that only one parameter,

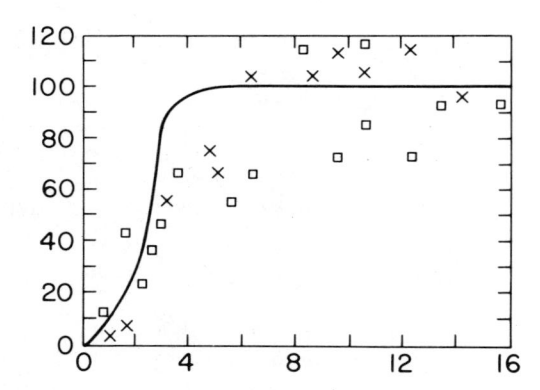

Figure 2.3 The dynamics of *P. aurelia* and *P. caudatum* in percent of the equilibrium level when grown separately. Points are taken from Gause (1934); curves are from the model.

2.7 Two-Species Ecosystems 45

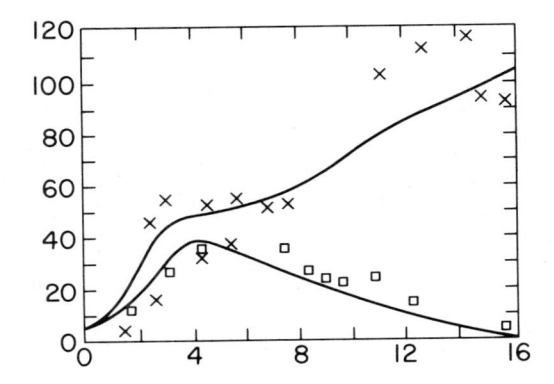

Figure 2.4 Competition between the P. aurelia and P. caudatum. Points are taken from Gause (1934); curves are generated by the model.

α, was chosen to fit the data; however, both ε and γ were obtained from the independent experiments.

The curve of the prey-predator interaction is plotted in Figure 2.5. Here the prey is the *Paramecium caudatum* and the predator is *Didinium nasutum*. The curve is calculated from our model with $\varepsilon_1 = 3.0$, $\varepsilon_2 = 4.0$, $\alpha = 7.5$, and $\gamma = 2.6 \times 10^{-2}$. We have a good qualitative fit. The theory gives a somewhat higher rate of elimination for the predators than occurs in reality. This is probably due to some special properties of *Didinium* not taken into account by the model. The problem may be that *Didinium* continues to reproduce for some time in the absence of food.

Though the results are presented in terms of actual population numbers, the calculations were done in terms of biomasses. We assumed the average biomass for *P. caudatum* to be 0.002 mg and for *D. nasutum* to be 0.0009 mg (Chorick, 1968). The hypothesis of neutrality was accepted for the predators since their population size is small compared to the carrying capacity of the ecosystem. For *P. caudatum*, this is not the case, and we must take density-dependent effects into account.

Models of Lotka-Volterra type do *not* yield all the types of dynamical behavior that we have described with our model. An interesting question is whether we can get the limit-cycle behavior for the prey-predator ecosystem within the framework of our parametric model.

Consider the fitness functions for the prey-predator model in the general form:

$$\left. \begin{array}{l} f_1 = \varepsilon_1 - \alpha_1 p_2 - \gamma_{11} N_1 - \gamma_{12} N_2 \\ f_2 = -\varepsilon_2 + \alpha_2 p_1 - \gamma_{21} N_1 - \gamma_{22} N_2 \end{array} \right\}$$

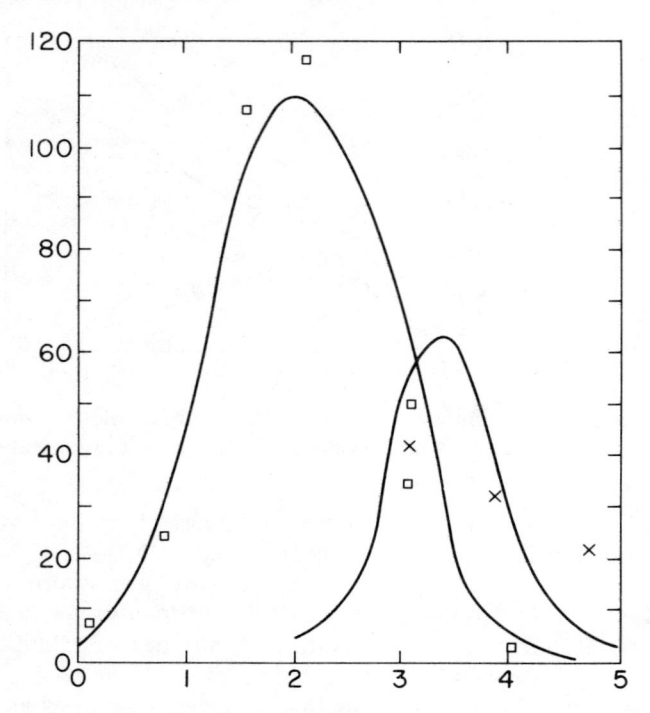

Figure 2.5 Predator-prey dynamics (*P. caudatum* and *D. nasutum*). Points are taken from Gause (1934); curves are generated by the model.

Let us assume the following (Castilla, 1977):

1. Both species have a limiting action on the growth of prey population, though self-limitation should be small; $\gamma_{12} \neq 0$, $\gamma_{11} \neq 0$, and γ_{11} is small.
2. There exists a steady state where small disturbances tend to be amplified; $\alpha_2 - \alpha_1 > 0$.
3. Food is sufficient to support the predator; $\alpha_2 - \varepsilon_2 > 0$.

We have to analyze three equilibrium points; the origin, $(\varepsilon_1/\gamma_{11}, 0)$, and (N_1, N_2). Under the conditions we have imposed, the three equilibria are unstable. From Figure 2.6 we can see that all trajectories enter area D, so according to the Poincaré-Bendixon theorem there must exist inside D either a stable equilibrium or a limit cycle. The latter occurs. Though theoretically it is known that there could exist a finite number of limit cycles, we need only establish that we will have periodic behavior of both populations.

A full nonlinear analysis of this model yields a stable limit cycle. From Figure 2.6 we can verify that there is a steady state for

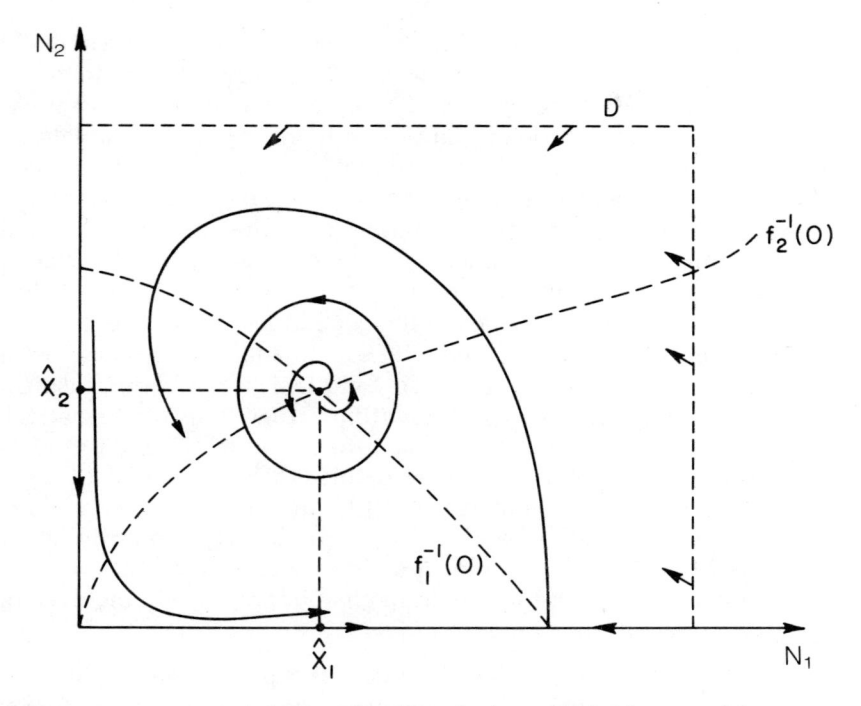

Figure 2.6 Limit cycle behavior within the framework of our model.

the prey alone, but no matter how small the number of predators is, the latter tend to increase. Also observe that no matter how small the populations are, we will never have the situation where both die out.

To summarize the results of this section, we emphasize that within the proposed parametric models, we get a large variety of dynamical behavior. Practically all types of behavior for two-species ecosystems that we can imagine exist here, and there is no need to turn to the general qualitative models of the Kolmogorov type in order to describe them. All the parameters are clearly interpretable and allow a biologically meaningful classification of the different types of dynamical behavior.

2.8 Problems and Discussion

1. The equations of population dynamics that are suggested in this chapter are models of intermediate complexity between oversimplified Lotka-Volterra models and overgeneralized qualitative models of the Kolmogorov type. The suggested parametric form also includes models of natural selection. We have succeeded, therefore,

in combining the two different classes of models described in the introduction. This allows us to interpret results obtained in one of the two fields in terms of the other field, and it also opens the way for combining evolutionary and population dynamics models. In fact, nothing prevents us from formulating the coevolutionary models in the same way by setting our interaction matrices in block form, where each block will describe evolutionary processes within a population, and interactions between blocks will correspond to interactions between species.

This approach leads to the general family of models, which has not been analyzed. Although such an analysis presents mathematical problems of considerable complexity, the main reason for not doing it in this book is scientific rather than mathematical. The number of parameters we need to introduce in such models is so high that we fear falling into the Ptolemaic trap and describing "everything" without really explaining anything. Any progress in this direction will depend on our ability to narrow down the problems by making biologically meaningful, simplifying assumptions. Such progress may be of great importance in the development of coevolutionary models.

2. The inverse problem of estimating parameters of the model (or ranges of parameters) from a given list of possible coexisting subsets of populations was mentioned in Section 2.6. The problem could have been formulated on the narrower basis of the traditional Lotka-Volterra equations. In many cases data are insufficient to estimate the parameters of species interactions; therefore, an expert opinion about the list of possible coexisting combinations of species is sometimes the only source of information. Such a list may greatly limit the ranges for the interaction parameters, which then can be used for global analysis of the system. This is an important problem, which has not received sufficient attention from theoreticians.

3 Models of Natural Selection

This chapter reviews the results pertaining to the classical model of natural selection for one locus with multiple alleles. The new results suggest the relationship of this model to the models of population growth and investigate the case of multiple loci when the number of loci is large. Surprisingly, when the number of loci is large enough, the multiple loci model behaves, from the point of view of population dynamics, very similarly to a much simpler one-locus model. This should have important implications for mixed ecological-genetical models.

3.1 Equilibria and Stability

Here we will briefly review the results on equilibrium and stability for the multiple-allele selection model that was presented in the introductory chapter (Section 1.2). Using what we learned in Chapter 2, most of these results also allow an ecological interpretation. The distinctive feature of this model, which makes it a special case from the ecological point of view, is the symmetry of the fitness matrix, $W_{ij} = W_{ji}, i, j = 1, \ldots, n$. This symmetry results from an important assumption: Selection operates only on the level of zygotes, and not on the level of gametes. Gametic selection plus zygotic selection would lead to asymmetric fitness matrices, make the model more

Chapter 3: Models of Natural Selection

general, and bring it closer to its ecological analogue (see Section 3.8, Problems and Discussions).

Let us rewrite equations (1.4):

$$\dot{p}_i = p_i(W_i - \overline{W}), \qquad i = 1, \ldots, n$$
$$\dot{N} = \overline{W} N \tag{3.1}$$

where

$$W_i = (W_{i.}, \mathbf{p}), \qquad i = 1, \ldots, n$$
$$\overline{W} = (\mathbf{p}, W\mathbf{p})$$

We are continuing to use the vector-matrix notations introduced in the previous chapter, so that $W_{i.}$ is the ith row of the fitness matrix and W is the matrix itself.

The analysis of equilibrium and stability is similar to the one we have already performed for the ecosystem models in Chapter 2, except for additional results deriving from the important symmetry property of the fitness matrix.

In the classical case of constant fitnesses, we ignore the last equation of (3.1). That is what we have referred to as *balanced growth* in the ecosystem model.

The equilibrium equations

$$p_i(W_i - \overline{W}) = 0, \qquad i = 1, \ldots, n \tag{3.2}$$

can again have up to $2^n - 1$ solutions lying in all possible faces of the frequency simplex. These equilibria correspond to all monomorphisms, dimorphisms, trimorphisms, and so on—up to a possible full polymorphism with all n alleles present. The formula for such a full polymorphism is

$$\mathbf{p}^* = \frac{W^{-1}\mathbf{e}}{(\mathbf{e}, W^{-1}\mathbf{e})} \tag{3.3}$$

We have assumed here that $\det W \neq 0$, and the formula has a biological meaning only if all components of $\mathbf{p}^*$ are nonnegative. An analogous formula works for every subset of alleles. It would, of course, use the corresponding submatrix of the full fitness matrix.

In the case of two alleles, expression (3.3) reduces to the familiar formulas for the equilibrium frequencies under selection:

$$p_1^* = \frac{W_{12} - W_{22}}{2W_{12} - W_{11} - W_{22}}$$

$$p_2^* = \frac{W_{12} - W_{11}}{2W_{12} - W_{11} - W_{22}}$$

3.1 Equilibria and Stability

The equilibria defined by formula (3.3) and its lower-dimensional analogs need not be stable. In fact, in many cases the majority of them are unstable. We will discuss this problem in more detail in the next chapter. Full necessary and sufficient conditions of the complete polymorphism are well known and can be expressed either in terms of the signs of the principal minors of the fitness matrix (Mandel, 1959) or in terms of the eigenvalues of the fitness matrix (Kingman, 1961).

If we introduce a notation for the rth principal minor of the fitness matrix as

$$W\begin{pmatrix}1,2,\ldots,r\\1,2,\ldots,r\end{pmatrix} = \det\begin{vmatrix}W_{11} & \cdots & W_{1r}\\ W_{12} & \cdots & W_{2r}\\ \vdots & & \vdots \\ W_{r1} & \cdots & W_{rr}\end{vmatrix}$$

Mandel's criteria for stability are

$$(-1)^r W\begin{pmatrix}1,2,\ldots,r\\1,2,\ldots,r\end{pmatrix} < 0, \quad r = 1,2,3,\ldots,n$$

Kingman's eigenvalue criterion is that the matrix W should have one positive and $n-1$ negative eigenvalues.

Both of these results are based on the symmetry of the fitness matrix, which allows interpretation of the stability conditions in these relatively simple and clear forms. I say "relatively simple," because principal minors are quite complicated functions of the elements and checking out these criteria requires extensive calculations, plus a knowledge of all the elements of the fitness matrix. In practice we rarely, if ever, have numerical values for fitnesses in multiallelic systems. Some limited conditions of stability (necessary but not sufficient conditions) that allow simpler interpretation will be discussed in the next chapter.

The stability conditions for the boundary equilibria are also similar to the ones we have considered in the previous chapter for the case of an arbitrary (nonsymmetric) matrix. If some of the frequencies are zero at the equilibrium point $p_i^* = 0$, the stability condition means that the ith allele cannot invade the population:

$$(W_{i\cdot\cdot}, \mathbf{p}^*) > (\mathbf{p}^*, W\mathbf{p}^*)$$

This is, of course, in addition to the Mandel-Kingman stability condition, which corresponds to the positive components of the equilibrium.

All of the results in this section are well known and can be found in any complete text on population genetics. We have reviewed them here only for completeness and for references in the following chapters.

3.2 Conservation of Allelic Fitnesses

One very simple algebraic identity related to the classical selection models has escaped the attention of most authors. In addition to being an interesting invariant of the evolutionary process by itself, it is very useful when analyzing the relationship of selection to population growth (Chapter 5).

Consider formula (3.3) for the complete polymorphism, $\mathbf{p}^*$. Let us relax the assumption of $\mathbf{p}^*$ being a fully positive vector. In other words, consider the vector $\mathbf{p}^*$ defined by formula (3.3) whether or not it is a biologically meaningful polymorphism. This vector is the unique solution of the algebraic system

$$(W_{i\cdot},\mathbf{p}^*) = (\mathbf{p}^*, W\mathbf{p}^*), \qquad i = 1,\ldots,n \qquad (3.4)$$

The uniqueness follows from the assumption that $\det|W| \neq 0$.

Let us multiply the ith equation of the system in (3.4) by p_i and add, to obtain

$$(\mathbf{p}, W\mathbf{p}^*) = \left(\sum_{i=1}^n p_i\right)(\mathbf{p}^*, W\mathbf{p}^*) = (\mathbf{p}^*, W\mathbf{p}^*)$$

Now, using the symmetry of the fitness matrix,

$$(\mathbf{p}^*, W\mathbf{p}) = (\mathbf{p}^*, W\mathbf{p}^*)$$

or, in scalar form,

$$\sum_{i=1}^n p_i^* W_i(\mathbf{p}) = \sum_{i,j=1}^n p_i^* p_j^* W_{ij} = \overline{W}^* \qquad (3.5)$$

The weighted (by the p_i^*'s) sum of allelic fitnesses is identically constant and equal to $\overline{W}^*$, independent of the particular allelic frequencies, $\mathbf{p}$. Remember, allelic fitness, W_i, is a function of gene frequencies; it is not a constant and may increase or decrease during the process of evolution. However, the weighted sum in (3.5) remains constant and equal to the equilibrium value of the average fitness, $\overline{W}^*$. That is what suggests the name *conservation of allelic fitnesses*. It has a particularly interesting interpretation when p^* is in fact a biologically meaningful polymorphism. Then, $p_i^* > 0$ and alleles "exchange" fitnesses, preserving the weighted sum in the course of natural selection. One of the consequences is, for instance, that the allelic fitnesses cannot all increase or decrease at the same time.

Another interpretation comes from the fact that the allelic fitness, W_i, is the "Malthusian parameter" of the ith allele; that is,

$$W_i = \frac{1}{N_i} \dot{N}_i = (\ln \dot{N}_i),$$

where N_i is the absolute number of ith alleles in the population as a function of time. This gives

$$\sum_{i=1}^{n} p_i^*(\ln \dot{N}_i) = \bar{W}^* = \text{constant}$$

or, with one more differentiation,

$$\sum_{i=1}^{n} p_i^*(\ln \ddot{N}_i) = 0 \qquad (3.6)$$

In the case of two alleles this has a particularly clear form,

$$p_i^*(\ln \ddot{N}_i) = -p_2^*(\ln \ddot{N}_2)$$

which reminds one of the Newtonian law of action and reaction that describes mechanical interactions between two bodies. We will use the absolute numbers of alleles, as well as their frequencies, a number of times in this book for purposes of interpretation. We have the freedom to do this because our fitnesses are always absolute fitnesses. Continuing the mechanical analogy, the conservation of allelic fitnesses is similar to the conservation of momentum law in physics. The equilibrium frequencies play the role of "masses," but can also be negative. Note that stability of the equilibrium is not required; p^* is just the unique solution of the algebraic system (3.4) and is not necessarily a stable solution.

Establishing conservation rules, or finding scalar invariants of multidimensional evolutionary processes, is an intuitively satisfying exercise. Whether or not our physical analogy has any deeper meaning is not clear. We will return to this problem in Chapter 7.

3.3 Fisher's Theorem and Wright's Principle

Fisher's fundamental theorem of natural selection and Wright's adaptive topography are two parts of the point of view on natural selection that have dominated the intuition of population biologists for a long time.

The proof of the Fisher theorem is very simple if we use the continuous model in (3.1). The statement we would like to prove is that the average fitness of the population, $\bar{W}$, never decreases in the

Chapter 3: Models of Natural Selection

course of natural selection. This generalizes the Darwinian survival-of-the-fittest principle for the diploid case, which is probably the reason why the theorem is said to be fundamental.

Consider the derivative, $\dot{\bar{W}}$:

$$\dot{\bar{W}} = \sum_{i=1}^{n} \frac{\partial \bar{W}}{\partial p_i} \dot{p}_i = \sum_{i=1}^{n} (2W_i) \dot{p}_i \tag{3.7}$$

Substituting $\dot{p}_i$ from equations (3.1), we have

$$\dot{\bar{W}} = 2 \sum_{i=1}^{n} W_i p_i (W_i - \bar{W}) \tag{3.8}$$

Note that now $\sum_{i=1}^{n} \dot{p}_i \equiv 0$, which implies

$$\sum_{i=1}^{n} p_i (W_i - \bar{W}) \equiv 0 \tag{3.9}$$

Subtracting the expression (3.9) multiplied by $2\bar{W}$ (effectively subtracting zero), we obtain

$$\dot{\bar{W}} = 2 \sum_{i=1}^{n} p_i (W_i - \bar{W})^2 \geq 0 \tag{3.10}$$

which is the statement of the theorem. It is clear from expression (3.10) that $\dot{\bar{W}} = 0$ only at the equilibrium points—that is, at solutions of equations (3.2). Therefore, except for the equilibria,

$$\dot{\bar{W}} > 0$$

The average fitness of the population increases as a result of natural selection until the population reaches an equilibrium.

Note that the symmetry of the fitness matrix is essential for this result. In the first line of the proof, (3.7), we wrote

$$\frac{\partial \bar{W}}{\partial p_i} = 2W_i$$

which is true because of the symmetry. For the general nonsymmetric matrix, instead of (3.10) the result would be

$$\dot{\bar{W}} = 2 \sum_{i=1}^{n} p_i ((W_{i.}, p) - \bar{W})((W_{.i}, p) - \bar{W})$$

where $W_{i.}$ and $W_{.i}$ are rows and columns of the fitness matrix. It becomes a covariance rather than a variance, and in general its sign is not definite. It is important, therefore, to realize that the statement of the theorem is not only the consequence of *one-locus* models, but also of the assumption of zygotic selection.

In a generic case the average fitness, which is a quadratic form of gene frequencies, has a number of local maxima typically located on low-dimensional boundaries of the simplex. Depending on the initial conditions, the evolutionary trajectory will climb one of these peaks of the average fitness and stabilize at the peak. The topography of the average fitness, $\overline{W}$, in the space of gene frequencies is thus an important argument in predicting the behavior of evolutionary trajectories. This is called *Wright's adaptive topography*. It is not, however, the only factor. The distribution of the attraction zones of different local peaks is still not clearly understood. We know that it is not correct, for instance, that the highest peak always has the largest attraction zone (Karlin and Feldman, 1981). The size of attraction zones correlates with some measure of diversity of the attracting equilibrium rather than with the value of average fitness at the equilibrium. Why this is so will become somewhat clearer later in this chapter (see also Problems and Discussion). It is important to realize that, except for the case of just two alleles (when the adaptive landscape is one-dimensional), Wright's topography does not uniquely define evolutionary trajectories.

Coming back to the statement of Fisher's theorem, let us rewrite it in terms of the dynamics of population size. From the last equation of (3.1), we have

$$\overline{W} = \frac{1}{N(t)} \frac{d}{dt} N(t) = \frac{d}{dt} (\ln \cdot N(t))$$

Fisher's theorem says, therefore, that the logarithm of population size under natural selection always has a nonnegative acceleration:

$$\frac{d^2}{dt^2} (\ln N(t)) \geq 0 \qquad (3.11)$$

This interesting reformulation of the theorem can be constrasted with statement (3.6) of the previous section. While some weighted sum of allelic accelerations stays identically zero, the overall population size has a positive acceleration except at an equilibrium. Note that all sizes are measured on a log scale, which of course is a consequence of the multiplicative character of the population growth process.

3.4 Recombination

It has been known for a long time that neither Fisher's theorem nor the adaptive landscape concepts are applicable when we consider

Chapter 3: Models of Natural Selection

two or more loci. The reason is that recombination—a random, nondirectional force—may create lower fitness genotypes from the higher fitness ones. This may bring the average fitness of the population down and sometimes overcome the influence of natural selection. To understand how the recombination terms influence the evolutionary trajectory, consider the simplest case of two loci with two alleles at each locus. The equations that describe the population dynamics have the following form:

$$\begin{aligned}\dot{p}_1 &= p_1(W_1 - \overline{W}) - W_{14}rD(p) \\ \dot{p}_2 &= p_2(W_2 - \overline{W}) + W_{14}rD(p) \\ \dot{p}_3 &= p_3(W_3 - \overline{W}) + W_{14}rD(p) \\ \dot{p}_4 &= p_4(W_4 - \overline{W}) - W_{14}rD(p) \\ \dot{N} &= \overline{W}N\end{aligned} \qquad (3.12)$$

where p_1, p_2, p_3, and p_4 are the frequencies of four alternative gametotypes, AB, Ab, aB and ab; r is the probability of recombination between two loci ($0 \leq r \leq \frac{1}{2}$); and $D(p) = p_1 p_4 - p_2 p_3$ is the so-called linkage disequilibrium function. In this case, $\|W_{ij}\|$ is a 4×4 fitness matrix containing all possible genotypic fitnesses.

In addition to the usual symmetry $W_{ij} = W_{ji}$, there is one more relationship resulting from the usual assumption of the phenotypic equivalency of two double heterozygotes

$$\frac{A\ B}{a\ b} \quad \text{and} \quad \frac{A\ b}{a\ B}$$

This leads to $W_{14} = W_{23}$. All W_i, $i = 1, \ldots, 4$ are gametotypic fitnesses and are defined in the same way as allelic fitnesses in a one-locus model. Also, $\overline{W}$ is the average fitness of the population.

Clearly, with $r = 0$ (no recombination), the model is equivalent to a one-locus, four alleles system. The general case of arbitrary fitnesses and $r \neq 0$ presents a difficult mathematical problem and is not yet completely understood, although substantial progress has been made (see Karlin (1975) and Ewens (1979) for a full review of results on two-locus systems).

Possible equilibria of the system are defined by the set of four algebraic equations, and the solution p^*, in general, depends on r. The case of $D(p^*) = 0$ is an exception.

In reality, for weak selection we expect the values of $D(p^*)$ to be rather small unless linkage is very tight (r is close to zero). Let us prove this statement and show that the product of $r|D(p^*)|$ should be on the order of the selection intensity. Consider the equilibrium system

$$P_1(W_1 - \overline{W}) = W_{14}rD$$
$$p_2(W_2 - \overline{W}) = -W_{14}rD$$
$$p_3(W_3 - \overline{W}) = -W_{14}rD$$
$$p_4(W_4 - \overline{W}) = W_{14}rD$$

Multiplying the first equation by p_4, the second by $-p_3$, the third by $-p_2$, and the fourth by p_1, we obtain, by summation,

$$W_{14}rD(p) = p_1^* p_4^* (W_1 + W_4 - 2\overline{W}) - p_2 p_3 (W_2 + W_3 - 2\overline{W})$$

We can assume now without loss of generality that $D(\mathbf{p}^*) > 0$— that is, $p_1^* p_4^* > p_2^* p_3^*$ (the case of $D(\mathbf{p}^*) < 0$ is completely analogous). Then W_2 and W_3 do not exceed $\overline{W}$ and we can estimate the product $p_2 p_3$ by the greater number $p_1 p_4$. We have

$$W_{14} rD(\mathbf{p}^*) < p_1^* p_4^* (W_1 + W_4 - W_2 - W_3)$$

The expression in the right-hand parentheses is linear in **p** and has the following form:

$$\begin{aligned} W_1 + W_4 - W_2 - W_3 &= (W_{11} - W_{21} - W_{31} + W_{41}) p_1^* \\ &+ (W_{12} - W_{22} - W_{32} + W_{42}) p_2^* \\ &+ (W_{13} - W_{23} - W_{33} + W_{43}) p_3^* \\ &+ (W_{14} - W_{24} - W_{34} + W_{44}) p_4^* \end{aligned}$$

This expression certainly does not exceed the greatest of four coefficients. A crude estimate can be obtained if we introduce a parameter S, defining the strength of selection. Let us assume that

$$W_{14} = 1, \quad |W_{ij} - 1| \leq S, \quad i, j = 1, \ldots, 4$$

Each one of the four coefficients of our last expression clearly cannot exceed 4S. In reality, because of our additional symmetry $W_{14} = W_{23}$, it cannot exceed 3S. The product $p_1^* p_4^*$, like any product of two frequencies, does not exceed $\frac{1}{4}$. We have, therefore

$$r |D(\mathbf{p}^*)| < \tfrac{3}{4} S \tag{3.13}$$

This estimate is very crude. The more precise result has been obtained numerically by Hastings (1981):

$$r |D(\mathbf{p}^*)| < \tfrac{1}{10} S$$

The exact numerical value for the constant is not important in our context. The significant conclusion is that when selection is weak (small S), we expect the equilibrium values of $D(\mathbf{p}^*)$ to be very small unless r is very small (tightly linked loci).

Chapter 3: Models of Natural Selection

This result explains why many attempts to measure linkage disequilibrium in natural populations have indicated that it is very close to zero. Weak enough selection may well be the cause.

Let us demonstrate now why the average fitness does not necessarily increase in a two-locus system. By calculating the derivative,

$$\dot{W} = \sum_{i=1}^{n} \frac{\partial W}{\partial p_i} \dot{p}_i$$

and by taking into account equations (3.12) and following the same sequence of steps as in the previous section, we will have

$$\dot{W} = 2 \sum_{i=1}^{4} p_i (W_i - \overline{W})^2 + 2W_{14} r D(p)(W_2 + W_3 - W_1 - W_4)$$

We see that the rate of change of the average fitness can be expressed as the sum of two terms: the selection-induced term (identical to the one-locus expression), which is always nonnegative, and the second term involving both selection and recombination parameters. The second term is zero when $r = 0$, so this expression is a generalization of the one-locus result. Note, by the way, that the second term also vanishes along the surface $D(\mathbf{p}) \equiv 0$. This will become important later, when we consider the case of multiple loci.

Since the sign of the second term is in general not defined, the statement of Fisher's theorem is not applicable. The sign of the second term may be either negative or positive depending on the particular gene frequencies. An exception would be the case when

$$W_2 + W_3 - W_1 - W_4 \equiv 0$$

This is equivalent to the following set of conditions.

$$W_{11} - W_{21} - W_{31} + W_{41} = 0$$
$$W_{12} - W_{22} - W_{32} + W_{42} = 0$$
$$W_{13} - W_{23} - W_{33} + W_{43} = 0$$
$$W_{14} - W_{24} - W_{34} + W_{44} = 0$$

This very strict set of conditions is satisfied, for instance, when fitnesses are additive. Fisher's theorem will therefore be a correct statement even for a multiple-locus system in some special cases. We are not going to deal with such cases. The theory of the two-locus and multiple-locus systems, with a number of specific, more or less general assumptions about fitnesses, is a large field of study by itself with major contributions made by S. Karlin and collaborators. At the same time there are very few results for unrestricted fitnesses even in the two-locus case.

Returning to our population-dynamics interpretation of Fisher's theorem: In general, population size may accelerate or decelerate during the course of natural selection involving multiple-locus systems. Of course, the absence of recombination ($r = 0$) or some very specific assumptions about the fitnesses may save the theorem, which is not generally applicable.

Let us now discuss the case of an arbitrary number of loci. With m loci the system analogous to (3.12) will involve 2^m equations, since there are 2^m gametes (assuming two alleles at each locus). What is more important, the number of the linkage-disequilibrium terms, analogous to the term $W_{14}rD(p)$ in system (3.12), grows even faster with the number of loci. An asymptotic estimation for large m gives of the order of $(\frac{1}{2})3^m$ linkage disequilibrium terms in the system. All of these terms will consist of a fitness for a particular heterozygote genotype, a probability for a particular recombination event, and an expression of the sort $p_1p_4 - p_2p_3$, which indexes gametes that can be produced by this specific recombination event. I would prefer not to go into the details of introducing all the necessary indexes and notations here. They can be found in Karlin (1977) and Ginzburg and Braumann (1980). It is clear that there is not much one can do with such complex systems. The ways out of the difficulties are either to assume tight linkage so that one can analyze what is, effectively, a one-locus system (with very large numbers of "alleles"), or to assume something specific about the way fitnesses are assigned (additive, multiplicative, generalized symmetric, and so on). Both ways have been employed (Karlin 1977, 1978, 1979, and Karlin and Liberman 1979a, b). The largest number of loci for which explicit equations have been analyzed is three (Feldman, Franklin, and Thompson, 1974, Feldman et al., 1975, and Franklin and Feldman 1977). Writing equations for many loci is such hard work that even computer simulations of these systems have been very limited. The latest reviews of results in multilocus selection theory can be found in Karlin (1978) and Hedrick, Jain, and Holden (1978).

The difficulties of the exact analysis of multilocus systems have led to a feeling that a radical change in point of view should be attempted. The very questions we ask about the behavior of multilocus systems should differ from the usual questions we ask when analyzing low-dimensional dynamic systems. We have attempted to make such a change (in Ginzburg and Braumann 1980). The end of this chapter briefly summarizes results of this work. The idea behind the work is based on some interesting geometric properties of the frequency simplex in cases of high dimension. We will consider these properties and then apply the results to the model of selection in the case of a large number of loci.

3.5 Linear and Quadratic Functions on the Standard Simplex of Growing Dimension

It is not generally surprising that the case of dimensions tending to infinity is mathematically more tractable than the case of a finite number of dimensions. In the last century statistical physics began to use this approach to deal with interactions between large numbers of particles. We are trying to apply the same basic idea to our multidimensional system describing changes in gametotypic frequencies. Consider a variable space in our system, which is a set of n frequencies ($n = 2^m$), $p_1, \ldots, p_n$, which belong by definition to the standard simplex

$$\delta_n = \{p_i \geq 0, \sum_{i=1}^{n} p_i = 1\}$$

This set is a line segment when $n = 2$, a triangle when $n = 3$, and a tetrahedron when $n = 4$ (Figure 3.1). The possibility of drawing pictures on two-dimensional paper stops there. Central points of the simplex

$$\frac{1}{n}\mathbf{e} = \left(\frac{1}{n}, \frac{1}{n}, \ldots, \frac{1}{n}\right)$$

are marked on the pictures. They are $(\frac{1}{2}, \frac{1}{2})$, $(\frac{1}{3}, \frac{1}{3}, \frac{1}{3})$ and $(\frac{1}{4}, \frac{1}{4}, \frac{1}{4}, \frac{1}{4})$.

The first basic property of a high-dimensional simplex is the measure-concentration effect. It states that when $n \to \infty$, most of the measure of the simplex is concentrated near the central point $(1/n, \ldots, 1/n)$. To prove that, consider the projection $\delta_{(k,n)}(p_i, \ldots, p_k)$ of the uniform distribution on δ_n on the subsimplex δ_k of the first k components of the vector $\mathbf{p}$, $k < n$. The density function is

$$\delta(k, n)(p_i, \ldots, p_k) = (n-1) \cdots (n-k)(1 - p_1 - \cdots - p_k)^{n-k-1}$$

We can calculate all the moments of this distribution (Ginzburg and Braumann, 1980):

$$E[p_1^{l_1} \cdots p_k^{l_k}] = \frac{l_1! \cdots l_k!(n-1)!}{(l_1 + \cdots + l_k + n - 1)!}$$

($l_1, \ldots, l_k$ are nonnegative integers). In particular, for the first and

3.5 Linear and Quadratic Functions

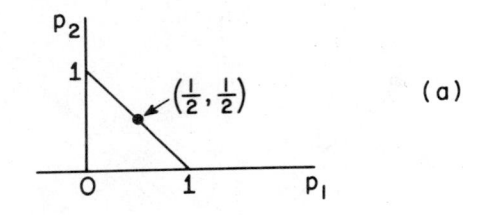

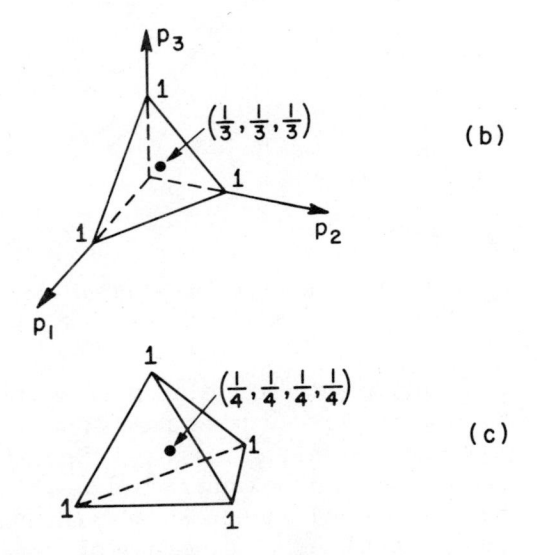

Figure 3.1 Standard simplices with their centers shown.
(a) $n = 2$. (b) $n = 3$. (c) $n = 4$.

second moments we have

$$E[p_i] = \frac{1}{n}$$

$$E\left[\left(p_i - \frac{1}{n}\right)^2\right] = \frac{n-1}{n^2(n+1)}$$

$$E\left[\left(p_i - \frac{1}{n}\right)\left(p_j - \frac{1}{n}\right)\right] = -\frac{1}{n^2(n+1)}, \quad i \neq j$$

Let us now calculate the expected value of the square of the distance between any point on the simplex and the center. This yields

$$E\left[\sum_{i=1}^{n}\left(p_i - \frac{1}{n}\right)^2\right] = \frac{n-1}{n(n+1)} \approx \frac{1}{n} \quad \text{as } n \to \infty$$

Chapter 3: Models of Natural Selection

$$\left(\frac{1}{n}, \frac{1}{n}, \ldots, \frac{1}{n}\right)$$

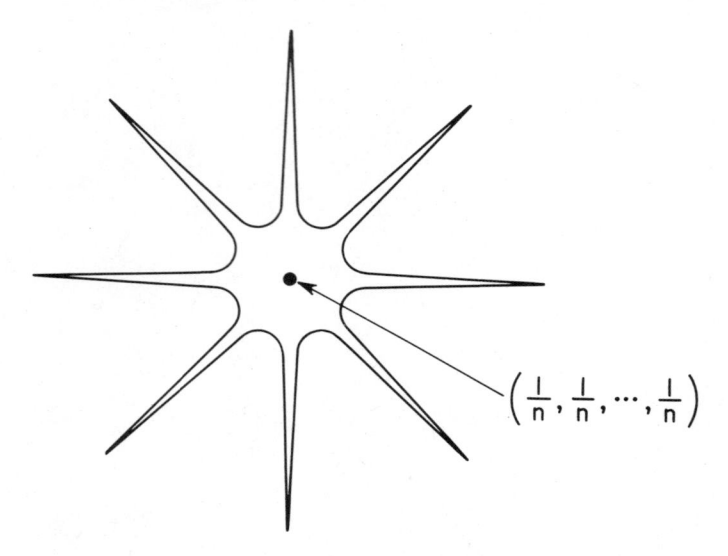

Figure 3.2   The two-dimensional "image" of an n-dimensional simplex when n is very large.

This is a very important relationship. It shows that even though the central point stays a finite distance away from any fixed-dimensional subsimplex when $n \to \infty$, the "majority" of points on the simplex δ_n are concentrated around the center when $n \to \infty$. In other words, the measure (n-dimensional volume) of a small neighborhood of the center almost equals the total measure of the simplex.

Now, let me disclose a secret. I have my own image of a high-dimensional simplex—which is, of course, wrong. One cannot draw such pictures in two dimensions. I would still like to share this image with you since it may help you to understand the idea (Figure 3.2). The picture demonstrates that most of the volume of this body is concentrated around the center, although some points stay at the fixed distance.

Let me explain this phenomenon in yet another way. If you consider a randomly chosen, high-dimensional frequency vector, it is very improbable that a few components will add up to almost unity and all the rest will be very small. A randomly chosen (uniformly on the simplex!) vector typically will be much closer to the central point $(1/n, \ldots, 1/n)$ than to the corners $(1, 0, \ldots, 0) \ldots$, $(0, \ldots, 0, 1)$ or to any fixed low-dimensional boundaries.

Consider now the linear functions $f_2, f_3, \ldots$, defined correspondingly on the simplices $\delta_2, \delta_3, \ldots$:

$$f_n(\mathbf{p}) = \sum_{i=1}^{n} \alpha_i p_i$$

3.5 Linear and Quadratic Functions

Keeping in mind our future applications to the genetic model, it will be sufficient to consider the case when all coefficients α_i are bounded. In this case, the mean

$$\mathbf{E} f_n(\mathbf{p}) = f_n\left(\frac{1}{n}\mathbf{e}\right) = \frac{1}{n}\sum_{i=1}^n \alpha_i$$

will also be bounded. Let us calculate the variance of our linear function over the simplex. We have

$$\left[f_n(\mathbf{p}) - f_n\left(\frac{1}{n}\mathbf{e}\right)\right]^2 = \sum_{i=1}^n \alpha_i^2 \left(p_i - \frac{1}{n}\right)^2 + \sum_{i \neq j} \alpha_i \alpha_j \left(p_i - \frac{1}{n}\right)\left(p_j - \frac{1}{n}\right)$$

Using the formula for the second-order moments, we obtain

$$\mathbf{E}\left[f_n(\mathbf{p}) - f_n\left(\frac{1}{n}\mathbf{e}\right)\right]^2 \sim \frac{\sigma_n^2}{n} \quad \text{as } n \to \infty$$

where

$$\sigma_n = \left[\frac{1}{n}\sum_{i=1}^n \left(\alpha_i - \frac{1}{n}\sum_{j=1}^n \alpha_j\right)^2\right]^{1/2}$$

is the standard deviation of the sequence α_i, which is also bounded since the α's are bounded.

We see, therefore, that although f_n covers the range

$$\min_{i=1,\ldots,n} \alpha_i \leq f_n(\mathbf{p}) \leq \max_{i=1,\ldots,n} \alpha_i$$

In most cases when n is large, the value of the function can be estimated by its value at the central point. We can repeat all the necessary calculations for the sequence of quadratic functions

$$F_n(\mathbf{p}) = \sum_{i,j}^n \beta_{ij} p_i p_j$$

with bounded coefficients. The only difference from the linear case is that we will need all the fourth-order moments. Omitting calculations, we present only the asymptotic result:

$$\mathbf{E}\left[F_n(\mathbf{p}) - F_n\left(\frac{1}{n}\mathbf{e}\right)\right]^2 \sim \frac{4\gamma_n^2}{n} \quad \text{as } n \to \infty$$

where

$$\gamma_n = \left[\frac{1}{n}\sum_{i=1}^n \left(\frac{1}{n}\sum_{j=1}^n \beta_{ij} - \frac{1}{n^2}\sum_{ij}^n \beta_{ij}\right)^2\right]^{1/2}$$

is the standard deviation of the row averages of the matrix $\|\beta_{ij}\|$ from their mean value.

The same statement is therefore valid for quadratic functions. The same method of proof, using higher-order moments, is applicable for any fixed-power polynomial, not just for linear and quadratic ones. All of these functions concentrate near their central values when $n \to \infty$. In other words, for most of the simplex δ_n, these functions will be close to constants. They can differ significantly from the constant only in the neighborhood of low-dimensional subsimplices, but these neighborhoods all together have a negligible measure when n is large enough.

It is clear that boundedness of the coefficients is too restrictive an assumption. The convergence of some series would be sufficient to obtain the same result. The uniformity of measure also is not a necessary assumption; we use the uniform measure because we are interested in that portion of the simplex where certain properties hold. The effect of concentration is a basic property of the geometry of the simplex rather than of a concrete function and measure. It is not our purpose here to formulate the most general theorem describing this important effect with minimal assumptions. Since genotypic fitnesses in our genetic model are naturally bounded and we are always dealing with fixed power polynomial functions of gametic frequencies, the results presented here are sufficient for our purposes and we will apply them to our model in the next section.

3.6 Relative Importance of Selection and Recombination

Consider the general form of a multiple-locus selection recombination system:

$$\dot{p}_i = p_i(W_i - \overline{W}) + \psi_i, \qquad i = 1, \ldots, n \qquad (3.14)$$

Here $n = 2^m$, where m is the number of loci and ψ_i are complicated functions involving terms of the linkage disequilibrium form from our two-locus model in (3.11):

$$\psi_i = \ldots W_{lk} r_l (p_k p_l - p_{k'l'}) \ldots \qquad (3.15)$$

We will be concerned with the analogy of Fisher's theorem for systems involving many loci. Let us calculate, therefore, the rate of change of the average fitness, $\overline{W}$, taking into account system (3.15). The calculations are completely analogous to what has been done in cases of one locus and two loci. We will obtain

$$\dot{\overline{W}}(\mathbf{p}) = 2 \sum_{i=1}^{n} p_i (W_i - \overline{W})^2 + \Phi(\mathbf{p})$$

where $\Phi(\mathbf{p})$ is the sum of a large number of terms, each of the form

$$\ldots (W_k + W_l - W_{k'} - W_{l'}) W_{kl} r_{kl} (p_k p_l - p_{k'l'}) \ldots$$

3.6 Relative Importance of Selection and Recombination

When the number of loci is large ($n \to \infty$), for most of the simplex we can approximate our functions of frequencies, which are polynomials, by their values at the center. What is important to notice is that

$$\Phi\left(\frac{1}{n}\mathbf{e}\right) = 0$$

All linkage disequilibrium terms vanish at the center of the simplex. The center is, of course, the intersection of all linkage equilibrium surfaces for all possible pairs of loci. The accuracy of approximating $\Phi(p)$ by zero grows with the number of loci as was explained in the previous section. At the same time, the first term in the expression of $\dot{W}$ induced by selection has some positive value at the center of the simplex, so that

$$\dot{W}\left(\frac{1}{n}\mathbf{e}\right) = \frac{2}{n}\sum_{i=1}^{n}\left(\frac{1}{n}\sum_{j=1}^{n}W_{ij} - \frac{1}{n^2}\sum_{i,j=1}^{n}W_{ij}\right)^2 > 0$$

The variance,

$$\mathbf{E}\left[\left(\dot{W}(\mathbf{p}) - \dot{W}\left(\frac{1}{n}\mathbf{e}\right)\right)^2\right] = o\left(\frac{1}{n}\right) \to 0 \quad \text{as } n \to \infty$$

so that the larger the number of loci, the higher is the proportion of points, p, of the simplex for which $\dot{W} > 0$; however, there are always some points at which this inequality is not true.

In other words, by choosing the vector of gametic frequencies at random, we can state that

$$\text{prob}\{\dot{W}(\mathbf{p}) > 0\} \to 1 \quad \text{as } n \to \infty$$

In most cases the average fitness will grow under an arbitrary selection-recombination mechanism. In fact, since the contribution of recombination is going to be small, we can state it another way. The relative contribution of recombination to the change in average fitness will be small compared to the contribution of selection. To clarify the meaning of this statement mathematically, let us introduce notations for the rate of change of average fitness due to selection, $\dot{W}_s$, and due to recombination, $\dot{W}_R$. We have

$$\dot{W}_s = \sum_{i=1}^{n} p_i(W_i - \dot{W})^2$$

$$\dot{W}_R = \Phi(\mathbf{p})$$

$$\dot{W} = \dot{W}_s + \dot{W}_R$$

Chapter 3: Models of Natural Selection

For every $\varepsilon > 0$,

$$\text{prob}\left\{\left|\frac{\dot{W}_R}{\dot{W}_s}\right| < \varepsilon\right\} \to 1 \quad \text{as } n \to \infty \tag{3.16}$$

In intuitive terms this means that for a large number of loci, recombination terms usually balance each other in terms of generating fitness imbalance, while selection is still doing its work as if there were no recombination.

The rate with which the proportion of the simplex with

$$\left|\frac{\dot{W}_R}{\dot{W}_s}\right| < \varepsilon$$

converges to 1 is an important question. This rate will give us an idea of how many loci are actually needed to predict with sufficient accuracy the prevalence of selection over recombination. To obtain this estimate, let us introduce two parameters: the overall selection intensity, s, and the overall effective recombination intensity, r_e. There are a number of ways we can define these macroparameters, which are designed to characterize the degree to which the elements of the fitness matrix differ and the typical chance of recombination between two adjacent loci. We will define

$$s = \frac{1}{n}\sum_{i=1}^{n}\left|\frac{1}{n}\sum_{j=1}^{n}W_{ij} - \frac{1}{n^2}\sum_{i,j}W_{ij}\right|$$

and

$$r_e = 1 - (1 - r^*)^{1/(m-1)}$$

where r^* is the overall probability of some recombination. If one considers (we do not) the special case of no interference with the same recombination fraction (or crossover probability), $\bar{r}$, between any two neighboring loci, then $\bar{r}$ and r_e coincide. We can, therefore, interpret r_e as a kind of "average" recombination fraction between all pairs of neighboring loci.

With these two parameters, we can now give a crude estimate of the rate of convergence (Ginzburg and Braumann, 1980):

$$\text{prob}\left\{\left|\frac{\dot{W}_R}{\dot{W}_s}\right| < \varepsilon\right\} = 1 - 2\Phi\left(-\varepsilon\frac{s}{r_e}C(n)\right) \to 1 \quad \text{as } n \to \infty$$

with

$$C(n) = \frac{(n+5)^4}{4n^3(n-m)(m-2)}(n+5)^{1/2} \to \infty \quad \text{as } n \to \infty$$

Here

$$\Phi(x) = \frac{1}{\sqrt{2\pi}}\int_{-\infty}^{x}e^{-y^2/2}\,dy$$

3.6 Relative Importance of Selection and Recombination

which is the distribution function of a standard normal variable. By inverting, we may determine crude confidence intervals $(-\varepsilon, \varepsilon)$ for $|\dot{W}_R/\dot{W}_S|$. For example, the 95% confidence interval is given by

$$\varepsilon = 1.96 \frac{r_e}{s} \frac{1}{C(n)}$$

We see that the larger the number of loci m and the larger the ratio

$$\theta = \frac{s}{r_e}$$

between the "strength" of selection and recombination, the less important the effect of recombination on the rate of change of the average fitness. The two limiting cases are trivial. If there is no recombination, Fisher's theorem holds identically for all p's, since we are dealing with essentially one-locus systems. If there is no selection (all W_{ij}'s are equal to each other), there is no change in $\bar{W}$ at all ($\dot{W} \equiv 0$). As soon as we have some selection and recombination, their relative strengths, θ, plus the number of loci, m, define the proportion of the simplex for which the theorem holds.

To illustrate, let us present some numerical values (Tables 3.1 and 3.2), assuming $m = 15$ loci, r_e is within the range 0.1% to 1.0%, and s is within the range 5% to 15%. The range of r_e corresponds to closely linked loci only on the average, and does not rule out the possibility that some of them may be loosely linked. For those who like to think in terms of nonepistatic selection schemes, the suggested range of s corresponds to a 1% to 3% average absolute selective differential per locus; irrespective of any specific fitness scheme, it seems to correspond to small to moderate selection intensities. We can only guess the typical genotypic selection intensities in natural populations, but it appears obvious that they should be higher in a multilocus model context than in single-locus models.

TABLE 3.1 Estimates of prob $\{|\dot{W}_R/\dot{W}_S| < 5\%\}$ for 15 loci and several values of r_e (effective recombination fraction between two neighboring loci) and s (average selective differential).

	\multicolumn{4}{c}{s}			
r_e	5%	7.5%	10%	15%
0.1%	100.00%	100.00%	100.00%	100.00%
0.5%	91.86%	99.10%	99.95%	100.00%
1.0%	61.64%	80.88%	91.86%	99.10%

TABLE 3.2 Estimates of ε for the 95% confidence interval $(-\varepsilon, \varepsilon)$ of $|\dot{W}_R/\dot{W}_S|$ for 15 loci and several values of r_e and s.

		s		
r_e	5%	7.5%	10%	15%
0.1%	1.12%	0.75%	0.56%	0.37%
0.5%	5.62%	3.75%	2.81%	1.87%
1.0%	11.25%	7.50%	5.62%	3.75%

Certainly, any decrease in recombination or increase in selection intensity will only strengthen the effect. On the contrary, if selection is very weak, recombination will likely become an important evolutionary force. This effect is illustrated in Figure 3.3. If selection intensity is small compared to recombination (see the curves $\theta = s/r_e = 1$ and $\theta = 5$, for example) and if the number of loci is small, then the portion of the simplex (probability) for which the recombination effect is negligible (less than 5%) compared to the effect of selection is small. Only for a number of loci of 20 to 25 does that portion of the simplex approach 100%. On the other hand, if the selection intensity is somewhat higher than the recombination rate

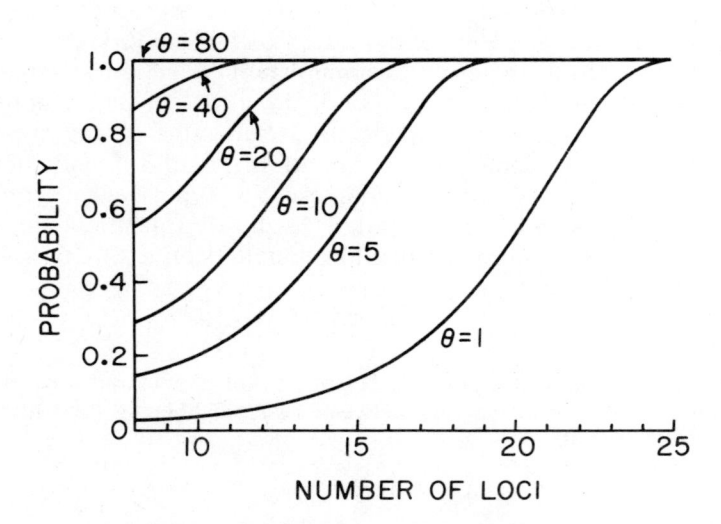

Figure 3.3 Probability $\{|\dot{W}_R/\dot{W}_S| < 5\%\}$ (that the effect of recombination on the change in the average fitness is less than 5% of the effect of selection) as a function of the number m of loci considered for several ratios $\theta = s/r_e$ (s = selection intensity and r_e = effective recombination fraction).

(see curves $\theta = 40$ and $\theta = 80$), even with very few loci, then the effect of recombination compared to that of selection is negligible (less than 5%) in almost 100% of the simplex. Note that nowhere in this book do we assume anything explicit about fitness values.

3.7 Evolutionary Interpretations

Returning to our original idea of gaining simplicity from the fact that the number of loci under selection is high, we have partly reached our goal. Many loci are in a sense similar to one locus, from the point of view of the change in average fitness, or the acceleration in population size. In most cases the system behaves as if it were in complete linkage equilibrium; although this last statement needs to be qualified.

First, equilibrium points of multilocus systems are just those points where our mean estimates do not work. At these points selection and recombination balance each other so that both forces are of the same order. Our result means that the areas (including all the neighborhoods of equilibria) where selection balances recombination constitute a negligible proportion of the simplex. Being of small measure, these "balance zones" are just the places where evolutionary trajectories stop. We can expect, therefore, that the statement of Fisher's theorem most probably will be wrong near the end of any evolutionary trajectory. From what we know about the measure-concentration effect, we may suggest for any reasonable fitness structure that these zones will be attached to very low-dimensional subsimplices. This means that we should expect very few gametotypes at equilibria or, in other words, that a lot of loci should be essentially monomorphic.

Second, for all the interpretations above or below, counterexamples using a particular fitness scheme can easily be constructed. A principle suggested by Turner (1971), that "the mathematical interest of a system of viabilities is inversely proportional to its biological probability" seems to apply here. I will therefore reject such counterexamples on "Turner's principle." The example developed by Franklin and Lewontin (1970) and analyzed by Karlin (1978), where each locus is over-dominant and the fitnesses are multiplicative among loci, is the counterexample for the last statement. Two complementary gametotypes coexist in this case at a stable equilibrium so that all loci are polymorphic. Since I do not believe, a priori, in any advantage of being a heterozygote per se (see discussion in Section 4.3 of the next chapter), the fitness set used in this last example seems atypical.

In a slowly changing environment, there can be an even more pronounced effect of the proposed modification of Fisher's theorem for multiple loci. The movement of the equilibrium points (and balance zones attached to them) will increase the chances for a population to stay in the zone of "typical" behavior. Mutations in a multilocus system will also act as a factor that strengthens this effect. A mutation appearing in a monomorphic locus changes the number of gametotypes (dimension of our dynamic system) from n to $2n$. In the single-locus case, the dimension changes from n to $n+1$. Aside from the dimension effect, mutations acting epistatically with other loci can change the location of the equilibrium points and the surrounding balance zones, and thus keep the population again in the zone of typical behavior.

Wright's principle, as an exact fitness maximization at an equilibrium, is certainly not valid in a multilocus context. However, since for "most of the simplex" selection is prevalent over recombination, the equilibria typically are expected to be close to Wright's peaks. How far in the frequency space (or in the direction of mean fitness difference) these equilibria will be from the peak depends on the details of fitness and recombination structure and cannot be answered in a general context. The counterexample of the equilibrium point of a two-locus system right in the saddle point of the mean fitness surface is well known (Karlin, 1978).

Quantitative genetics dealing with traits controlled by a large number of loci gives some interesting evidence that supports our result. Experiments in artificial selection (Falconer, 1981) show quite monotonic change in the mean value of a trait followed by irregular oscillations near a plateau. This behavior is consistent with our results. The modified Fisher's theorem may work initially, until the population reaches the balance zone, where recombination is responsible for the fluctuations around the plateau. A multiplicity of possible equilibria and surrounding balance zones explains the different outcomes of selection in different cases. The initial response to selection is more typical than the asymptotic behavior, which is in complete agreement with our analysis. The asymmetry of response between upward and downward selection is explainable by epistatic interactions. Fitness matrices for upward and downward selection will be very different with epistasis, and thus a symmetry of response should be a rare exception. The above interpretation should be taken cautiously, since frequency dependence may be involved, and this has not been covered by our model.

This last interpretational remark I would like to make relates to the validity of one-locus selection models. Of course, with epistatic interactions, the marginal fitnesses of one-locus genotypes depend on gene frequencies at other loci, and the consideration of evolution on a locus by locus basis is not exactly correct. Still, with a large number of epistatically interacting loci, the one-locus fitnesses will be functions of a great many such frequencies and our concentration idea may work again. One would need some kind of assumption on the statistical equivalency of loci in order to employ the averaging. If two loci make all the difference in fitness and the others add only slight modifications, then no averaging idea will work. With a lot of reasonably equally influential loci, however, a locus-by-locus consideration may be applicable in most cases. The old idea of a locus on a randomized genetic background may not be as bad as it first seems. This problem clearly needs much more careful consideration than we can present now; however, keeping this possibility in mind makes me feel more comfortable when I go back to one-locus theory in the next chapter.

3.8 Problems and Discussion

1. In the first section of this chapter I mentioned that the symmetry of the fitness matrix is due to the assumption that there is only zygotic selection. Gametic selection leads to a fitness matrix, which is a product of the diagonal matrix of gametic fitnesses and a symmetric matrix of zygotic fitnesses.

An interesting result for this system was obtained in Gimelfarb, et al. (1974). The existence of polymorphism in such a system is defined by the full nonsymmetric matrix, but as long as an equilibrium exists, its stability is fully defined by the symmetric part alone; that is, by the zygotic fitnesses. This follows from the fact that the eigenvalues of a symmetric matrix do not change signs when the matrix is multiplied by a positive diagonal.

2. The following is a group selection argument which may suggest why genes manifested in a zygote are often not the same ones which are expressed during the gametic life stage. The property of $\dot{W}$ being positive is an advantageous property, since it shows adequate response of populations to selection. For purely zygotic selection, Fisher's theorem is correct. It is also trivially correct for purely gametic selection. In this case we deal basically with haploid systems where the "best survives." Fisher's theorem is not correct when we have both zygotic and gametic selection operating on the same locus. Separate phenotypic expressions of the loci "responsible" for the gametic and zygotic stages of the life cycle will benefit the population in the sense that it will always respond adequately ($\dot{W} > 0$) to environmental changes.

Chapter 3: Models of Natural Selection

3. A constant degree of inbreeding can be formulated as a modification of the fitness matrix. The new matrix, again, will not be symmetric. It would be interesting to see how simple (one-parametric) inbreeding, introduced to a one-locus model, changes the general conclusions about the selective process.

4. Even in its ideal form (one locus, constant zygotic selection), Wright's principle presents a number of interesting problems. The relative size of the attraction zones for different fitness peaks is not a clear issue. In a recent paper (Karlin and Feldman, 1981), it has been shown that the size of the attraction zone does not correlate with the height of the peak but rather with some measure of the heterozygosity at equilibrium. This result becomes intuitively clear in light of the measure of concentration effect considered in this chapter. Actually, the most diverse equilibrium is the one closest to the center of the simplex, but that is where most of the simplex is. With random initial conditions, most evolutionary trajectories will most often end at the equilibrium where one special trajectory ends. This one originates at the center $(1/n, \ldots, 1/n)$. Indeed, for dimensions 2 through 8, about two-thirds of all trajectories follow this rule in spite of very many other equilibria, which combined have attracted the other one-third of the trajectories. This work was done with randomly and independently generated fitnesses. My guess is that the correlation between heterozygote and homozygote fitnesses, which is a biologically more-reasonable assumption, will increase the proportion of the largest attraction zone from two-thirds towards one. It may turn out that in a more realistic setup the vast majority of initial conditions are evolutionarily attracted to a single peak, although not necessarily to the highest one. I think additional research in this area may significantly change a common intuition; the response to selection may be more "unique" than it is thought to be at present.

5. Simulations are often done with large numbers of alleles. Their authors, of course, mean a large number of loci but are unable to write down equations with an astronomical number of recombination forms. Even if we think of a very tight linkage ($r \approx 0$), our "one-locus" fitness matrix has additional symmetries that arise from the fact that it is generated by the underlying multiple-locus model. My simulations for a two-locus, two-allele model, where $W_{14} = W_{23}$ is an additional constraint, gave, for instance, much higher chances of polymorphism than the four-allele model without constraints (Lewontin, Ginzburg, and Tuljapurkar, 1978).

6. Karlin (1979) has suggested a number of very interesting principles that describe equilibria in multilocus, selection-recombination

systems. (By principles, he means plausible statements that are proved to be correct in a number of special cases but which have not been proved in general.) One of the principles suggests that a selectively maintained polymorphic equilibrium cannot be destroyed by any degree of recombination. I recommend studying Karlin's work in this area. It is the major contribution to existing theory and a stimulus for new developments.

4 Polymorphism and Natural Selection

The more we learn about the genetic structure of natural populations, the more variation we discover. Nobody would have thought 20 years ago that it would be possible to detect dozens of alleles in a locus while looking at a sample of a few hundred genes. But with widespread use of electrophoretic techniques, this is no longer surprising. Modifications of electrophoresis designed to increase resolution generally identify even more alleles in the same sample. There is hope that the tendency to find more and more allelic variants of the same loci will level off. In any case, theoreticians are already faced with a problem in understanding the maintenance of such a high number of allelomorphs in virtually all species studied, ranging from plants to man.

Two competing theories—the neutralist and the selectionist—have attempted to resolve this problem. The truth probably lies somewhere between. In fact, nobody likes to be called either a neutralist or a selectionist any more. The discussion is now moving on to the more difficult problems of gauging relative importance. The purpose of this chapter is to give you a feeling for the role of selection as a mechanism influencing allelic variation.

4.1 The Triangle Inequalities

Unfortunately, the perception of most biologists about the ways in which natural selection operates at the level of one locus is still based on the classical case of two alleles. In this restricted case, heterozygote superiority in fitness is both necessary and sufficient for the maintenance of two alleles in a population. Although it was noticed many years ago that beginning with the three-allelic case, there is no direct relationship between full polymorphism and heterosis, this information was viewed by many biologists as an esoteric mathematical exercise. In most books on population genetics, the chapter on selection for multiple alleles is unappealing. It usually shows how to generalize from two to n alleles using the notation of matrix algebra and stresses similarities rather than distinctions.

Is there a real qualitative difference between the cases of two and many alleles? First of all, are the cases of two and three alleles much different? We will show in this section that they are.

A widespread heuristic principle says that what is true for $n = 3$ is true for any $n > 3$. Strangely, it often works—not because it is correct, but because we often notice in n dimensions only those features we can see in three. This principle therefore describes the limitations of the mind rather than those of the real world. In the case under discussion, however, even this intuitive observation is wrong. Since allelic frequencies are normalized so that $p_1 + p_2 + \cdots + p_n = 1$, we always consider one dimension less than the number of alleles. The transition from the case of two to that of three alleles therefore corresponds to a change from one to two dimensions.

Let us start with a simple example, with the following fitness matrix in the case of three alleles.

$$\begin{array}{c} \\ A_1 \\ A_2 \\ A_3 \end{array} \begin{pmatrix} A_1 & A_2 & A_3 \\ 1 & 1+s & 1+s \\ 1+s & 1 & 1+s \\ 1+s & 1+s & 1 \end{pmatrix} \quad s > 0 \quad (4.1)$$

From the symmetry it is clear that the point $p_1{}^* = p_2{}^* = p_3{}^* = \tfrac{1}{3}$, at the center of the simplex, is an equilibrium point. At this point all the marginal fitnesses are equal, which is the only property required for a point to be an equilibrium. We know that there can be only one fully polymorphic equilibrium point (Section 3.1), so that this is a unique polymorphism. It is also globally stable, which is easy to establish using the criterion from Section 3.2. There are six other unstable equilibria, at the three points of monomorphism and on each two-allele boundary, with the third allele absent (Figure 4.1).

Chapter 4: Polymorphism and Natural Selection

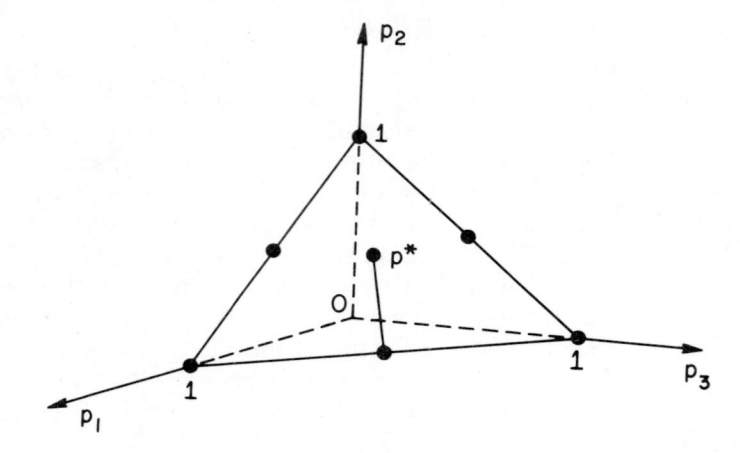

Figure 4.1 Circles mark unstable equilibria. The solid point corresponds to the central globally stable equilibrium. The straight line shows the path of this equilibrium as W_{13}, the fitness of one of the heterozygotes, increases.

This is a clear case of full polymorphism with all heterozygotes superior in fitness.

Let us try now to increase the fitness of one of the heterozygotes, such as $A_1 A_3$. What will happen to the position of our central polymorphism as we increase W_{13}? At first the point **p*** will move along a line in the direction of the two-allele boundary $p_1 + p_3 = 1$, $p_2 = 0$. In other words, the heterozygote $A_1 A_3$ will prevail in competition with the two heterozygotes of lower fitness, increasing the frequencies of the alleles constituting the fittest heterozygote (see Figure 4.1). The immediate question is whether at some point, when fitness W_{13} is high enough, the central equilibrium will coalesce with the two-allelic boundary and full polymorphism will disappear. This is indeed what happens. For this example, it is not difficult to calculate the threshold value of W_{13} such that stable coexistence of three alleles will be replaced by stable coexistence of only two alleles, A_1 and A_3; A_2 will be excluded.

Instead of just going through this individual calculation, let us ask a more general question. In an arbitrary 3×3 fitness matrix, what are the restrictions on fitnesses that permit all three alleles to coexist stably? Although the exact result can easily be deduced from general criteria (it is only a two-dimensional problem!), we will present a partial, but easily interpretable, answer. For a 3×3 fitness matrix to allow the stable coexistence of all three alleles, it is necessary that heterozygote fitnesses satisfy the following inequalities:

$$W_{12} < W_{13} + W_{23}$$
$$W_{13} < W_{12} + W_{23} \quad (4.2)$$
$$W_{23} < W_{12} + W_{13}$$

Any one of the heterozygote fitnesses should not exceed the sum of the two others (as though they were sides of the same triangle). The analogy suggests the name *triangle inequalities*.

The Proof

Since we need a necessary condition, let us assume that there is a globally stable equilibrium point $\mathbf{p}^* > 0$. From the previous chapter, we know this implies that the average fitness $W(\mathbf{p})$ is a convex function, with its maximum at the point $\mathbf{p}^*$. Both of these properties will be used in the proof.

First, from the conservation of fitness identity (Section 3.2), we have

$$p_1{}^* W_1(\mathbf{p}) + p_2{}^* W_2(\mathbf{p}) + p_3{}^* W_3(\mathbf{p}) = W^* \quad (4.3)$$

where W_1, W_2, and W_3 are the marginal allelic fitnesses. We will prove the second of the triangle inequalities in (4.2). The validity of the other two inequalities will follow from symmetry.

Consider the two-allelic boundary, given by the equations:

$$p_1 + p_3 = 1, \qquad p_2 = 0$$

Since $W(\mathbf{p})$ is a convex quadratic function, it has a maximum point along this line (the point does not necessarily lie within the simplex; either p_1 or p_2 could be negative). Let us denote this point by

$$\mathbf{p}^+ = (p_1{}^+, 0, p_3{}^+)$$

At that point $W_1(\mathbf{p}^+) = W_3(\mathbf{p}^+) = W(\mathbf{p}^+)$. Substituting $\mathbf{p}^+$ into equation (4.3) we obtain

$$p_2{}^* W_2(\mathbf{p}^+) = W^* - (p_1{}^* + p_3{}^*) W(\mathbf{p}^+) \quad (4.4)$$

Subtracting $p_2{}^* W(\mathbf{p}^+)$ from both sides of the equation, we have

$$p_2{}^* (W_2(\mathbf{p}^+) - W(\mathbf{p}^+)) = W^* - W(\mathbf{p}^+)$$

The expression on the right is positive, since W^* is the maximal value of the quadratic forms W, constrained by the normalizing equation $p_1 + p_2 + p_3 = 1$. Therefore

$$W_2(\mathbf{p}^+) > W(\mathbf{p}^+)$$

We can evaluate these expressions using the well-known results of

Chapter 4: Polymorphism and Natural Selection

the two-allelic theory (Chapter 3). We substitute

$$p_1^+ = \frac{W_{13} - W_{33}}{2W_{13} - W_{11} - W_{33}}, \qquad p_3^+ = 1 - p_1^+$$

on both sides of the inequality. This yields

$$W_{12}(W_{13} - W_{33}) + W_{23}(W_{13} - W_{11}) > W_{13}^2 - W_{11}W_{33}$$

Solving this quadratic inequality, we obtain

$$W_{13} < \frac{W_{12} + W_{23}}{2} + \sqrt{\left(\frac{W_{12} + W_{23}}{2}\right)^2 - Z} \qquad (4.5)$$

where

$$Z = W_{12}W_{33} + W_{13}W_{22} - W_{11}W_{33}$$

We already know from the previous section that

$$W_{ij} < \frac{W_{ii} + W_{jj}}{2}, \qquad i,j = 1, 2, 3$$

Therefore

$$Z > W_{22}\left(\frac{W_{11} + W_{33}}{2}\right)$$

and so is necessarily positive. As a result we can obtain, from (4.5),

$$W_{13} < W_{12} + W_{23}$$

Note that up to (4.5) we had an exact result. We have replaced it by the weaker, but more tractable, inequality.

The set of triangle inequalities limits the variability of heterozygote fitnesses, not letting any one be much larger than another. The largest of heterozygote fitnesses cannot, for instance, be twice as large as the next-largest one. The same sort of proof works in the more general case of n alleles (Lewontin, Ginzburg, and Tuljapurkar, 1978). The convexity of the average fitness $W(\mathbf{p})$ and its maximization at the equilibrium point allows us to formulate the following generalization: For a full stable polymorphism to exist in the case of n alleles, it is necessary that for any genotype $A_i A_j (i \neq j)$ there exist an allele $A_k (k \neq i, j)$ such that

$$W_{ij} < W_{ik} + W_{kj}, \qquad i, j = 1, \ldots, n$$

This too is a statement that limits the variability of heterozygote fitnesses as a necessary condition for polymorphism. What is happening in the case of multiple alleles is analogous in a sense to competition, not among alleles, but among subsets of alleles. The magnitude of the variation for heterozygote fitnesses is important

4.2 Why Should Heterozygotes Often Be Superior in Fitness?

because if the variation is too high, one of the subsets will tend to pull the equilibrium away from full polymorphism. Only if all heterozygote fitnesses are relatively close to each other can we expect this competition to result in the stable coexistence of a large number of alleles.

Remember that triangle inequalities are a necessary—but not sufficient—condition for polymorphism. How far from sufficient they are is not clear. The exact necessary and sufficient conditions are well known (Chapter 3) but are not very useful, since they are expressed in terms of determinants of the fitness matrix, which are high-power polynomials in W_{ij}. The only application for these easily obtained but not so easily interpreted conditions is to check whether they are satisfied for a particular set of fitness values. Unfortunately, we rarely have reliable values for fitnesses that might permit us to employ these exact formulas. We are forced, therefore, to look for practical necessary or sufficient conditions, such as the triangle inequalities.

4.2 Why Should Heterozygotes Often Be Superior in Fitness?

We will continue in the same way to obtain other useful relationships among fitnesses as necessary conditions of polymorphism. First, we will show that the arithmetic average of the heterozygote fitnesses should exceed the arithmetic average of homozygote fitnesses:

$$\frac{1}{n(n-1)} \sum_{i \neq j}^{n} W_{ij} > \frac{1}{n} \sum_{i=1}^{n} W_{ii}$$

The Proof

We know from Section 2.2 that convexity of the average fitness as a function of allelic frequencies implies

$$W_{ij} > \frac{W_{ii} + W_{jj}}{2}, \qquad i, j = 1, \ldots, n$$

If we sum up all such inequalities for all i and j, we have

$$\sum_{ij}^{n} W_{ij} > n \sum_{i=1}^{n} W_{ii}$$

This is equivalent to

$$\sum_{i \neq j}^{n} W_{ij} + \sum_{i=1}^{n} W_{ii} > n \sum_{i=1}^{n} W_{ii}$$

$$\sum_{i \neq j}^{n} W_{ij} > (n-1) \sum_{i=1}^{n} W_{ii}$$

Chapter 4: Polymorphism and Natural Selection

Dividing both sides by $n(n-1)$, we obtain the desired result:

$$\frac{1}{n(n-1)} \sum_{i \neq j}^{n} W_{ij} > \frac{1}{n} \sum_{i=1}^{n} W_{ii}$$

To illustrate the necessary but not sufficient character of this result, we borrow two examples from the paper by Lewontin, Ginzburg, and Tuljapurkar (1978).

The first is an example in which all heterozygotes are superior to all homozygotes with no stable three-allelic polymorphism.

$$\begin{array}{c} & A_1 & A_2 & A_3 \\ A_1 & \begin{pmatrix} 0.6563 & 0.7462 & 0.8861 \\ A_2 & 0.7462 & 0.2817 & 0.7654 \\ A_3 & 0.8861 & 0.7654 & 0.6121 \end{pmatrix} \end{array}$$

In the second example, one of the heterozygotes is inferior to one of the corresponding homozygotes. There exists a full stable polymorphism.

$$\begin{array}{c} & A_1 & A_2 & A_3 \\ A_1 & \begin{pmatrix} 0.2358 & 0.8457 & 0.7482 \\ A_2 & 0.8457 & 0.1837 & 0.3927 \\ A_3 & 0.7482 & 0.3927 & 0.3954 \end{pmatrix} \end{array}$$

$$p_1^* = 0.4297, \quad p_2^* = 0.1938, \quad p_3^* = 0.3764$$

These illustrate the extent to which two-allele intuition fails to work in the case of three alleles. Our problem, therefore, is to create a new image of what we can and cannot expect in the case of multiple alleles.

Before we attempt that, let us formulate another inequality relevant to the problem of average heterozygote superiority. Suppose we sample genotypes from a population where different alleles are represented in different frequencies. We define the sampled average heterozygote fitness as

$$\overline{W}_{\text{het}}(\mathbf{p}) = \frac{\sum_{i \neq j}^{n} W_{ij} p_i p_j}{\sum_{i \neq j}^{n} p_i p_j}$$

and the sampled average homozygote fitness as

$$\overline{W}_{\text{hom}}(\mathbf{p}) = \frac{\sum_{i=1}^{n} W_{ii} p_i^2}{\sum_{i=1}^{n} p_i^2}$$

4.2 Why Should Heterozygotes Often Be Superior in Fitness?

We can show that at the equilibrium frequency, $\mathbf{p}^*$, the following relationship holds:

$$\overline{W}_{\text{het}}(\mathbf{p}^*) > \overline{W}_{\text{hom}}(\mathbf{p}^*)$$

The Proof

Since $W(\mathbf{p})$ is maximized at the equilibrium point,

$$\overline{W}(\mathbf{p}) < \overline{W}(\mathbf{p}^*), \qquad \mathbf{p} \neq \mathbf{p}^*$$

Substituting points of monomorphism, we obtain

$$\overline{W}_{ii} < \overline{W}(\mathbf{p}^*), \qquad i = 1, \ldots, n$$

Averaging all these inequalities for all the homozygotes, we have

$$\overline{W}_{\text{hom}}(\mathbf{p}) < \overline{W}(\mathbf{p}^*)$$

Now,

$$\overline{W}(\mathbf{p}^*) = \overline{W}_{\text{hom}}(\mathbf{p}^*) \sum_{i=1}^{n} (p_i^*)^2 + \overline{W}_{\text{het}}(\mathbf{p}^*) \sum_{i \neq j}^{n} p_i^* p_j^*$$

Therefore, we have

$$\overline{W}_{\text{hom}}(\mathbf{p}^*) < W(\mathbf{p}^*) < \overline{W}_{\text{het}}(\mathbf{p}^*)$$

and the desired inequality is proved.

We now assume that the populations we observe in nature have already gone through some selection process. If selective forces are responsible for the maintenance of polymorphism, we should see that heterozygotes on the average are superior in fitness to homozygotes. This would be the property of the subset of alleles chosen by natural selection from a larger set of possible alleles.

Summarizing, we might say that the usual explanation—based on two-allelic intuition—that polymorphism is a consequence of heterozygote superiority is basically wrong. Heterozygote superiority, either individually or on an average, is not sufficient for polymorphism (except in the case of two alleles). What is correct is that heterozygote superiority and polymorphism are a *joint consequence* of natural selection (Ginzburg, 1979).

A well-established experimental phenomenon is the overall average fitness depression as a result of inbreeding. This phenomenon could serve as a macroscopic confirmation of our result. With inbreeding, we have an increased percentage of homozygotes that should be less fit on the average. The problem with this kind of evidence, of course, is that inbreeding affects a whole genome rather than just one locus, and more theoretical work is required to bring

Chapter 4: Polymorphism and Natural Selection

about a complete understanding (see Section 4.6, Problems and Discussion).

Consider now a system of n independently evolving loci. The necessary and sufficient condition of the independent evolution is that fitnesses are multiplicative between loci. We will assume, as in the one-locus case, that our population is at evolutionary equilibrium. We also assume a sufficient amount of recombination, so that the equilibrium fitness is the product of one-locus fitnesses (Ewens, 1979). Consider a set of n polymorphic loci. Let us arrange the set of all n-locus genotypes in a system of subsets in the following manner. The zero set will include all the single heterozygotes (monomorphic in any set of $n-1$ loci out of n), the second set will include all the double heterozygotes (monomorphic in any set of $n-2$ loci out of n), and so on. The last, nth set will include all the n-locus heterozygotes.

Let us show that the average fitness calculated in every set should make a growing sequence. The average homozygote fitness is

$$\prod_{i=1}^{n} \overline{W}_{\text{hom}}^{(i)}$$

where $\overline{W}_{\text{hom}}^{(i)}$ is the average homozygote fitness in the ith locus $(i = 1, \ldots, n)$. The average single heterozygote fitness is

$$\frac{1}{n}\left(\overline{W}_{\text{het}}^{(1)} \prod_{i=2}^{n} \overline{W}_{\text{hom}}^{(i)} + \cdots + \overline{W}_{\text{het}}^{(n)} \prod_{i=1}^{n-1} \overline{W}_{\text{hom}}^{(i)}\right) \quad \textbf{(4.6)}$$

Every term in the sum is greater than the average homozygote fitness since we have an average heterozygote superiority at every locus. Calculations are similar for any number of loci. For double heterozygotes, for instance, we will have C_n^2 terms involved in averaging. They can be grouped into n terms, where every group will exceed a corresponding term in (4.6). A similar proof for the weighted fitnesses can also be obtained (Turelli and Ginzburg, 1982).

It should be stressed again that this statement does not relate to individual fitnesses, so that a particular double heterozygote can be less fit than a particular single heterozygote, for instance. The statement is correct only on the average; thus we can say that at an evolutionary stable state a "typical" double heterozygote has a greater fitness than a "typical" single heterozygote.

4.3 Allowable Variability in Heterozygote Fitness

Although average or even total heterosis is insufficient to provide stable polymorphism in a case of multiple alleles, some fitness

4.3 Allowable Variability in Heterozygote Fitness

assignments do provide such stability. It will certainly happen in the case of a fitness matrix with all heterozygote fitnesses equal to 1 and all homozygote fitnesses equal to $1-s$, where s is the average heterozygote superiority $(0<s<1)$. Clearly, with n alleles, an equilibrium must exist at $p_i^* = 1/n$ by symmetry, and this equilibrium is stable according to the criteria of Section 3.1. Starting with this degenerate case, we can explore fitness matrices around it by allowing some variation in fitnesses among heterozygotes and among homozygotes. If the variation is not too great, the fitness matrices so produced should have stable equilibria. The problem is how much variability in fitnesses there can be before the coexistence of all the alleles is no longer preserved.

The answer to this question was given in Lewontin, Ginzburg, and Tuljapurkar (1978) and is summarized here and in the following section. The fitnesses were chosen in the form

$$W_{ij} = 1 + \delta_{ij}, \quad i \neq j$$
$$W_{ii} = 1 - s + \varepsilon_i \tag{4.7}$$

where δ_{ij} and ε_i are independent random variables with means of zero and standard deviations of σ_δ and σ_ε, respectively. The question then was what values of s, σ_δ, and σ_ε would make a fully stable polymorphism likely.

In answering this question, we first chose the standard deviations σ_δ and σ_ε to be equal ($\sigma_\delta = \sigma_\varepsilon = \sigma$) and later examined the effect of differences between them. Based on the necessary conditions in the last two sections, we made the following preliminary guesses. First, from the simple observation that multiplication of all fitnesses by a constant does not change either locations or stability of equilibria, the chances of stable polymorphism should depend only on the ratio σ/s. Second, the triangle inequalities should limit the variability of heterozygote fitnesses. Third, the chances of polymorphism should decrease as the number of alleles grows, since in a higher-dimensions matrix there is increased opportunity for competition among heterozygotes to reduce the polymorphism by violating, for instance, one of the triangle inequalities.

A computer simulation was devised to check the validity of these guesses, which proved correct. The results of that simulation are given in Table 4.1. The fitnesses were chosen independently from the uniform distribution, in agreement with expressions (4.7). One thousand matrices were generated in each case.

Table 4.1 shows the effect of increasing σ/s from 0.1 to 0.2; there is a drastic reduction in the chances for polymorphism. The uniform distribution has range $\pm\sqrt{12}\sigma$, so when $\sigma/s = 0.2$ there is nearly 30% overlap between homozygote and heterozygote fitnesses;

TABLE 4.1 The effect of number of alleles and the ratio σ/s on the chances of the existence of a full, stable polymorphism.

Number of alleles	$\sigma/s = 0.1$	$\sigma/s = 0.15$	$\sigma/s = 0.20$
2	1.000	1.000	1.000
3	1.000	1.000	0.998
4	1.000	0.999	0.952
5	1.000	0.975	0.829
6	1.000	0.938	0.673
7	1.000	0.869	0.453
8	0.998	0.747	0.259
9	0.981	0.601	0.146
10	0.972	0.461	0.063
11	0.937	0.312	0.024
12	0.893	0.197	0.004
13	0.822	0.099	0.001
14	0.769	0.057	0
15	0.666	0.020	0
16	0.598	0.001	0
17	0.489	0.002	0
18	0.417	0.001	0
19	0.324	0	0
20	0.257	0	0

when $\sigma/s = 0.1$, there is no overlap at all and total heterozygote superiority is guaranteed.

We next looked into the effect of variations in heterozygote and homozygote fitnesses, by considering different values of σ_δ and σ_ε. These results are given in Table 4.2. This table shows that the probability of polymorphism is much more strongly controlled by heterozygote fitness variability σ_δ than by homozygote fitness variability σ_ε. Increasing σ_ε fourfold while holding σ_δ at 0.01 has a rather small effect, but a drastic reduction in the probability of polymorphism occurs when the opposite change is made.

An exact analytic definition of the set of matrices that give a high probability of polymorphism is difficult. The following necessary condition is also given in Lewontin, Ginzburg, and Tuljapurkar (1978):

$$\frac{\sigma_\delta}{s} < \frac{1}{2\sqrt{n}} \tag{4.8}$$

Although not exact, this expression gives the correct impression of the qualitative role of all three parameters: the average heterozygote superiority, s, the variability of fitnesses, σ_δ, and the number of alleles, n.

TABLE 4.2 The effect of changing the variation among the homozygote fitnesses, σ_ε, and among heterozygote fitnesses, σ_δ, on the chances of the existence of a full stable polymorphism.

Number of alleles	$s = 0.1$ $\sigma_\delta = \sigma_\varepsilon = 0.01$	$s = 0.1$ $\sigma_\delta = 0.01,\ \sigma_\varepsilon = 0.04$	$s = 0.1$ $\sigma_\delta = 0.04,\ \sigma_\varepsilon = 0.01$
2	1.000	1.000	1.000
3	1.000	1.000	0.760
4	1.000	0.990	0.350
5	1.000	0.982	0.138
6	1.000	0.947	0.025
7	0.999	0.903	0.002
8	0.997	0.841	0
9	0.988	0.768	0
10	0.979	0.687	0
11	0.949	0.599	0
12	0.913	0.433	0
13	0.863	0.402	0
14	0.798	0.316	0
15	0.733	0.227	0
16	0.642	0.162	0
17	0.543	0.102	0
18	0.442	0.069	0
19	0.350	0.032	0
20	0.286	0.018	0

It is clear from condition (4.8) that in order to achieve stable polymorphism for a large number of alleles, the mean difference between heterozygote and homozygote fitnesses must be much larger than the variation among heterozygote and among homozygote fitnesses.

We began our analysis in this section with the degenerate case of complete heterosis with no variation in fitnesses and then looked at the effect of small variations around these conditions. What if we formulated the question differently, asking instead: what are the chances of polymorphism given all possible combinations of fitnesses, without assuming any a priori constraints? We will address this question in the next section.

4.4 Chances for Coexistence of Multiple Alleles

For n alleles we have $n(n+1)/2$ distinct genotypes, and we can scale all their fitnesses into the interval $[0, 1]$. We may then represent any set of fitnesses of all genotypes as a point in a unit $[n(n+1)/2]$-dimensional hypercube. With this geometric image in mind, there are two questions we may ask.

86   Chapter 4: Polymorphism and Natural Selection

First, what is the size of the region corresponding to stable polymorphisms within this fitness space? In one case, we know the answer. For $n = 2$, the fitness space is three-dimensional and the heterozygote is superior over both homozygotes in one-third of the cube. In other words, the probability that one random number will be greater than two others drawn independently from the same distribution is $\frac{1}{3}$. It is simple in the case of two alleles, because here heterozygote superiority is both a necessary and a sufficient condition for polymorphism.

The second question asks what the shape of the "polymorphic" region is, and how the measure of this region changes as the number of alleles grows. We do not have a complete answer to this question, but we did find one "center of concentration" for such fitness configurations in the previous section.

Let us look at the first question. One numerical method of investigation would be to make a regular lattice of points in the hypercube and to test each one for polymorphism. This is clearly an unreasonable task; even with the help of a computer. For ten alleles we are dealing with a 55-dimensional hypercube, and even if we space our points at every tenth from 0 to 1 for each fitness dimension, there would be 11^{55} such points (matrices) to check. The alternative is to throw points into the cube at random and use the resulting proportion of polymorphic cases to characterize the relative measure of the polymorphic subset within the total set of possible fitness configurations. This is what was done in Lewontin, Ginzburg, and Tuljapurkar, (1978).

We used three different computer simulations, each based on checking 100,000 fitness matrices for different dimensions (numbers of alleles). First, all fitnesses W_{ij} were independently sampled from the uniform distribution to explore all the fitness space. The results are presented in Table 4.3. For $n = 2$, the empirically observed proportion is close to the exact theoretical expectation of $\frac{1}{3}$; thereafter, the frequency decreases rapidly as the number of alleles

TABLE 4.3 The proportion of fitness matrices providing a stable polymorphism over all fitness space.

Number of alleles	Proportion
2	0.33466
3	0.04237
4	0.00240
5	0.00006
6	0.00000
7	0.00000
8	0.00000

increases. Indeed, out of the 100,000 cases tried, there was not a single case of polymorphism for six alleles. This result cannot be used to make general statements about the probability of occurrence of polymorphism because such statements would require assumptions about the distribution of fitnesses in nature. The random generation of fitnesses is a simple device for estimating the measure of polymorphic regions in the parameter space. This estimate can, however, be used in conjunction with assumptions about the nature of fitness determination to decide whether selective polymorphisms with a given number of alleles are likely to be found.

The second simulation experiment analyzed the part of the fitness space constrained by the condition of pairwise heterosis— that is, $W_{ii} < W_{ij}$ and $W_{ij} > W_{jj}$ for all i and j. Based on the triangle inequalities, this constraint should not significantly increase the proportion of polymorphic cases. The third experiment dealt with the case of total heterosis, where all heterozygotes are assigned superiority over all homozygotes. The results for these last two experiments are given in Table 4.4. For two alleles, of course, all cases are polymorphic, since $W_{11} < W_{12}$ and $W_{12} > W_{22}$ is the necessary and sufficient condition. As the number of alleles increases, the proportion of stable polymorphisms again decreases rapidly, so that even under total heterosis there were no cases of eight alleles in the 100,000 replicates examined. Neither pairwise nor total heterosis is, therefore, sufficient to significantly increase the probability of selective polymorphism for multiple alleles.

The conclusion is obvious. The large amounts of genetic polymorphism observed cannot be attributed to selection based on a model of panmixia among constant-fitness populations—at least not unless we are willing to suppose that nature chooses fitnesses in some very peculiar way (for instance, around the degenerate case considered in Section 4.3). Should we therefore abandon either our

TABLE 4.4 The proportion of fitness matrices providing a stable polymorphism in the regions of fitness space restricted by the conditions of pairwise or total heterosis.

Number of alleles	Pairwise heterosis	Total heterosis
2	1.0000	1.0000
3	0.5224	0.7120
4	0.1259	0.3433
5	0.0116	0.1091
6	0.0003	0.0137
7	0.0000	0.0011
8	0.0000	0.0000
9	0.0000	0.0000

search for a tractable and realistic selective model or the idea that selection contributes very much to existing patterns of polymorphism? The answer is in the next section.

4.5 Selection and Neutrality As Complementary Explanations of Genetic Polymorphism

As we saw in the previous section, pure selection theory with constant fitnesses predicts the typical occurrence of two or three alleles at a locus. The addition of frequency-dependence or time-dependence to selective models (Gillespie, 1977) can account for many more alleles, but requires a great many parameters. Though plausible, such models cannot compete in simplicity with those based on neutral theory, which in the classical version (Kimura, 1968; King and Jukes, 1969) uses only one free parameter: the product of the effective population size and the neutral mutation rate.

Pure neutral theory adequately accounts for the observed number of alleles, but does not explain their observed frequency distributions. Real data show a pronounced skewness toward rare alleles, which is inconsistent with predictions from pure neutral theory. A number of authors have modified the classical theory to include mutations to slightly deleterious alleles; this brings neutral predictions into closer conformity with the data (Ohta, 1973, 1975, 1976; Watterson, 1978). These modifications assume no dominance.

I believe that it is unacceptable to assume a total absence of dominance. I hope to show here that a compromise theory, which allows the possibility of selective dominance within a "neutralistic" system, can give a better fit to the observed data.

From the abundant electrophoretic data on polymorphism, we have selected two sets of results. The first is from Ayala et al. (1974) and Harris, Hopkinson, and Robson (1974), as summarized in Ohta (1975); the second is from Chakraborty, Fuerst, and Nei (1980). The spectra of allele frequencies, lumped into five frequency classes, are shown in Tables 4.5 and 4.6. An interesting feature of these data is the slight intermediate maximum in the middle of the spectra around 0.5, which is clearly present in six of the eight species samples listed.

Spectra derived from neutral theory tend to be relatively flat, often with a minimum in the range of intermediate frequencies. If the true overall allele frequency distribution were flat in intermediate regions, each of the three central classes in our lumped spectra would have an equal probability of being the largest. The a priori probability of getting this many central maxima is about 0.02.

4.5 Selection and Neutrality

TABLE 4.5 The observed number of alleles in various frequency classes (after Ohta (1975)).

Allele frequency	Drosophila willistoni	Drosophila tropicalis	Drosophila equinoxialis	Homo sapiens
<0.2	132	75	103	67
0.2–0.4	3	2	3	4
0.4–0.6	4	4	5	5
0.6–0.8	2	3	3	3
>0.8	25	24	25	37

Although this is not a strict statistical test, we believe the data suggest the general presence of a small intermediate maximum in allele frequency spectra.

The intermediate maxima suggest that the data may include some heterotic selection. This problem can be posed as a question. Is there a difference between a set of ideally neutral loci and a set which is neutral only on the average, where selection may operate in each locus in a different random direction? We will show that there is a difference in the expected spectrum, and that this difference reflects the observational phenomenon described above. The model to accommodate this theory will be developed in two steps. We will begin by describing a simple deterministic selection model with fitnesses drawn from a statistical ensemble and then relax our assumptions to allow finite population size and mutations.

Suppose that the mutation rate for selectively different alleles is much lower than the mutation rate for neutral alleles, so that at any given time the population is segregating for only a few selective classes and a larger number of alleles that are neutral within a class.

Consider a locus where only one selective class (A) is present, and a new selectively different mutant (a) appears. There are three possibilities. The fitness of the heterozygote Aa could be less than the fitness of AA. In this case a is eliminated, unless the drift

TABLE 4.6 The observed number of alleles in various frequency classes (after Chakraborty, Fuerst, and Nei (1980)).

Allele frequency	Macaca fuscata	Taricha rivularis	Zoarces viviparus	Drosophila heteroneura
<0.2	26	12	15	39
0.2–0.4	0	2	2	3
0.4–0.6	0	6	6	3
0.6–0.8	0	4	2	4
>0.8	29	33	28	20

variance is quite large. When the fitness of Aa is greater than that of AA, the result could be either fixation of a (if the fitness of aa is greater than that of Aa) or selective polymorphism (if the fitness of aa is less than or equal to that of Aa). The probabilities for these three cases depend on the exact probability distribution of the fitnesses. If the mutation rate is higher—so that more than two selective classes may be segregating at once—the picture is more complex, though qualitatively similar.

We assume that only one selectively different mutation appears in a homozygous locus, and that the destiny of this mutation is determined by the relative fitnesses of the two homozygotes, W_{AA} and W_{aa}, and the heterozygote W_{Aa}, as in the standard deterministic model. Since we are interested not in the particular locus, but in a typical locus representing an overall genome, our three fitnesses form a random triple of numbers drawn from an ensemble described by a three-dimensional distribution. We have chosen this ensemble to be a trivariate normal distribution with equal expectations for all three fitnesses—$E(W_{AA}) = E(W_{Aa}) = E(W_{aa})$—and the following variance-covariance matrix:

$$\begin{array}{c|ccc} & W_{AA} & W_{Aa} & W_{aa} \\ \hline W_{AA} & \sigma^2 & r\sigma^2 & 0 \\ W_{Aa} & r\sigma^2 & \sigma^2 & r\sigma^2 \\ W_{aa} & 0 & r\sigma^2 & \sigma^2 \end{array}$$

This distribution has equal means and variances for all three fitnesses and a special covariation structure where the heterozygote has a positive correlation coefficient, r, with both homozygotes. The heterozygote has one allele in common with each homozygote, implying some positive correlation between their fitnesses. Homozygotes do not have alleles in common and their fitnesses are assumed to be uncorrelated.

Let us clarify the biological meaning of the parameter r. In any particular sample from this distribution, the heterozygote may be overdominant, intermediate, or underdominant. The degree of dominance in fitness for a given set of fitnesses may be measured by

$$d = W_{Aa} - \frac{W_{AA} + W_{aa}}{2}$$

which is the deviation of the heterozygote fitness from the midrange of the two homozygote fitnesses. Thus the probability distribution of the fitnesses defines a probability distribution of d.

Define D to be

$$D = \frac{1}{\sigma} [\mathbf{E}(d^2)]^{1/2}$$

4.5 Selection and Neutrality

Since $E(d) = 0$, D^2 is just the variance of d, scaled by the variance of the fitnesses.

Then

$$D^2 = \frac{3 - 4r}{2}$$

That is, D^2 is linearly related to the correlation parameter r so that higher values of r imply lower average degrees of dominance.

Note that the acceptance of the above correlation structure among fitnesses implies

$$r \leq \frac{\sqrt{2}}{2} \approx 0.707$$

Any r beyond $\sqrt{2}/2$ implies a correlation between homozygote fitnesses. Therefore, our range of r-values, $0 \leq r \leq \sqrt{2}/2$, will imply the following range for D-values:

$$0.293 \leq D \leq 1.225$$

Since the degree of dominance makes more sense as a biologically significant parameter, we will present all results in terms of D rather than r.

Before calculating the distribution of the allelic frequencies at the equilibrium produced by our ensemble, notice that the *equilibrium distribution will depend neither on the mean value of fitnesses nor on the value of the fitness variance*, σ^2. This follows immediately from the formula for the equilibrium frequency of the A-allele,

$$q^* = \frac{W_{Aa} - W_{aa}}{2W_{Aa} - W_{AA} - W_{aa}}$$

which is invariant with respect to any linear transformation of fitnesses. Therefore, the only free parameter in our model is D (or r). The variance of fitnesses, σ^2, which is a measure of the strength of selection, is important if we want to consider a population in a transient state or the effect of finite population size. Since here we are concerned only with equilibrium predictions, the variance σ^2 can be any positive value (in practice, probably very low (Lewontin, 1974)). Thus we are left with one parameter, D. Later it will become clear that even this parameter has little effect.

Omitting calculations, let us present the results. The probability of polymorphism, P, which can be thought of as the likely proportion of polymorphic loci in a genome, is

$$P = \frac{1}{\pi} \arctan(D\sqrt{2})$$

Chapter 4: Polymorphism and Natural Selection

and the density function of q^* is

$$f(q^*) = \frac{\sqrt{2}D}{\pi[1 + 2D^2 - 8D^2 q^*(1-q^*)]} \\ + \frac{(1-P)}{2}\delta(1-q^*) + \frac{(1-P)}{2}\delta(q^*) \quad (4.9)$$

where δ is the Dirac delta function. The probability of monomorphism is $1 - P$. The first term in (4.9) shows the distribution of polymorphic frequencies, which has a sum of P, so that

$$\int_0^1 f(q^*)\,dq^* = P + \frac{1-P}{2} + \frac{1-P}{2} = 1$$

Figure 4.2 shows the behavior of $f(q^*)$ for several values of D. The proportion of polymorphic loci P varies between 12.5% and 33%, increasing with the average degree of dominance. The distribution of q^* has a maximum at $\frac{1}{2}$.

We would like to write the allele frequency spectrum (expected number of alleles in a given frequency range) for a more realistic model. This would include mutation (to alleles both within the same selective class and in another class), finite population size, sampling, and the fitness ensemble described in the last section. Unfortunately, we cannot. Instead, we will limit ourselves to qualitative discussion. We will show that the intermediate maximum is expected to persist for some range of the effective population size and mutation rates.

First of all, with infinite population size and no mutation, the spectrum of allele frequencies over the ensemble of loci with

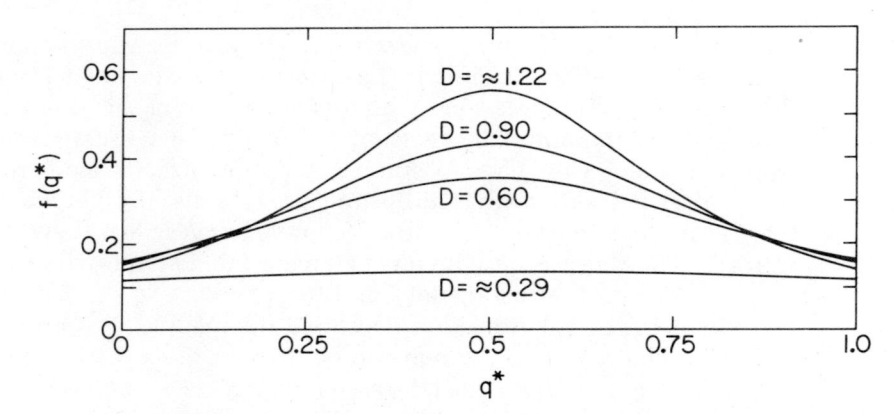

Figure 4.2 Distributions of the equilibrium frequency, $0 < g^* < 1$, under the assumption of the model with different values of D.

4.5 Selection and Neutrality

fitnesses W_{AA}, W_{Aa}, and W_{aa} generated as described above is (*) with δ-functions at the ends and a unimodal distribution in the middle of the frequency range. Now allow mutation to occur. There must be two mutation rates: μ_n, the probability per generation that a gene will mutate to another allele in the same selective class, and μ_s, the probability that a gene will mutate to an allele in a second selective class (Figure 4.2). To be more specific, we assume an arbitrary number of alleles, $A_1, A_2, \ldots$, in the first selective class and an arbitrary number of alleles, $a_1, a_2, \ldots$, in the second selective class. Fitnesses of all genotypes $A_i A_j$ are equal to each other, and the same is true within the set of all possible genotypes $a_i a_j$. Heterozygotes between selective classes, $A_i a_j$, have equal fitnesses too. In other words, for all i and j,

$$\left. \begin{array}{r} W_{A_i A_j} = W_{AA} \\ W_{a_i a_j} = W_{aa} \\ W_{A_i a_j} = W_{Aa} \end{array} \right\}$$

where a triple of fitnesses, W_{AA}, W_{Aa}, and W_{aa}, is randomly assigned to each locus, as described in the above model. We let μ_n be the same for each allele and μ_s be the same for each selective class. Consider at first finite population size and no neutral mutations, $\mu_n = 0$, $\mu_s \neq 0$. We are still dealing with two alleles at each locus with fitnesses of the triple of genotype varying from locus to locus. The shape of the spectrum remains similar to (*), but is "smeared." That is, the δ function at 0 and 1 will be spread out to spikes at 0 and 1 extending towards neighboring frequencies, and, depending on actual values of $N_e \mu_s$, the central part of the spectrum will be more or less flattened. The important point to recognize is that the spectrum with $\mu_n = 0$ is symmetric around $\frac{1}{2}$, with a mode at $\frac{1}{2}$. To show this, consider that the probability distribution for any given q^* will give rise to a symmetric spectrum with modes at q^* and $1 - q^*$. The overall spectrum is a sum of such spectra weighted by the distribution of q^*, given by (*). Since (*) is symmetric, the resulting spectrum must be symmetric. The mutation rate, μ_s, and population size will affect the strength of the mode at $\frac{1}{2}$, but not its position.

Allowing neutral mutations to come into play, $\mu_n \neq 0$, basically subdivides our lumped frequencies into subclasses of alleles which are neutral within our selective classes. Now we have more than two alleles per locus. We assume that we see all the alleles, but as far as selection is concerned, they are lumped at each locus into only two selectively different classes $\{A_1, A_2, \ldots\}$ and $\{a_1, a_2, \ldots\}$. Let us use the notation $F(x, q^*)\Delta x$ for the expected number of alleles in a given frequency class, $x \leq q \leq x + \Delta x$, conditioned on the deterministic selective equilibrium at q^* at a particular locus. Population

Chapter 4: Polymorphism and Natural Selection

size and the neutral mutation rate are parameters of this distribution. Based on the suggested model, the observed spectrum $\phi(x)$ should be the integral of F weighted by the distribution of q^* over loci.

$$\phi(x) = \int_0^1 F(x, q^*) f(q^*) \, dq^*$$

It is a difficult problem to obtain exact expressions for F, which would enable us to calculate the desired spectrum. Instead, we will limit ourselves to a qualitative discussion. We will attempt to show that the intermediate maximum in the selective frequency distribution f will produce an intermediate maximum in the spectrum, ϕ.

Let us picture qualitatively the behavior of the function $F(x, q^*)$ for a few characteristic values of q^*. For a locus with high q^* (close to 1), subdivision should lower the mass of the distribution, at the same time adding to the lower end of the spectrum so that $F(x, q^*)$ will have a bimodal U-shaped form. For a locus with low q^* (close to zero), the "neutral subdivision" will move the mass of the spectrum even lower, sharpening the increase of $\phi(x)$ when $x \to 0$. For loci with intermediate values of q^*, we will have a general lowering of the mass with the corresponding addition at the lower end of the spectrum. Therefore, with such a subdivision, the mass of the spectrum generally moves towards the smaller frequency range. The mode around 0 becomes higher than the mode around 1, so that the symmetry of the spectrum is destroyed and the mode at $\frac{1}{2}$ could be shifted to a lower value. With high enough mutation rate and low population size, the mode will probably be obliterated. However, by continuity, the spectrum of allelic frequencies will continue to have a mode near the center of the frequency range, at least for large values of effective population size and low neutral mutation rates. This mode is a reflection of the underlying selective processes.

We have striven to show in our model that the possibility of heterosis must be allowed in theories attempting to explain genetic polymorphism. In doing so, we have emphasized alleles of intermediate frequencies to the exclusion of rare alleles. In any one case, the existence of the hump in the empirical frequency spectrum is not statistically significant, but the existence of a similar hump in the same place in a number of different spectra is at least highly suspicious.

We do not claim that the majority of enzyme polymorphisms are being maintained by selection. We believe that mutation and drift are the important factors in determining the large numbers of alleles observed at some loci and the overall shape of the allele frequency distribution. What we suggest is that an appropriate description of the processes determining gene frequencies must include selection, and in such a manner that heterotic allele combinations are possible. The question is, What proportion of the total amount of heterozygosity is attributable to segregation of neutral alleles and how much to heterotic alleles?

Our model of only two possible selective classes is admittedly simple. The allele frequency distributions quoted above suggest that this assumption is not so bad. As the number of alleles held in strictly selective polymorphism grows, the expected value of the frequency of an allele drops, as does the mode. For two alleles the mode is $\frac{1}{2}$. The central small mode of the observed frequency distributions is around $\frac{1}{2}$. In fact, if the mode were displaced from $\frac{1}{2}$ by very much, it would be difficult to see it at all, because it would be swamped in the general increase of rare alleles.

Sensitivity of the results to the exact form of the fitness ensemble is another question which needs to be answered. In any case, we feel that the statistical approach to the description of fitness parameters, allowing for some form of dominance as well as neutral mutations and drift, will be a necessary component of any explanation for the observed genetic polymorphisms.

4.6 Problems and Discussion

1. Samuel Karlin suggested that the average heterozygote superiority and the triangle inequalities might be the only necessary conditions for polymorphism expressed as linear inequalities in terms of fitnesses. The problem of studying models with multiple alleles and formulating other interpretable necessary or sufficient conditions for polymorphism is still important because of its relationship to multilocus theory. Actually, in the absence of recombination, one can consider multilocus gametotypes as "alleles" in a multiallelic model. A number of results for the case of tight linkage (low recombination fraction) have been obtained (Karlin, 1975), based on understanding the limiting case of no recombination (multiple alleles).

2. The problem of the shape of the polymorphic region in the fitness space is not completely resolved. One "center of concentration" of such selective regimes is discussed in Section 4.3. Are there others, or is this the only one?

3. The models discussed in this chapter did not include any mechanism for mutations, which would randomly try different combinations of alleles. Would we expect a higher number of alleles in a selection-mutation polymorphism? A computer simulation

carried out in collaboration with R. W. Setzer (unpublished) gave a basically negative answer, but we had tried only specific fitness distributions over a range of mutation rates.

4. The measurement of fitnesses with respect to whole chromosomes, not loci, has been performed in some cases (Dobzhansky and Spassky, 1963; also see the discussion in Lewontin, 1974). They have demonstrated an average chromosomal heterozygote superiority and also a lower variance of the heterozygote fitnesses, as compared to homozygote fitnesses. What is the relationship between chromosomal and one-locus heterozygote superiority? Karlin (1975) has shown that stable polymorphism in multilocus systems with tight linkage produces heterozygote superiority for the marginal one-locus fitnesses averaged over the rest of the loci. Alan Hastings has recently demonstrated that in general this statement is incorrect (personal communication). There are a number of other important results obtained in a multilocus context by Karlin and his collaborators (Karlin, 1979) that are relevant to the problem of explaining the maintenance of polymorphism by selection.

5. We have demonstrated (Section 4.2) that in a simple model with independently evolving loci, the average fitness of a genotype should grow with its degree of heterozygosity when the population is at selective equilibrium. I would like to make a few comments on how other modes of evolution affect this statement.

(a) *Density-dependent selection*: If selection is density-dependent—that is, all fitnesses W_{ij} depend on the population size N—the equilibrium fitness configuration can be characterized by the values of fitnesses calculated at the equilibrium density level, $W_{ij}(\mathbf{N}^*)$. As will be shown in Chapter 6, the fitness matrix $W_{ij}(\mathbf{N}^*)$ satisfied the same necessary conditions of stability as the constant fitness matrix. Thus it should have no effect on our results, provided the fitnesses are measured at the equilibrium density level.

(b) *Neutral loci*: If all the loci we look at are ideally neutral, obviously the fitness will not change with the degree of heterozygosity. If some of the loci are neutral, it will lower both the rate of increase of fitness as a function of degree of heterozygosity and the fitness variance. The possibility that some of the loci are neutral does not, therefore, contradict our basic statement.

(c) *Frequency-dependent selection*: It was shown in one of the earliest papers on frequency-dependent selection (Lewontin, 1958) that heterozygote inferiority at a stable equilibrium is possible. So, in principle, frequency-dependent selection could work against our main statement. However, a very specific mechanism of frequency-dependence is needed to get such an effect. The majority of the mechanisms of frequency-dependence, which were reviewed recently by Clarke (1979), imply either complete or partial heterozygote dominance. This assumption can be written as

$$\min\{W_{ii}(\mathbf{p},\mathbf{N}), W_{jj}(\mathbf{p},\mathbf{N})\} \leq W_{ij}(\mathbf{p},\mathbf{N}) \leq \max\{W_{ii}(\mathbf{p},\mathbf{N}), W_{jj}(\mathbf{p},\mathbf{N})\}$$

Under this condition, the fitnesses are necessarily all equal to each other at equilibrium (Chapter 6), so that the loci affected by possible heterozygote inferiority will be effectively neutral at the equilibrium point. Therefore, frequency-dependence—together with the assumption of complete or partial dominance—does not contradict our statement. The only effect it might have is to lower the rate at which fitness increases with increasing heterozygosity.

(d) *Epistasis*: Multiplicativity of fitnesses between loci was an important assumption in our arguments. To consider epistatic models, we should reject this assumption and assign fitnesses directly to the multilocus genotype without specifying a rule for combining fitnesses among loci. Being unable to obtain results analytically, we used the computer simulations in this chapter. In every case of complete polymorphism, we recorded the means of fitnesses for the homozygotes, single heterozygotes, and one double heterozygote. The vast majority of the simulated cases did not lead to polymorphism. Out of 1000 runs, we obtained only 74 polymorphic cases (1.4%). Out of those 74 polymorphic cases, in 59 (80%) the mean single heterozygote fitness exceeded the mean homozygote fitness, and in 64 (85%) the fitness of the double heterozygote was greater than the average fitness of the single heterozygotes. Additional simulation work on two- and three-locus models, which has been performed by Mike Turelli (Davis) at my suggestion, shows that the effect is strengthening with the increased number of loci (Turelli and Ginzburg, 1982).

There is much more work to be done along this line. For example, we can consider multiple-allele models, try multilocus models, or follow the influence of recombination fractions more closely. The conclusion I want to draw now is that simulations basically support our statement, if we add the qualifier *in most cases* instead of *always* for no epistasis.

We can also expect the other phenomena to offset any epistatic effects. If the number of polymorphic loci is large, then the number of possible pairs, triples, and so on is very high; epistatic effects should average out over those sets, resulting in a net average fitness increase with growing heterozygosity for the sequence of genotypic sets.

6. In relation to the necessary conditions of polymorphism obtained in this chapter I would like to discuss a more general question which

I will state in a very informal way: If we are not able to obtain, or cannot interpret, the exact necessary and sufficient conditions for a phenomenon, which knowledge is preferable, that of necessary or that of sufficient conditions?

This is a very ill-posed question since the answer clearly depends on what you need. In applied sciences, however, this question appears all the time. If you are building an airplane and analyze the stability of its structure under certain flight conditions as a function of parameters of your choice, which knowledge will be preferred? Without doubt, since you worry about the stability, you will be satisfied only with the sufficient conditions that guarantee the stability if your parameters are within certain limits. You might overdo it a little if you are not guided by an exact result, but it is better to be on the safe side. Necessary conditions are of no use in this case. This kind of logic has influenced people's thoughts for a long time, and I believe that if we were to poll many scientists' responses to my odd question, sufficient conditions would win over necessary ones by a wide margin.

I would like to argue now that in population biology at its present stage, we are not actively creating things but rather trying to understand what is going on in populations that have already evolved; therefore, necessary conditions are very useful. If we observe a population in a polymorphic state and want to check the hypothesis that selection is the force that brought about what we see, we will benefit from a theory giving us the necessary conditions. Of course, if we were able to measure fitnesses, we would use the exact necessary and sufficient result. Since we are unable to measure fitnesses, we can at least reject hypotheses based on the necessary conditions.

5 "Exponential" Growth with Selection

When natural selection is operating, the growth of a population cannot be exactly exponential unless the population is in equilibrium with respect to its genetic composition. When the population is not at equilibrium, its growth trajectory will wander away from the exponential curve, although it might tend toward a simple exponential curve when gene frequencies tend to an equilibrium. Therefore, we can expect that the population growth curve in some way reflects the underlying processes of change in gene frequencies. It is obviously easier to deal with the one-dimensional population growth curve than with the multidimensional dynamics of gene frequencies. Thus it would be interesting to find out what properties of the natural selection process can be seen macroscopically, by simple observations of population size.

This chapter is a study of these relationships, based on a multiple-allele model with constant fitnesses.

5.1 Selective Delay

Consider a population growing in a constant unlimited environment. If the gene frequencies are in equilibrium, the population will

Chapter 5: "Exponential" Growth with Selection

grow exponentially, with the exponent $W^* = W(\mathbf{p}^*)$:

$$N(t) = N_0 \exp\{W^* t\},$$

where N_0 is the initial population size, $N(0) = N_0$ (see Figure 5.1, curve I).

Now let us assume that the initial population size is the same N_0, but the initial gene frequencies differ from the equilibrium: $\mathbf{p}_0 \neq \mathbf{p}^*$. If the initial frequencies are in the attraction zone of this equilibrium, we will have

$$\mathbf{p}(t, \mathbf{p}_0) \to \mathbf{p}^*, \quad \text{as } t \to \infty$$
$$W(t, \mathbf{p}_0) \to W^*, \quad \text{as } t \to \infty$$

In this case the population growth curve, $N(t)$, will not be exponential (see curve II, Figure 5.1), but will take the form

$$N(t) = N_0 \exp\left\{\int_0^t W(\zeta)\, d\zeta\right\}$$

which will asymptotically approach an exponential curve given by

$$N(t) = N_1 \exp\{W^* t\}$$

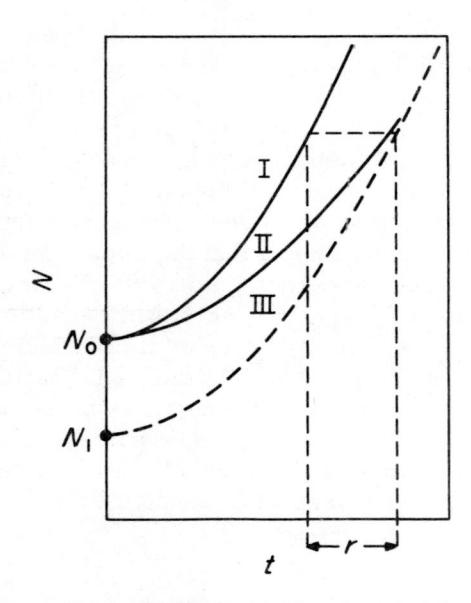

Figure 5.1 The growth of a population in the course of the natural selection process. Curve I, the growth of a population with the initial number N_0 and the structure p^*; curve II, the growth of a population with the initial number N_0 and the structure $\mathbf{p} \neq \mathbf{p}$; curve III, the exponential to which the curve II asymptotically tends.

where $N_1 < N_0$ (Figure 5.1, curve III). This last curve lags behind the original curve (curve I) by an interval of time τ. We will call this time interval the *selective delay*. This delay is a measure of the distance between the equilibrium and initial gene frequencies modified by the strength of selection. It is intuitively clear that the selective delay will be higher for initial frequencies more distant from the equilibrium than for the ones which are close to it. The exact meaning of this distance will become clear later.

We can define the selective delay more precisely:

$$\tau(\mathbf{p}_0, \mathbf{p}^*) = \frac{1}{W^*} \ln \frac{N_0}{N_1} = \frac{1}{W^*} \int_0^\infty [W^* - W(\zeta)] \, d\zeta \qquad (5.1)$$

To arrive at this formula, we simply transform the population-size axis of Figure 5.1 to a logarithmic scale and notice that the slope of the straight line representing the exponential growth is W^*.

There are some obvious properties of selective delay:

1. $\tau(\mathbf{p}^*, \mathbf{p}^*) = 0$. There is no delay if the population is at the equilibrium point from the beginning.

2. $\tau(\mathbf{p}_0, \mathbf{p}^*) > 0$ for all $\mathbf{p}_0 \neq \mathbf{p}^*$. This follows from Fisher's theorem of natural selection. Actually, since W can only grow, it will not exceed W^*, so we can have only positive delays.

Another useful graphical representation is the curve describing the dynamics of the average fitness (Figure 5.2). The product $W^*\tau$ represents the area above the curve $W(t)$ in Figure 5.1. This curve has sometimes been called the *adaptation curve*, since it shows the rate with which the average fitness approaches its maximum value (Maynard Smith, 1976).

5.2 Entropy Distance

We introduce the distance between the initial and the equilibrium gene frequency vectors in the following way:

$$H(\mathbf{p}, \mathbf{p}^*) = -\sum_{i=1}^n p_i^* \ln \frac{p_i}{p_{i*}} \qquad p_i^* > 0, \quad i = 1, \ldots, n$$

This distance between two frequency distributions is well known in information theory (Kullback, 1960). It was first used in population genetics in Ginzburg (1972), because it has some specific properties pertinent to evolutionary models. Before we consider these properties, let us analyze the behavior of this distance as a function of gene frequencies.

It is easy to see that $H(\mathbf{p}^*, \mathbf{p}^*) = 0$. Let us show that $\mathbf{p} = \mathbf{p}^*$ is also a minimum point of this function, so that $H(\mathbf{p}, \mathbf{p}^*) > 0$ for

Chapter 5: "Exponential" Growth with Selection

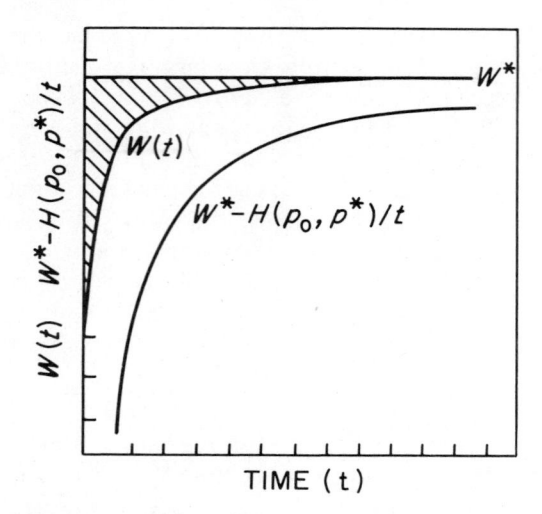

Figure 5.2 Shaded area between the graph of $W(t)$ and W^* is the genetic distance $H(\mathbf{p}_o, \mathbf{p}^*) = \int (W^* - W(t))\,dt$.

all $\mathbf{p} \neq \mathbf{p}^*$. Consider the optimum equations on the simplex $\sum_{i=1}^{n} p_i^* = 1$:

$$\frac{\partial}{\partial p_i}\left[H(\mathbf{p},\mathbf{p}^*) + \lambda\left(\sum_{i=1}^{h} p_i - 1\right)\right] = 0, \qquad i = 1,\ldots,n$$

where λ is the Lagrange multiplier. We obtain

$$p_i^*/p_i = \lambda, \qquad i = 1,\ldots,n$$

Taking into account the normalizing conditions, we have

$$p_i = p_i^*$$

The second derivatives at the point $\mathbf{p}^*$ have the form

$$\frac{\partial^2}{\partial p_i^2} H(\mathbf{p},\mathbf{p}^*) = \frac{2}{p_i^*} > 0, \qquad i = 1,\ldots,n$$

$$\frac{\partial^2}{\partial p_i \partial p_j} H(\mathbf{p},\mathbf{p}^*) = 0, \qquad i \neq j$$

We have shown, therefore, that $\mathbf{p} = \mathbf{p}^*$ is the minimum point of the function H, and thus H is a positive function of $\mathbf{p}$ when $\mathbf{p} \neq \mathbf{p}^*$.

It is also easy to see that $H(\mathbf{p},\mathbf{p}^*) \to \infty$ when $\mathbf{p}$ tends to the boundary of the simplex—that is, when at least one of the frequencies tends to zero.

5.2 Entropy Distance

Although we have used the word *distance*, $H(\mathbf{p}, \mathbf{p}^*)$ is not really a distance in the usual sense. For instance,

$$H(\mathbf{p}, \mathbf{p}^*) \neq H(\mathbf{p}^*, \mathbf{p})$$

Generally, the triangle inequality does not hold. Provided that this is understood, we will keep the term *distance* and use it to mean that $H(\mathbf{p}, \mathbf{p}^*)$ is a positive function that equals zero only when $\mathbf{p}$ equals $\mathbf{p}^*$; in addition, we will make the boundary points of the simplex infinitely far from the internal points.

The behavior of this function is qualitatively illustrated in Figure 5.3 in the case of two alleles. Simplex $p_1 + p_2 = 1$ is represented by the segment in the (p_1, p_2) plane and H is shown as a function of $\mathbf{p}$ with a fixed $\mathbf{p}^*$. The boundary points $(p_1 = 1, p_2 = 0)$ and $(p_1 = 0, p_2 = 1)$ are therefore infinitely far, in the sense described, from the point $\mathbf{p}^*$.

The function H has a number of important properties for the description of the evolutionary process. All of them stem from the fact that the rate of change of this function is related to the average fitness imbalance. To demonstrate this, let us calculate the time derivative of H, taking into account the equation of evolution, (3.1). We have

$$\frac{dH}{dt} = \sum_{i=1}^{n} \frac{\partial H}{\partial p_i} \frac{dp_i}{dt} = -\sum_{i=1}^{n} \frac{p_i^*}{p_i} p_i(W_i - W)$$

$$= -\sum_{i=1}^{n} p_i^*(W_i - W) = W - \sum_{i=1}^{n} p_i^* W_i$$

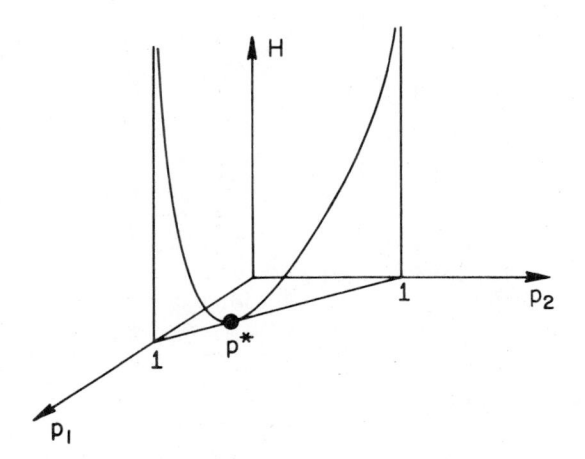

Figure 5.3 Qualitative behavior of the entropy distance $H(\mathbf{p}, \mathbf{p}^*)$.

Chapter 5: "Exponential" Growth with Selection

Using the conservation-of-fitness rule (3.5), we obtain

$$\frac{dH}{dt} = W - W^* \tag{5.2}$$

where W is the average fitness of a population and W^* is its value at the equilibrium point. Note that $H(\mathbf{p}, \mathbf{p}^*)$ can be considered as a Lyapunov function for our evolutionary system in (3.1). If the average fitness is maximized at an equilibrium $W - W^* \leq 0$, so that $dH/dt \leq 0$, this proves the global stability of the equilibrium.

This is not really important in the context of one-locus theory, since the average fitness itself can serve as a Lyapunov function. What is important is that the average fitness is nothing but the Malthusian parameter in (1.4):

$$\frac{d}{dt}(\ln N) = W \tag{5.3}$$

We can thus relate our distance H to the population-size dynamics.

Let us denote

$$H(t) = H(\mathbf{p}(t), \mathbf{p}^*)$$

and integrate equation (5.2) from 0 to t. We will have

$$H(t) - H(0) = \int_0^t W(t)\, dt - W^* t$$

Substituting $W(t)$ from (5.3), we have

$$H(t) - H(0) = \ln N(t) - \ln N(0) - W^* t$$

Now, let $t \to \infty$. Then $H(t) \to 0$ because $\mathbf{p}(t) \to \mathbf{p}^*$. Also, $\ln N(t) \to \ln N_1 = W^* t$. Consequently,

$$-H(0) = \ln N_1 - \ln N_0$$

Since $\ln N_1 - \ln N_0 = W^* \tau$ (see definition (5.1)), we obtain the following result:

$$H(\mathbf{p}, \mathbf{p}^*) = W^* \tau \tag{5.4}$$

This result connects the concept of selective delay introduced in the beginning of this chapter with the specific formula that measures the distance between the initial and the final frequency configurations. The important feature of this formula is that both parameters on the right-hand side can be observed from the population size dynamics alone, so that we can basically measure $H(\mathbf{p}, \mathbf{p}^*)$ without knowing either $\mathbf{p}$ or $\mathbf{p}^*$. In this sense the relationship can be regarded as macroscopic; that is, the information about the changes in gene frequencies may be extracted from the population growth curve.

5.3 Rate of Adaptation

One of the properties of the adaptation curve $W(t, \mathbf{p}_0)$ is known as Fisher's fundamental theorem of natural selection (Fisher, 1930; see Chapter 3 of this book). It states that the average fitness tends to its equilibrium value monotonically:

$$\frac{d}{dt} W(t, \mathbf{p}_0) \geq 0$$

Therefore, the average fitness at any instant of time, t, lies between the initial and final fitness values:

$$W(0, \mathbf{p}_0) \leq W(t, \mathbf{p}_0) \leq W^*$$

This is a trivial consequence of Fisher's theorem. One may ask whether there exists a nontrivial, time-dependent estimate of the adaptation rate, or whether it can assume any value. Let us formulate the problem by fixing one of the parameters, namely, $\mathbf{p}^* > 0$. This means in the final analysis that we fix some of the properties of the environment as they are expressed in terms of fitness values and, consequently, the position of the equilibrium frequency vector. The question now is whether the population can move from the initial genetic composition $\mathbf{p}_0$ to the equilibrium composition $\mathbf{p}^*$ at any preassigned rate. The answer is no. In reality, knowledge of the initial and final points restricts possible rates of adaptation. It will also be shown that this restriction is expressed in the entropy distance between the initial and equilibrium frequency vectors, $H(\mathbf{p}_0, \mathbf{p}^*)$ defined in the previous section.

Integrating equation (5.2) from 0 to ∞, we have

$$\int_0^\infty (W^* - W)\, dt = H(\mathbf{p}_0, \mathbf{p}^*) \tag{5.5}$$

Let us now show that

$$W(t) \geq W^* - \frac{H(\mathbf{p}_0, \mathbf{p}^*)}{t} \tag{5.6}$$

To prove it, consider an arbitrary time t_0 and write the integral as a sum:

$$\int_0^\infty (W^* - W)\, dt = \int_0^{t_0} (W^* - W)\, dt + \int_{t_0}^\infty (W^* - W)\, dt$$

Assume the opposite;

$$W(t_0) < W^* - \frac{H(\mathbf{p}_0, \mathbf{p}^*)}{t_0}$$

Then it should also be true for all time $0 \leq t < t_0$ because of Fisher's theorem. Therefore,

$$\int_0^\infty (W^* - W)\, dt > \int_0^{t_0} (W^* - W)\, dt > H(\mathbf{p}_0, \mathbf{p}^*)$$

This contradicts the original equation, (5.5). Since our assumption was incorrect, then for all time

$$W(t) \geq W^* - \frac{H(\mathbf{p}_0, \mathbf{p}^*)}{t}$$

The hyperbola that bounds all possible adaptation curves $W(t)$ is shown in Figure 5.2, in which the shaded area is equal to $H(\mathbf{p}_0, \mathbf{p}^*)$.

5.4 Experimental Confirmation

There are two relationships proposed in this chapter that can be verified experimentally. One is equation (5.4), which relates the entropy distance between the initial and the equilibrium gene frequencies to the selective delay; the other is inequality (5.6), which bounds all possible adaptation curves by hyperbolas. Note that in neither case do we need to know the gene frequencies during the course of evolution. We need them only to calculate the entropy distance at the beginning and at the end of the process. All of the other parameters can be measured directly from the population growth curve.

Such verification has been performed (Costantino, Ginzburg, and Moffa Scully 1977; Ginzburg and Costantino, 1979). Let us first discuss the experiments directed towards the verification of equation (5.4). Populations of the flour beetle *Tribolium castaneum* Herbst that segregate at the unsaturated fatty acid sensitive locus (symbolized by *cos*, for corn oil sensitive) were studied. A general review of the biology of the *cos* mutant is beyond the scope of this book (see Costantino, Bell, and Rogler, 1967, 1968; Costantino and Rowe, 1972; and Moffa Scully and Costantino, 1975.) It is sufficient to note here that for the *cos/cos* genotype, larval viability is approximately 8%, compared to 70% for the +/+ genotype and 80% the +/*cos* genotype. Other measures of fitness, such as days to sexual maturity and eggs produced per 24-hour interval, also forecast a stable genetic polymorphis at this locus.

Cultures were established in which the initial allele frequency of *cos* ranged from 0 to 1 in 0.1 increments. Five replicates were maintained for each of the initial allele frequencies 1, 0.9, 0.7, 0.6, and 0.5; three replicates were maintained for each of the remaining allele frequencies. The initial genotypic array included only the

$+/+$ and cos/cos genotypes; the initial demographic array consisted of ten adult females and ten adult males. The populations were grown on 20 grams of corn oil media (percentage composition: 90% wheat flour, 5% dried brewer's yeast, and 5% liquid corn oil), which was changed every 2 weeks. The animals were cultured in chambers maintained at $33 \pm 1°C$ and $42 \pm 6\%$ relative humidity. The number of small and large larvae, pupae, and adults were counted every 2 weeks for 68 weeks using standard *Tribolium* techniques. We report here on the number of adults at 2, 4, and 6 weeks.

For each initial allele frequency, the Malthusian parameter for the mean number of adults at 2, 4, and 6 weeks was estimated by the method of least squares. The coefficients of determination, which measure the proportion of the corrected sums of squares that can be "explained" by fitting the form $\ln A = \ln A_0 + Wt$, ranged from 96.4% to 99.5%. The overall fit of the data was significant at the 0.01 probability level in each case.

The average fitness of the population at equilibrium was determined from data on 18 new cultures started with 20 randomly chosen adults of both sexes taken from the cultures at week 68. The estimated value of W^* was 0.713 ± 0.044. Genetic analysis revealed that the cultures initially segregating for the *cos* allele had converged to an equilibrium allele frequency of 0.25 ± 0.03.

It is impossible to find an exact value of the selective delay, since it is the asymptote as time tends to infinity. To estimate the parameter $\tau(\mathbf{p}_0, \mathbf{p}^*)$, we compared the time required for each initial nonequilibrium population to reach the number of adults predicted by the equilibrium culture at week 4. The experimental results are summarized in Table 5.1.

In general, the agreement between the observation and prediction is good. The hypothesis that the data fit the theoretical $H(\mathbf{p}_0, \mathbf{p}^*)$ was accepted using a chi-square test at the 0.05 level of

TABLE 5.1 Experimental check of $W^*\tau(\mathbf{p}_0, \mathbf{p}^*) = H(\mathbf{p}_0, \mathbf{p}^*)$.

$\mathbf{p}_0$	W	$\tau(\mathbf{p}_0, \mathbf{p}^*)$	$W^*\tau(\mathbf{p}_0, \mathbf{p}^*)$	$H(\mathbf{p}_0, \mathbf{p}^*)$
0.9	0.489 ± 0.061	1.828	1.303	1.191
0.8	0.610 ± 0.117	0.673	0.479	0.700
0.7	0.624 ± 0.071	0.567	0.404	0.429
0.6	0.634 ± 0.113	0.496	0.353	0.252
0.5	0.673 ± 0.048	0.234	0.167	0.130
0.4	0.712 ± 0.115	0.005	0.003	0.049
0.3	0.702 ± 0.065	0.061	0.043	0.006
0.2	0.676 ± 0.053	0.217	0.155	0.007
0.1	0.634 ± 0.104	0.498	0.355	0.092

$\mathbf{p}^* = 0.25$, $W^* = 0.713 \pm 0.044$

probability. It would appear that the macroparameter of the number of adults, together with the idea of selective delay compared to the fitness entropy, will yield some information about the genetic structure of a population. The data also reveal, however, a caution for this procedure. In our case of $\mathbf{p}^* = 0.25$, $H(\mathbf{p}_0, \mathbf{p}^*)$ ranges only from 0.130 to 0.092 for $\mathbf{p}_0$ between 0.5 and 0.1; consequently, it is difficult to discriminate among unknown populations in this rather wide range of allele frequencies.

Let us consider now the second set of experiments that were directed towards verification of inequality (5.6).

The experimental design centers on several cultures of the flour beetle *Tribolium castaneum* Herbst that were initiated with identical age structure but different frequencies of the unsaturated fatty acid sensitive allele. Demographic and genetic data of continuously growing populations were collected for 68 weeks. A complete discussion of these data is presented by Moffa and Costantino (1977). We will briefly review the experimental procedure and then focus attention on those data relevant to measuring the rate of adaptation.

Cultures were established in which the initial frequency of the unsaturated fatty acid sensitive allele (*cos*) range from 0 to 1 in increments of +/+ and *cos/cos* homozygotes; the initial demographic array consisted of ten newly emerged adult females and ten newly emerged adult males. Each population was grown on 20 grams of corn-oil medium, which was changed every 2 weeks. The beetles were cultured in chambers maintained at $33 \pm 1°C$ and $42 \pm 6\%$ relative humidity. The number of small and large larvae, pupae, and adults were counted every 2 weeks; in addition, the frequency of the sensitive allele and the genotypic array at this locus were estimated.

The measurement of the growth rate curves, $\hat{W}(t)$, was obtained by combining two data items: estimates of the total numbers of offspring (3.97, 54.32, and 46.53 for the *cos/cos*, +/*cos*, and +/+ genotypes, respectively) and the genotypic array data (see Table 3 in Moffa Scully, and Costantino, 1977). The predicted stable equilibrium frequency of the sensitive allele, based on the above estimates, was $\mathbf{p}^* = 0.13$. Experimentally, $\mathbf{p}^* = 0.25 \pm 0.03$. This discrepancy was discussed by Moffa Scully, and Costantino (1977), and it appears that the predicted value represents a lower boundary of $\mathbf{p}^*$; consequently, we used $\mathbf{p}^* = 0.25$ in our computations. The preceding theory applies to the continuous model. If S_i are the absolute fitnesses for the discrete case and W_i are the fitnesses in the continuous model, the relationship is $\exp(W_i t) = S_i > 0$, where t is generation time. We can take $t = 1$, so $W_i = \ln S_i$. Consequently, we have used W_i as the logarithms of the absolute fitnesses and calculated the average fitness with them.

We direct our attention now to inequality (5.6). The hyperbola that bounds the possible adaptation curves was computed with $W^* = 3.85$ and $H(\mathbf{p}_0, \mathbf{p}^*) = 0.25$. This lower bound and the experimental data are sketched in Figure 5.4. It is clear from the graphs that if the initial value of the average fitness, $W(0)$, is much less than W^*, the adaptation should go quickly. The closer $\mathbf{p}_0$ is to $\mathbf{p}^*$, the closer the adaptation curve should be to a step function. The data points were fitted to a function of the form $W(t) = \alpha - \beta/t$ by the method of least squares. The overall fit of the data was significant at the 0.05 probability level in each case. For the cultures with $\mathbf{p}_0 = 0.1$, 0.5, 0.7, and 0.9, $\hat{W}(t)$ is above the lower bound of $W^* - H(\mathbf{p}_0, \mathbf{p}^*)/t$. For the culture with $\mathbf{p}_0 = 0.3$, the data are below this bound. All populations definitely show a trend of convergence to W^*.

The general conclusion of this chapter is that the selective delay appears due to the action of the natural selection process in exponentially growing populations, and it can be described adequately by the entropy distance between the initial and final genetic structure of such populations. All considerations have been based on the assumption of constant fitnesses. More realistic models that involve density-dependent and frequency-dependent selection will be considered in the next chapter.

5.5 Problems and Discussion

1. One problem that can be formulated based on the results of this chapter is to generalize those results for the case of density-dependent selection. The objective would be to find a function of gene frequencies and population size such that its derivative could be expressed by the parameters of population-size dynamics without explicit influence of gene frequencies. The discovery of such a function could lead to useful equalities or inequalities (or both) that describe macroscopically the growth process with density-dependent selection, as was done in this chapter for the simpler case of constant selection. In a simple case of nonselective density-dependence, this was recently done by Desharnais and Costantino (1981).

2. Another problem is that of a generalization to the case of multiple loci. It is known already that in the two-locus case, we can have more than one stable equilibrium in the system. Therefore, we cannot expect a global Lyapunov function to exist in the case of multiple loci. It would be useful, however, to find at least local

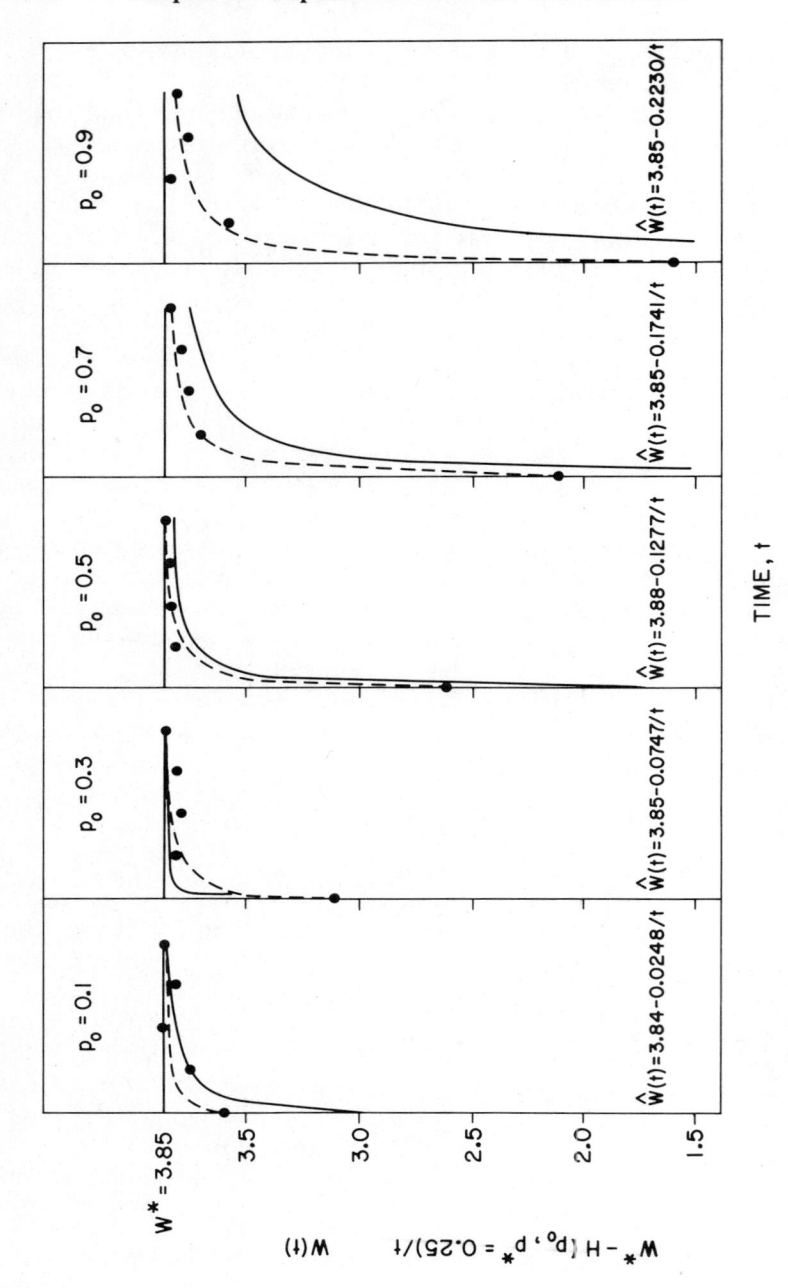

110 Chapter 5: "Exponential" Growth with Selection

Figure 5.4 A comparison of the interval between W^* and $W^* - H(\mathbf{p}_0, \mathbf{p}^* = 0.25)/t$; solid lines, with the experimental values of $W(t)$ and circles, for cultures with initial allele frequencies of 0.1, 0.3, 0.5, 0.7 and 0.9.

5.5 Problems and discussion

Lyapunov functions. This would help clarify problems of the size and shape of attraction zones and might also be useful in reaching a general understanding of the dynamics of multi-locus systems.

3. The use of the entropy distance H as a local Lyapunov function yields some useful results in the case of two loci. Consider the equations for the two-locus system involving selection and recombination in (3.12). The derivative of

$$H(\mathbf{p}, \mathbf{p}^*) = \sum_{i=1}^{4} p_i^* \ln \frac{p_i}{p_i^*}$$

has the following form:

$$\dot{H}(\mathbf{p}) = [W(\mathbf{p}) - W(\mathbf{p}^*)] - r[\Psi(\mathbf{p}^*, \mathbf{p}) - \Psi(\mathbf{p}, \mathbf{p}^*)]$$

where

$$\Psi(\mathbf{p}^*, \mathbf{p}) = \left(\frac{p_1^*}{p_1} + \frac{p_4^*}{p_4}\right) p_2 p_3 + \left(\frac{p_2^*}{p_2} + \frac{p_3^*}{p_3}\right) p_1 p_4$$

and r is the recombination fraction (see Section 3.4). It is easy to check that grad $\dot{H}(\mathbf{p})$ (within the simplex) vanishes at the equilibrium point $\mathbf{p} = \mathbf{p}^*$. If we assume (as in Karlin, 1979) that selection itself maintains polymorphism, then $W(\mathbf{p})$ is a convex function of frequencies, and thus the convexity of $\dot{H}(\mathbf{p})$ depends on the second term when $r \neq 0$. Consider the second-order approximation of the term containing r in the expression for $\dot{H}(\mathbf{p})$. The matrix of this second approximation has

$$\begin{pmatrix} -2p_2^*p_3^* & p_1^*p_4^* + p_2^*p_3^* & p_1^*p_4^* + p_2^*p_3^* & -2p_1^*p_4^* \\ p_1^*p_4^* + p_2^*p_3^* & -2p_1^*p_4^* & -2p_2^*p_3^* & p_1^*p_4^* + p_2^*p_3^* \\ p_1^*p_4^* + p_2^*p_3^* & -2p_2^*p_3^* & -2p_1^*p_4^* & p_1^*p_4^* + p_2^*p_3^* \\ -2p_1^*p_4^* & p_1^*p_4^* + p_2^*p_3^* & p_1^*p_4^* + p_2^*p_3^* & -2p_2^*p_3^* \end{pmatrix}$$

The eigenvalues of this matrix are $\lambda_1 = 0$, $\lambda_2 = 2D(\mathbf{p}^*)$, $\lambda_3 = -2D(\mathbf{p}^*)$, and $\lambda_4 = -4(p_1^*p_4^* + p_2^*p_3^*)$, where $D(\mathbf{p}) + p_1^*p_4^* - p_2^*p_3^*$ is the linkage disequilibrium function.

If $D(\mathbf{p}^*) = 0$, the whole expression is locally, nonpositively definite, so $H(\mathbf{p})$ is a Lyapunov function, and local stability is proved. Karlin's principle is therefore correct at least in the case of complete linkage equilibrium. This statement was also proved (Karlin, 1980) for a discrete time system. In general, when $D(\mathbf{p}^*) \neq 0$, the principle is clearly correct by simple continuity for small $|D|r$. Proving this for an arbitrary value of $|D|r$ would be another interesting problem.

6 Growth with Density- and Frequency-Dependent Selection

Most of the results on density-dependent selection, for the case of one population, have been summarized by Roughgarden (1979). Some of our considerations in this chapter will overlap with those results. We will be able to develop them a little further by using continuous-time models, which are easier to analyze. For instance, our generalization of Fisher's theorem for a density-dependent selection works only in continuous time, where we can avoid the oscillations and chaotic behavior which is characteristic for discrete-time models.

The theory of frequency-dependent selection remains considerably underdeveloped, as compared to the theory of density-dependence. The problems are not mathematical, but conceptual. We do not yet have a working idea of which classes of frequency-dependent fitnesses should be considered. I have chosen, therefore, to approach the problem from the point of view of necessary conditions, rather than to try setting up the entire system and then analyzing its behavior. This approach follows the logic of Chapter 4 (discussion section), where I argued for the utility of necessary conditions of polymorphism in the case of constant fitnesses. This logic also applies to density- and frequency-dependent selection.

6.1 Linear Density-Dependence

Here we consider the properties of equilibria and stability for density-dependent selection where the fitnesses W_{ij} are linear functions of population size. We will continue using the notation adopted in Chapter 2. The system we are interested in is the following (see 2.16):

$$\dot{p}_i = p_i(W_i - W), \quad i = 1, \ldots, n$$
$$\dot{N} = NW \tag{6.1}$$

where

$$f_i = \sum_{j=1}^{n} (\varepsilon_{ij} - \gamma_{ij}N)p_j = \sum_{j=1}^{n} W_{ij}(N)p_j$$

$$W = \sum_{i=1}^{n} p_i W_i$$

Matrices $\Sigma = ||\varepsilon_{ij}||$ and $\Gamma = ||\gamma_{ij}||$ are symmetrical.

Let us begin by proving the existence and uniqueness of the equilibrium. For the case of complete polymorphism, $p_i > 0$ ($i = 1, \ldots, n$), we have $W = 0$ from the last equation; therefore $W_i = 0$ ($i = 1, \ldots, n$). In other words,

$$(\Sigma - N\Gamma)\mathbf{p} = 0. \tag{6.2}$$

Now let us make two additional suppositions. First, assume that all γ_{ij} are positive, which means that all genotypes "feel" the effect of density (in general, we can speak of nonnegative γ_{ij}). Second, assume that the pencil of matrices $(\Sigma - N\Gamma)$ does not have double eigenvalues. Both assumptions are made only for the sake of simplicity. The second assumption is justified in Section 1.4 of the introduction.

We will now show that if problem (6.2) has a solution, it is unique. To prove this, assume the opposite: there are two solutions, $\{N_1 > 0, \mathbf{p}^{(1)} > 0\}$ and $\{N_2 > 0, \mathbf{p}^{(2)} > 0\}$. Thus

$$\left.\begin{array}{l}\Sigma \mathbf{p}^{(1)} = N_1 \Gamma \mathbf{p}^{(1)} \\ \Sigma \mathbf{p}^{(2)} = N_2 \Gamma \mathbf{p}^{(2)}\end{array}\right\} \tag{6.3}$$

Let us take the dot product of the first equation with $\mathbf{p}^{(2)}$ and of the second with $\mathbf{p}^{(1)}$ and then subtract one from the other:

$$(\mathbf{p}^{(2)}, \Sigma \mathbf{p}^{(1)}) - (\mathbf{p}^{(1)}, \Sigma \mathbf{p}^{(2)}) = N_1(\mathbf{p}^{(2)}\Gamma \mathbf{p}^{(1)}) - N_2(\mathbf{p}^{(1)}, \Gamma \mathbf{p}^{(2)})$$

Since both matrices are symmetrical, the bilinear forms are equal. We obtain

$$(N_1 - N_2)(\mathbf{p}^{(1)}, \Gamma \mathbf{p}^{(2)}) = 0$$

The bilinear form is positive because all $\gamma_{ij} > 0$. Therefore $N_1^* = N_2^*$; this contradicts the supposition about the eigenvalues of the pencil $(\Sigma - N\Gamma)$, so uniqueness is proved. Note that if we allow double eigenvalues, N_1 may be equal to N_2 and the following statement remains true: If there are two nontrivial equilibrium states $\{N_1, \mathbf{p}^{(1)}\}$ and $\{N_2, \mathbf{p}^{(2)}\}$, then $N_1 = N_2$. In other words, all equilibrium structures correspond to one and only one value of the population size.

As we already mentioned in Chapter 2, the number of equilibrium problems involving different equilibria for different subsystems is $2^n - 1$. Thus we can state that the number of equilibrium states does not exceed $2^n - 1$. The number is typically much less, since many subsets of alleles are not compatible.

Before we consider the stability problem, let us prove that all of the equilibrium points are extreme points of the average fitness of the population, given as a function of frequencies. We construct the Lagrange function for the conditional extremum:

$$W + \tilde{\lambda}\left(1 - \sum_{i=1}^{n} p_i\right) = (\mathbf{p}, (\Sigma - N\Gamma)\mathbf{p}) + \tilde{\lambda}\left(1 - \sum_{i=1}^{n} p_i\right)$$

Differentiation with respect of p_i gives

$$2(\Sigma - N\Gamma)\mathbf{p} = \tilde{\lambda}\mathbf{e}$$

Since $W = 0$ at the equilibrium point, we see that $\tilde{\lambda} = 0$, and then

$$(\Sigma - N\Gamma)\mathbf{p} = 0$$

So, the extremum frequencies satisfy the same set of equations as the equilibrium frequencies. It is easy to show that the boundary equilibrium points are the extreme points of the average fitness on the corresponding boundaries of the simplex $\Sigma_{i \in \bar{L}} p_i = 1$.

Let the equilibrium point be in the interior of the simplex $\{N^* > 0, \mathbf{p}^* > 0\}$. To analyze local stability, we need to construct the matrix of the linearized system. We have a situation analogous to the one considered as the second special case in the last section of Chapter 2, grad $F = 0$. Therefore, the matrix has the form

$$\begin{pmatrix} \mathbf{p}^*(\Sigma - N^*\Gamma) & \vdots & \alpha \\ \cdots\cdots\cdots\cdots\cdots & \vdots & \cdots\cdots \\ 0 \quad \cdot\cdot\cdot \quad 0 & \vdots & N^*\dfrac{\partial F}{\partial N} \end{pmatrix} \quad (6.4)$$

It is sufficient for stability that $\partial W/\partial N < 0$ and that all eigenvalues (except one which is always zero) of the matrix $\mathbf{P}^*(\Sigma - N^*\Gamma)$ be negative. Since $(\Sigma - N\Gamma)$ is a symmetrical matrix, the latter statement specifies the negative definiteness of that matrix on the simplex. The zero eigenvalue always exists because $\det(\Sigma - N\Gamma) = 0$. But this does not lead to the critical case of stability, since the system has $\sum_{i=1}^{n} p_i = 1$ as its first integral. The inequality $\partial W/\partial N < 0$ is satisfied automatically:

$$\frac{\partial W}{\partial N} = -\sum_{i,j=1}^{n} \gamma_{ij} p_i^* p_j^* < 0$$

The negative definiteness of the matrix $(\Sigma - N^*\Gamma)$ means that the equilibrium point is the maximum of the function W with respect to the frequencies. Finally, we conclude that the stability of the equilibrium $\{N^* > 0, \mathbf{p}^* > 0\}$ is equivalent to a maximization of the average fitness W with respect to the frequencies.

Now consider the boundary equilibria. Let $p_l^* = 0$ and $l \in L$. In our case, necessary conditions of stability (see Chapter 2) have the form

$$W_l(\mathbf{p}^*, N^*) = \sum_{j=1}^{n} (\varepsilon_{lj} - N^* \gamma_{lj}) p_j^* < 0, \qquad l \in L$$

Note that for symmetric matrices these conditions can be rewritten as

$$\frac{\partial W}{\partial p_l}(\mathbf{p}^*, N^*) < 0, \qquad l \in \overline{L} \tag{6.5}$$

which are the conditions of maxima at the boundary. It is simple to prove that the stability of the boundary equilibria is equivalent to inequalities (6.5) both for the zero frequencies and for the negative definiteness of the matrix $(\Sigma^{\bar{L}} - N^*\Gamma^{\bar{L}})$ on the corresponding subsimplex. Note that we mean only local asymptotic stability (see the discussion in Section 1.3). Finally, we see that the statement about maximization of the average fitness with respect to the frequencies is true for all stable equilibria, whether or not they are at the boundary.

Let us now reconsider the equilibrium problem for the interior of the simplex—that is, for the case of complete coexistence. It is easy to see that the matrix of the second partial derivatives $\partial^2 W / \partial p_i \partial p_j$ at the equilibrium point coincides with the matrix $2(\Sigma - N^*\Gamma)$. At the same time, the stability conditions are nothing more than the convexity conditions for the function W with respect to frequencies near the equilibrium point. Remembering the classification of interaction types from Chapter 2, we see that the stability of the equilibrium is equivalent to the limited and mutualistic case. The presence of the competitive term is the sufficient condition of instability.

Chapter 6: Growth with Density- and Frequency-Dependent Selection

Let $\phi(\mathbf{p})$ be a function representing the population size at equilibrium if we keep the genetic structure constant:

$$\phi(\mathbf{p}) = \frac{(\mathbf{p}, \Sigma \mathbf{p})}{(\mathbf{p}, \Gamma \mathbf{p})} \tag{6.6}$$

Multiplying (6.2) by $\mathbf{p}$, we note that $N = \phi(\mathbf{p})$. Next we consider the extremal points of this function on the simplex δ_n. The Lagrange function has the form

$$\phi(\mathbf{p}) + \tilde{\lambda}\left(1 - \sum_{i=1}^{n} p_i\right)$$

Setting up the system of equations for the extremi, we obtain

$$\frac{\partial \phi}{\partial p_i} = \tilde{\lambda}, \quad i = 1, \ldots, n$$

As an homogeneous function (by definition (6.6)), ϕ satisfies the Euler identity:

$$\sum_{i=1}^{n} p_i \frac{\partial \phi}{\partial p_i} = 0$$

Therefore, $\tilde{\lambda} = 0$. Calculating the partial derivatives, we get

$$(\Sigma - \phi(\mathbf{p})\Gamma)\mathbf{p} = 0$$

So, at any equilibrium point $\{N^*, \mathbf{p}^*\}$, the function $\phi(\mathbf{p})$ is at an extremum. The opposite is also true. Every extremal point of the function ϕ, where $\phi(\mathbf{p}^*) > 0$, is an equilibrium point. Equilibria belonging to the boundary $\{N^* > 0, \mathbf{p}^* \geq 0\}$ are also extremal points of the function $\phi(\mathbf{p})$ on the corresponding subsimplices $p_l = 0, l \in \overline{L}$.

$$\left(\frac{\partial^2 \phi}{\partial p_i \partial p_j}\bigg|_{\mathbf{p}^*}\right) = \frac{2}{(\mathbf{p}^*, \Gamma \mathbf{p}^*)} - (\Sigma - N^*\Gamma)$$

That is, this matrix is proportional to the matrix of the first approximation system defining the stability. It is easy to see that for the boundary equilibria, (6.5) is just a necessary condition for maxima of this function. The stability of equilibria in the interior of the simplex is equivalent to maximization of function (6.6) at the corresponding interior point.

We now arrive at the following result: The equilibrium state $\{N^*, \mathbf{p}^*\}$ is stable if and only if the point $\mathbf{p}^*$ is the local maximum of the function $\phi(\mathbf{p})$. All the stable equilibrium points are maximum points of the function $\phi(\mathbf{p})$, where $\phi(\mathbf{p}^*) > 0$. At these points, $N^* = \phi(\mathbf{p}^*)$.

6.1 Linear Density-Dependence

Note that we can easily formulate the conditions of uniqueness of the stable equilibrium for all the simplex, including the boundaries. The sufficient condition is that the function $\phi(\mathbf{p})$ be convex; that is, that for any two frequency vectors $\mathbf{p}$ and $\mathbf{q}$ and for any $0 \leq \lambda \leq 1$, we should have

$$\Phi(\lambda \mathbf{p} + (1-\lambda)\mathbf{q}) \geq \lambda\phi(\mathbf{p}) + (1-\lambda)\phi(\mathbf{q})$$

The uniqueness of the maximum follows from the convexity of the function defined on the convex set δ_n. As a bounded function on a closed set, $\phi(\mathbf{p})$ always reaches its maximum. Therefore, at least one stable equilibrium always exists (if $\phi(\mathbf{p}^*) > 0$).

The necessary and sufficient conditions for the existence of a stable polymorphism for the case of two alleles can easily be obtained (Ginzburg and Konovalov, 1974). They are a generalization of the classical advantage of heterozygotes,

$$\frac{\varepsilon_{11}}{\gamma_{11}} < \frac{\varepsilon_{12}}{\gamma_{12}} \quad \text{and} \quad \frac{\varepsilon_{12}}{\gamma_{12}} > \frac{\varepsilon_{22}}{\gamma_{22}}$$

It is hard to find interpretable conditions of the same type in terms of the elements of the matrices $\Sigma = ||\varepsilon_{ij}||$ and $\Gamma = ||\gamma_{ij}||$ for n alleles; however, some questions can be answered. For example: Are there density-dependent factors (matrix γ) that provide a stable polymorphism independently of the values of density-independent fitnesses (matrix Σ)? The answer is yes, when the heterozygotes are not affected by density:

$$\begin{cases} \gamma_{ij} = 0, & i \neq j, \quad i,j = 1,\ldots,n \\ \gamma_{ii} > 0, & i = 1,\ldots,n \end{cases}$$

When Γ is a diagonal matrix, the equilibrium equations

$$(\Sigma - N\Gamma)\mathbf{p} = 0$$

can be reduced to the form

$$(\Gamma^{-1/2} \Sigma \Gamma^{-1/2} - N\mathbf{I})(\Gamma^{1/2})\mathbf{p} = 0$$

where $\mathbf{I}$ is the unit matrix. An equilibrium state for $\varepsilon_{ij} \geq 0$ exists and is unique, by a corollary to the Perron-Frobenius theorem (Gantmacher, 1959). Stability is guaranteed by the same theorem.

This result shows that the advantage of heterozygotes, especially in their sensitivity to density, might sometimes be the determining factor in allowing polymorphism where we would not expect it based on classical density-independent considerations.

For the purpose of interpretation, it is interesting to consider two cases: one with density-independent selection ($\gamma_{ij} = \gamma$, $i,j = 1,\ldots,n$) and one with selection that is only density-dependent

($\varepsilon_{ij} = \sigma$, $i, j = 1, \ldots, n$). In the first case,

$$\phi = \frac{1}{\gamma} \sum_{i,j=1}^{n} \varepsilon_{ij} p_i p_j$$

and we obtain Fisher's well-known result: maximization of the average fitness at a stable equilibrium. In the second case

$$\phi = \frac{\sigma}{\sum_{i,j=1}^{n} \gamma_{ij} p_i p_j}$$

and the result is a minimization of the effect of density-dependent factors on the population at the stable equilibrium. Therefore, the general case must represent some compromise between these two tendencies.

6.2 General Density-Dependence

We will generalize the results of the previous section for density-dependence by allowing the fitnesses to be arbitrary functions, not necessarily linear, of the population size. We assume that the average fitness $W(\mathbf{p}, N)$ is a decreasing function of the population size N; more precisely, we suppose that $\partial W/\partial N < 0$, and $W(\mathbf{p}, 0) < 0$, for all $\mathbf{p} \in \delta_n$. These assumptions reflect the influence of limiting factors upon the population. We also assume that for each $\mathbf{p} \in \delta_n$, the average fitness W is negative if N is large enough.

With these assumptions, the equation

$$W(\mathbf{p}, N) = \sum_{i,j=1}^{n} W_{ij}(N) p_i p_j = 0$$

has the unique root N for each fixed $\mathbf{p}$, so that for all $\mathbf{p} \in \delta$, there exists the implicit function $N = \phi(\mathbf{p})$ with

$$W(\mathbf{p}, \phi(\mathbf{p})) = 0$$

This function has the same meaning as before; it is the expected equilibrium population number, provided that the genetic structure $\mathbf{p}$ is fixed. We shall consider simultaneously the properties of the function ϕ with the equilibrium problem for the system.

Let us consider the equilibrium point $(\mathbf{p}^*, N^*)$ of a system in which $N^* > 0$. The equations of the equilibrium have the form $p_i W_i = 0$, $i = 1, \ldots, n$. Assume initially that there exists an equilibrium point with all $p_i^* > 0$ (polymorphism). In this case the equations are

$$\sum_{j=1}^{n} W_{ij}(N^*) p_j^* = 0, \quad i = 1, \ldots, n$$

6.2 General Density-Dependence

and the equilibrium point is just the eigenvector of the matrix $||W_{ij}(N^*)||$, corresponding to the "eigenvalue" N^*. Certainly at the equilibrium point, $N^* = \phi(\mathbf{p}^*)$.

Let us consider now the stationary points of the function $\phi(\mathbf{p})$ on the simplex δ_n. The Lagrange function for the constrained extremum problem is

$$\phi(\mathbf{p}) + \lambda \left(1 - \sum_{i=1}^{n} p_i\right)$$

and the necessary conditions of the extremum are $\partial \phi / \partial p_i = \lambda$, $i = 1, \ldots, n$. It is easy to show that, at the point $\mathbf{p}^*$,

$$\sum_{i=1}^{n} p_i \frac{\partial \phi}{\partial p_i} = 0$$

and so $\lambda = 0$. After the calculation of the partial derivatives for the implicit function ϕ, we obtain the conditions for the extremum:

$$\sum_{j=1}^{n} W_{ij}(\phi(\mathbf{p}^*)) p_j^* = 0, \qquad i = 1, \ldots, n.$$

Thus, the frequency component $\mathbf{p}^*$ of the equilibrium point $(\mathbf{p}^*, N^*)$ is the stationary point of the function $\phi(\mathbf{p})$ on the simplex δ_n. The deduction can easily be repeated for the equilibrium points on the boundary of the simplex (some p_i^* are zero). In these cases the result is also correct if we consider a stationary point on the minimal subsimplex containing the equilibrium point $\mathbf{p}^*$.

We now consider the local asymptotic stability of the equilibrium point $(\mathbf{p}^*, N^*)$ when $N^* > 0$, $p_i^* > 0$ $(i = 1, \ldots, n)$. The matrix of the linearized system for the nonlinear differential equations has the form

$$\begin{pmatrix} p_1^* & & & \\ & p_2^* & & 0 \\ & & \ddots & \\ 0 & & & p_n^* \\ & & & & N^* \end{pmatrix} \cdot \begin{pmatrix} W_{11}(N^*) & \cdots & W_{1n}(N^*) & \dfrac{\partial(W_1 - W)}{\partial N} \\ W_{21}(N^*) & \cdots & W_{2n}(N^*) & \dfrac{\partial(W_2 - W)}{\partial N} \\ \vdots & & \vdots & \vdots \\ W_{n1}(N^*) & \cdots & W_{nn}(N^*) & \dfrac{\partial(W_n - W)}{\partial N} \\ 0 & \cdots & 0 & \dfrac{\partial W}{\partial N} \end{pmatrix}$$

where all the partial derivatives are calculated at the point $(\mathbf{p}^*, N^*)$. As long as $\partial W / \partial N < 0$ and matrix $||W_{ij}||$ is symmetric, the sufficient

Chapter 6: Growth with Density- and Frequency-Dependent Selection

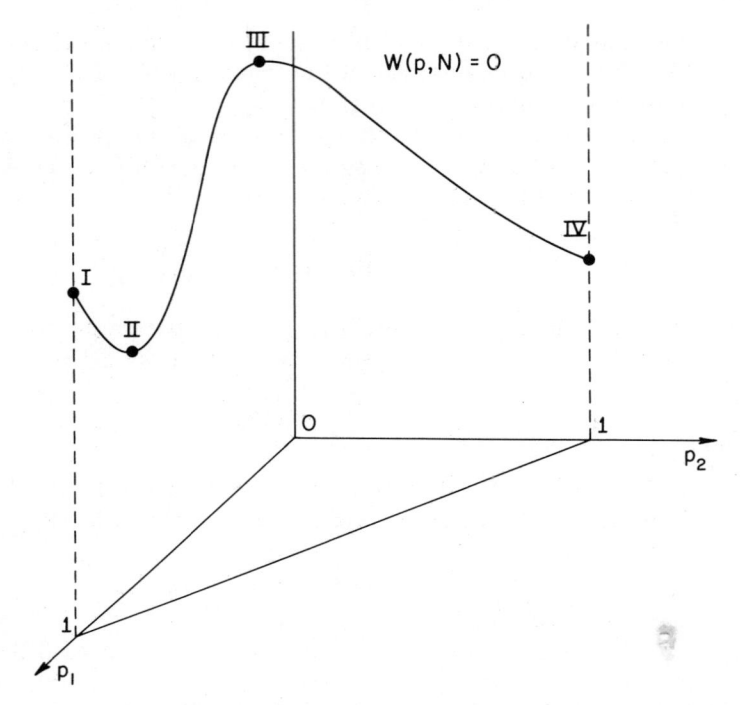

Figure 6.1 Qualitative behavior of the equilibrium surface with equilibria indicated. Points I and III are stable equilibria, while points II and IV are unstable.

condition for stability is the negative definiteness of the matrix $||W_{ij}(N^*)||$ on the simplex (Gantmacher, 1959)—or, in other words, the negativeness of all eigenvalues of this matrix except one (given the existence of the first integral of the system, $\sum_{i=1}^{n} p_1 = 1$).

Let us compare this result with the conditions for a maximum of the function $\phi(\mathbf{p})$ at the point $\mathbf{p}^*$. After some simple calculations, we obtain

$$\left(\frac{\partial^2 \phi}{\partial p_i \partial p_j}\bigg|_{\mathbf{p}^*}\right) = -\frac{2}{\frac{\partial W}{\partial N}\bigg|_{(\mathbf{p}^*, N^*)}} (W_{ij}(N^*))$$

It is clear that the conditions for a local maximum of the function ϕ at the point $\mathbf{p}^*$ are the same as the asymptotic stability conditions for the equilibrium point $(\mathbf{p}^*, N^*)$. This result is also correct for the boundary equilibrium points, although the proof is a little more complicated. If we do not take into account the critical

6.3 Density-Dependent Coevolution

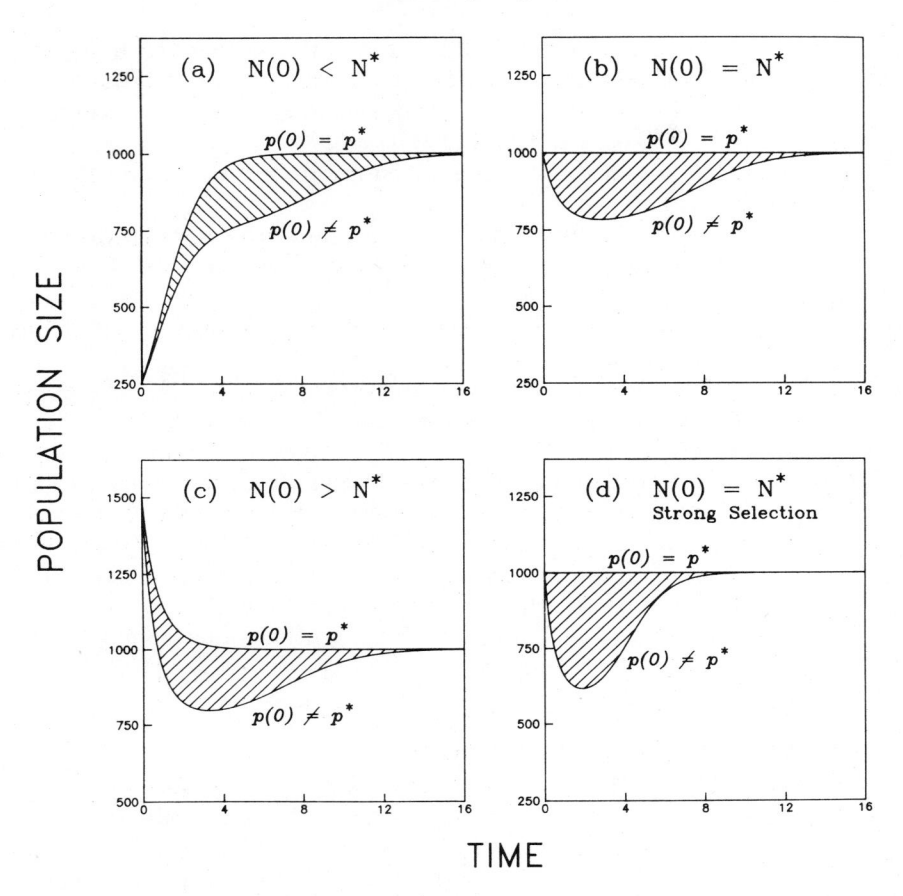

Figure 6.2 Comparison of the population-size trajectories of a population at genetic equilibrium, $\mathbf{p}^* = 0.5$, with populations initially at $\mathbf{p}_o = 0.01$, but which do eventually converge to $\mathbf{p}^*$ for the logistic model with density-dependent selection.

cases of stability that are parametrically unstable and thus not very interesting from a biological point of view, we have obtained the necessary and sufficient conditions of local stability. The equilibrium $(\mathbf{p}^*, N^*)$ is stable if and only if the point $\mathbf{p}^*$ is a local maximum of the function $\phi(\mathbf{p})$.

Now we will work out an analogue of Fisher's fundamental theorem of natural selection (Fisher, 1930) for the density-dependent case. The calculation of the derivative $\dot{W}$ gives

$$\dot{W} = 2 \sum_{i=1}^{n} p_i (W_i - W)^2 = \frac{\partial W}{\partial N} N W$$

If we assume that $W \geq 0$ at the initial moment $t = 0$ (for example, the initial population size is small enough), then $W \geq 0$ will continue for all time $0 \leq t < \infty$. If at any specified time t, the average fitness $W = 0$, it is easy to see that $\dot{W}(t) \geq 0$.

Thus $d/dt \,(\ln N) \geq 0$ at all times, except in the equilibrium case when $(\ln N)\dot{} = 0$.

If $W < 0$ at the moment $t = 0$ (the initial population number is large enough), then there may exist only one root of the function $W(t)$.

A qualitative phase portrait of the system in (6.1) is shown in Figure 6.1 for the case of $n = 2$.

It is interesting to note that even if $N(0) < N^*$, the curve $N(t)$ might decrease for a while and then increase, tending to the equilibrium level N^*. This effect can be very significant if the initial population structure $\mathbf{p}(0)$ is far enough from the equilibrium $\mathbf{p}^*$.

The experimental verification of this effect was attempted by Costantino and Desharnais (1980). Figure 6.2 shows that qualitative behavior of the population-size dynamics for a number of different initial conditions: with the initial population size above, below, or at the carrying capacity; and with the initial gene frequencies equal to or different from their equilibrium values.

6.3 Density-Dependent Coevolution

Consider a model of an ecosystem that consists of n interacting populations with numbers $N_1, \ldots, N_n$. Each population is under natural selection, and the genetic structure of each population is determined by m_i alleles ($i = 1, \ldots, n$) belonging to a single locus. (We use indices i or j or both to indicate a particular population in the ecosystem and other indices for different parameters within one population.) The basic equations of the model are

$$\begin{cases} \dot{p}_l^i = p_l^i(W_l^i - W^i), & i = 1, \ldots, n \\ \dot{N}_i = N_i W^i, & l = 1, \ldots, m_i \end{cases} \quad (6.7)$$

where p_l^i is the frequency of allele l in the ith population, W_l^i is the fitness of allele l in the ith population, and W^i is the mean fitness of the ith population, averaged over all genotypes. The functions W_l^i and W^i have the form

$$W_l^i = \sum_{k=1}^{m_i} W_{lk}^i p_k^i, \qquad W^i = \sum_{l=1}^{m_i} p_l^i W_l^i$$

where $||W_{lk}^i||$ is the fitness matrix of the genotypes (l, k) in the ith population. Here we consider density-dependent factors by allowing fitnesses to depend on the sizes of all the populations in the ecosystem

$$W_{lk}{}^i = W_{lk}{}^i (N_1, \ldots, N_n), \quad l, k = 1, \ldots, m_i, \quad i = 1, \ldots, n \qquad (6.8)$$

We do not admit the possibility of frequency-dependent selection here; that is, we do not allow the W_{lk} to depend on allelic frequencies. Note that the fitness matrices

$$W_{lk}{}^i = W_{kl}{}^i, \quad k, l = 1, \ldots, m_i, \quad i = 1, \ldots, n$$

are symmetric.

We assume that there exists an equilibrium state of the ecosystem which is polymorphic for each population. In other words, there are nonzero

$$N_i{}^* \quad (i = 1, \ldots, n), \qquad p^*{}_l{}^i \quad (l = 1, \ldots, m_i, \; i = 1, \ldots, n) \qquad (6.9)$$

that make the right-hand sides of (6.7) equal to zero. The further assumption that $N_i{}^*$, $p_l{}^{*i}$ are nonzero is introduced only for the sake of simplicity; all results can be generalized for boundary equilibria in which some of the population sizes or gene frequencies (or both) are zero (Levin and Udovic, 1977).

The equilibrium state of (6.9) will be called *ecologically stable* if the system

$$\dot{N}_i = N_i W^i(p_{m_i}{}^{*i}, \ldots, p_{m_i}{}^{*i}, N_1, \ldots, N_n), \qquad i = 1, \ldots, n$$

has the points $N_1{}^*, \ldots, N_n{}^*$ as a stable equilibrium. In other words, the matrix (computed at the equilibrium)

$$M = \begin{bmatrix} N_1{}^* & \cdots & 0 \\ \vdots & & \vdots \\ 0 & \cdots & N_n{}^* \end{bmatrix} \begin{bmatrix} \dfrac{\partial W^{*1}}{\partial N_1} & \cdots & \dfrac{\partial W^{*1}}{\partial N_n} \\ \vdots & & \vdots \\ \dfrac{\partial W^{*n}}{\partial N_1} & \cdots & \dfrac{\partial W^{*n}}{\partial N_n} \end{bmatrix} \qquad (6.10)$$

must have all eigenvalues with negative real parts. Generally speaking, ecological stability is neither a necessary nor a sufficient condition for the stability of the equilibrium state in (6.9), but in the case of density-dependent selection, it will be seen as a necessary condition for stability.

We use a special notation for the matrix of partial derivatives in (6.10),

$$E = (E_{ij}) = \left(\dfrac{\partial W^{*i}}{\partial N_j} \right)$$

and call it the *ecosystem matrix*. We consider the system under the assumption that it is ecologically stable.

Chapter 6: Growth with Density- and Frequency-Dependent Selection

At the equilibrium point (6.9), all derivatives $\dot{N}_i, \dot{p}_l^i$ are zero. Further, $W^i = 0$ for each $i = 1, \ldots, n$, and—in fact—

$$W_l^i = 0, \qquad l = 1, \ldots, m_i, \quad i = 1, \ldots, n$$

The equations involve only $\sum_{i=1}^{n} m_i$ equations with $\sum_{i=1}^{n} m_i + n$ variables, so to complete the system we must add the normalizing conditions

$$\sum_{l=1}^{n} p_l^i = 1, \qquad i = 1, \ldots, n$$

To consider the local stability problem, we calculate the matrix of the first approximation for system (6.7) at the equilibrium point (6.9). From the absence of frequency-dependent factors, we have

$$\frac{\partial W_l^i}{\partial p_k^j} = 0, \qquad \frac{\partial W^i}{\partial p_k^j} = 0$$

for all $j \neq i$ and arbitrary k. From the symmetry of the fitness matrices, we have

$$\frac{\partial W^i}{\partial p_l^i} = \frac{1}{2} W_l^i, \qquad l = 1, \ldots, m_i, \quad i = 1, \ldots, n$$

which are also zero at any equilibrium point. The matrix of the first approximation thus has the form

$$\begin{pmatrix} \boxed{V_1} & & & 0 & & \\ & \cdot & & & & \\ & & \cdot & & & U \\ & & & \boxed{V_{n-1}} & & \\ 0 & & & & \boxed{V_n} & \\ & & & & & M \end{pmatrix}$$

where M is given by (6.10), and each block V_1 is of size $m_i \times m_i$ and takes the form

$$V_i = \begin{pmatrix} p_1^{*i} & & \\ & \cdot & \\ & & \cdot \\ & & & p_{m_i}^{*i} \end{pmatrix} \begin{pmatrix} W_{1i}^{*i} & \cdots & W_{1m_i}^{*i} \\ \cdot & & \cdot \\ \cdot & & \cdot \\ W_{m_i 1}^{*i} & \cdots & W_{m_i m_i}^{*i} \end{pmatrix}, \qquad i = 1, \ldots, n$$

The matrix V consists of nonzero elements, but we are not interested

6.3 Density-Dependent Coevolution

in its structure because it has no influence on the stability conditions. In fact, it is clear (except for critical cases) that the equilibrium will be stable if and only if it is *ecologically stable*, and the matrices V_i are all stability matrices in which all eigenvalues have negative real parts. As a result of the symmetry of the fitness matrices, the conditions of stability for the matrices V_i are the same as for the fitness matrices $||W_{lk}^i||, i = 1, \ldots, n$, (that is, the negative definiteness of all these matrices on the corresponding simplexes).* This result means that all the fitness functions $W^i(p_1^i, \ldots, p_{m_i}^i)$ are maximized, subject to the constraint that population sizes are fixed at the values $N_1^*, \ldots, N_n^*$.

At the equilibrium point, all first derivatives of the functions W_i are zero and the matrix of second partial derivatives is a fitness matrix. This is a generalization of the corresponding result for the density-independent case, where the average fitness of the population is maximized at the equilibrium point.

If we introduce frequency-dependent factors that are "weak enough," the result will not change. Instead of zeros in the matrix, "small" elements will appear; these will not affect stability.

Consider now the equations corresponding to zero population growth for the n species

$$W^i(p_1^i, \ldots, p_{m_i}^i, N_1, \ldots, N_n) = 0, \qquad i = 1, \ldots, n \qquad (6.11)$$

These determine implicit functions

$$N_i = \phi_i(p_1^i, \ldots, p_{m_1}^1, \ldots, p_1^n, \ldots, p_{m_n}^n), \qquad i = 1, \ldots, n$$

in the neighborhood of a stable equilibrium point; indeed, all that is necessary for existence of that point is the condition $\det E \neq 0$. We will show that all the functions ϕ_i have extrema at the equilibrium point. Calculating partial derivatives from (6.11), we have

$$\frac{\partial W^i}{\partial p_l^k} + \sum_{j=1}^{n} \frac{\partial W^i}{\partial N_j} \frac{\partial \phi_j}{\partial p_l^k} = 0, \qquad i, k = 1, \ldots, n, \quad l = 1, \ldots, m_k$$

All derivatives $\partial W^i/\partial p_l^k$ at the equilibrium point are equal to zero, and therefore $\partial \phi_j/\partial p_l^k = 0$ for all j, k, l. To determine the nature of the extrema, we calculate second derivatives. Taking into account previous results, after a simple calculation we have

$$\frac{\partial^2 W^i}{\partial p_l^k \partial p_r^s} + \sum_{j=1}^{n} E_{ij} \frac{\partial^2 \phi_j}{\partial p_l^k \partial p_r^s} = 0 \qquad (6.12)$$

* There is always a zero eigenvalue for each matrix V_i. This means we do not have a critical case of stability, because of the constraints imposed by the normalizing conditions. However, if there is more than one zero eigenvalue, a critical case exists.

Chapter 6: Growth with Density- and Frequency-Dependent Selection

The only nonzero derivatives are for $k = s = i$, for which

$$\frac{\partial^2 W^2}{\partial p_l^s \partial p_r^s} = 2W_{lr}^s$$

Thus, multiplying (6.12) by p_l^k and p_r^s, summing on all k, l, s, and r, and using Taylor's theorem, we have an approximate explicit expression near the equilibrium point:

$$W^i(p_1^i, \ldots, p_{m_i}^i, N_1^*, \ldots, N_n^*) + \sum_{j=1}^{n} E_{ij}\phi_j = 0, \quad i = 1, \ldots, n \quad (6.13)$$

Inverting, we obtain

$$\phi_i = -\sum_{j=1}^{n} E_{ij}^{-1} W^j(p_1^j, \ldots, p_{m_j}^j, N_1^*, \ldots, N_n^*), \quad i = 1, \ldots, n$$

This is the approximate solution of equation (6.11) near the equilibrium point, where E_{ij}^{-1} are elements of the inverse matrix. Thus the nature of the extremum for each function ϕ_i depends on the signs of the corresponding elements of the inverse matrix E^{-1}. If, for example, all elements E_{ij}^{-1} are negative ($j = 1, \ldots, n$), then the function ϕ_i has a maximum at the equilibrium. If all elements in a row are positive, the corresponding function has a minimum point. In any case, we can determine the behavior of all the functions ϕ_i if we know the signs of the elements of the inverse ecosystem matrix.

This result can be of practical value if we want to predict changes in the equilibrium population sizes due to small changes in genetic structure.

The direction of change can often be predicted without any calculations. The result for the cases of self-influence (where we consider only the diagonal elements E_{ii}^{-1} of the inverse) and of two alleles ($m_i = 2, i = 1, \ldots, n$) is contained in Roughgarden (1976). An interesting interpretation of these cases in terms of feedback coefficients (Levins, 1974) has also been suggested.

As an illustration, consider coevolution between two interacting species. If the interaction between these species is competitive, all elements of the ecosystem matrix are negative. From the assumption of stability we have $\det E > 0$. Thus the elements of the inverse matrix have the following signs, which we indicate as shown:

$$\text{sign } E^{-1} = \begin{bmatrix} - & + \\ + & - \end{bmatrix}$$

This means that the functions ϕ_1 and ϕ_2 are maximized by their own genetic variables and minimized by the genetic structure of their competitors. Any change in the genetic structure of population 1

6.3 Density-Dependent Coevolution

near equilibrium will decrease the size of N_1 and increase the size of N_2.

In the mutualistic case, the ecosystem matrix has the sign structure

$$\text{sign } E = \begin{bmatrix} - & + \\ + & - \end{bmatrix}$$

and the inverse matrix will have the signs

$$\text{sign } E^{-1} = \begin{bmatrix} - & - \\ - & - \end{bmatrix}$$

The functions ϕ_1 and ϕ_2 are maximized at the equilibrium point, so that any change in the genetic structure of two mutualistic populations decreases the equilibrium population sizes.

Finally, for the predator-prey case, the ecosystem matrix signs are

$$\text{sign } E = \begin{bmatrix} - & - \\ + & - \end{bmatrix}$$

and the inverse matrix signs will be

$$\text{sign } E^{-1} = \begin{bmatrix} - & + \\ - & - \end{bmatrix}$$

The density of predators decreases as a result of any genetic change, but the prey population will decrease with a change in the structure of the prey itself and increase with a change in the structure of the predator population.

A most important point emerges; any change in the structure of one population implies a fixed direction of change for the sizes of all populations in the ecosystem. It is important to emphasize that this is not a dynamic result, but a simple property of the equilibrium equations; hence the interpretation is only quasi-static.

Generally, even under the restriction of stability, the signs of the elements of E^{-1} are not defined completely by the signs of the elements of E for $n \geqslant 3$. To obtain interpretable results for ecosystems with more than two components, we need to evaluate the interaction coefficients.

We will now try to find scalar functions that have a maximum at equilibrium and that are functions of all the genetic variables characterizing all the populations in the entire ecosystem. Certainly there are many such functions; we are interested only in those that are biologically significant. Let us multiply all equations (6.13) by

Chapter 6: Growth with Density- and Frequency-Dependent Selection

any positive χ_i and add them. We obtain

$$\sum_{i=1}^{n} \chi_i W^i(p_1{}^i, \ldots, p_{m_i}{}^i, N_1, \ldots, N_n) = - \sum_{i,j=1}^{n} \chi_i E_{ij} \phi_j$$

The function on the left-hand side is maximized at the equilibrium point. The same is true for the right-hand side. Remembering that ϕ_j are implicit functions in equations (6.11), we can formulate the following result. At the stable equilibrium the linear form

$$L = - \sum_{i,j=1}^{n} \chi_i E_{ij} N_j$$

with any positive $\chi_i (i = 1, \ldots, n)$ has a local maximum, under the restrictions $W^i = 0$, $i = 1, \ldots, n$. Conversely, all local maximum points of the linear form under the restrictions (6.11) are stable equilibria. Unfortunately, the matrix E_{ij} is calculated near the fixed equilibrium point, so that we cannot use the converse result directly (except in the case of Volterra-type systems, where the W^i are linear in $N_1, \ldots, N_n$ and the ecological matrix E does not depend on $N_1, \ldots, N_n$; here the converse principle becomes global and can be used for finding all equilibria).

In which cases is the sum of all population numbers maximized at the equilibrium point? In other words, in which cases does any genetic change in any population near the equilibrium decrease the general biomass of the ecosystem?* To answer this we set

$$L = \sum_{i=1}^{n} N_i$$

or

$$-\sum_{i=1}^{n} \chi_i E_{ij} = 1, \quad j = 1, \ldots, n$$

It is easy to see that this is true if and only if

$$\sum_{i=1}^{n} E_{ij}^{-1} < 0, \quad j = 1, \ldots, n \tag{6.14}$$

Hence, under the conditions of (6.14), the general biomass of the ecosystem will be maximized at the equilibrium.

We apply this result to the elementary two-population systems that we just considered.

$$E^{-1} = \frac{1}{\det E} \begin{pmatrix} E_{22} & -E_{21} \\ -E_{12} & E_{11} \end{pmatrix}$$

---
* Here we suppose that the biomass of a population is proportional to the population size. Without loss of generality we can interpret the values N_i as biomasses.

For the case of competition, all elements E_{ij} are negative. Conditions (6.13) mean that the self-competition intensity must be stronger than the interspecies competition intensity:

$$\left. \begin{aligned} E_{22} - E_{12} < 0 \\ E_{11} - E_{21} < 0 \end{aligned} \right\}$$

Under this restriction, which would be sufficient for ecological stability, the general biomass of the system $N_1 + N_2$ is maximized by the equilibrium genetic structures of both populations. In the case of mutualism, this fact is again true, since E^{-1} consists of negative elements. Finally, for the predator-prey case, we have E_{11}, E_{12}, and E_{22} negative and E_{21} positive. Thus, to satisfy conditions (6.14),

$$E_{11} - E_{12} < 0$$

must be true; self-competition in the prey population must be stronger than predation intensity. In this case the general biomass of the ecosystem $N_1 + N_2$ is maximized by the genetic structures of both predator and prey populations.

Our consideration of the equilibrium and stability problem has been local. When there is a way to solve equation (6.11) and find functions ϕ_i explicitly, these results become global. Another way to make the results global is to place certain restrictions on the ecosystem matrix that are considered as a function of all variables in the system. For this we need conditions of global solvability for system (6.11) that can be expressed in terms of some properties of the matrix E and its minors.

6.4 Frequency-Dependence

As we mentioned at the beginning of the chapter, frequency-dependence remains the least-developed part of the theory, although it has been suggested to be the most important cause of genetic polymorphism (Clarke, 1979). The problem with the theory is in choosing the specific functions that will describe how the fitnesses of different genotypes depend on their frequencies. With an arbitrary choice of functions and without any real possibility of measuring fitness in nature, frequency-dependence produces models of enormous complexity that allow nearly every imaginable kind of dynamic behavior. Such models are useless because they describe everything without explaining anything.

One way to gain explanatory (or rejectional) power is to concentrate on a more specific system, one in which the specificity arises from our biological understanding. An analysis of a few particular classes of natural selection regimes may prove to be more useful than a collection of diffuse generalized statements. We will consider, therefore, one specific class of selection regimes with complete or partial dominance. Such systems seem to be widespread in natural populations, and we will present some results that may be helpful in designing experimental tests to distinguish different kinds of selection for such systems.

Consider a locus with multiple alleles under natural selection. Our system has a standard form:

$$\begin{cases} \dot{p}_i = p_i(W_i - W), & i = 1, \ldots, n \\ \dot{N} = WN \end{cases} \quad (6.15)$$

We will assume fitnesses W_{ij} to be both frequency- and density-dependent:

$$W_{ij} = W_{ij}(\mathbf{p}, N), \quad i, j = 1, \ldots, n$$

Next we assume that the system exhibits complete or partial dominance with respect to fitness, or that every heterozygote fitness $W_{ij} (i \neq j)$ is either between the corresponding two homozygote fitnesses or equals one of them.

$$\min\{W_{ii}(\mathbf{p}, N), \ W_{jj}(\mathbf{p}, N)\} \leq W_{ij}(\mathbf{p}, N) \leq \max\{W_{ii}(\mathbf{p}, N), \ W_{jj}(\mathbf{p}, N)\}$$
$$i, j = 1, \ldots, n \quad (6.16)$$

This is not to be confused with the concept of phenotypic dominance, which may or may not coincide with the dominance in fitness described by (6.16). The two concepts will always coincide in the case of full phenotypic dominance, but for partial dominance (6.16) is a limitation that requires no selection for or against the intermediate type. Let us look for the necessary conditions of stable polymorphism in systems with complete or partial dominance.

The first statement we will prove is that frequency-dependent selection is necessary in such a system to provide a stable polymorphism. In other words, constant or density-dependent selection in such a system will always lead to a monomorphism. We consider the equilibrium equations, and assume that there exists a positive stable equilibrium $(N^*, \mathbf{p}^*)$; we have

$$W_i = W, \quad i = 1, \ldots, n \quad (6.17)$$

at the equilibrium point. Let us order the homozygote fitnesses in such a way that

$$W_{11}(\mathbf{p}^*, N^*) \geq \cdots \geq W_{nn}(\mathbf{p}^*, N^*)$$

and assume that they are not all equal to each other. Consider the first and last equations of system (6.17):

$$\begin{aligned} W_{11}p_1 + \cdots + W_{1n}p_n &= W \\ W_{n1}p_1 + \cdots + W_{nn}p_n &= W \end{aligned} \quad (6.18)$$

6.4 Frequency-Dependence

It follows from (6.16) that the coefficients in the last equation cannot exceed corresponding values in the first equation.

$$W_{ni} \leq W_{1i}, \qquad i = 1, \ldots, n$$

and at least one of the inequalities should be strict, since $W_{11} > W_{nn}$. Equations (6.18) are therefore contradictory, and one of the assumptions must be wrong. Either there is no such equilibrium point, or all homozygote fitnesses are equal to each other (and therefore equal to all the heterozygote fitnesses) at the equilibrium point. Thus the first necessary condition of polymorphism is that all fitnesses of all genotypes should be equal to each other. If we want population size, N, to be in equilibrium as well, we need $W = 0$; therefore,

$$W_{ij}(\mathbf{p}^*, N^*) = 0, \qquad i, j = 1, \ldots, n$$

In other words, systems with complete or partial dominance *at the polymorphic equilibrium point* are indistinguishable from neutral systems, because every genotype has the same fitness. This is a peculiar property of such systems and is not generally true; for example, it is not true if we allow heterozygote fitnesses to be more or less than homozygote fitnesses.

Let us show now that frequency-dependence is necessary for the stability of such an equilibrium. If the fitnesses of all genotypes are constant and equal to each other, all frequency configurations are equilibria and none of them is stable. The same is true for purely density-dependent selection. If

$$W_{ij}(N^*) = 0, \qquad i, j = 1, \ldots, n$$

all frequencies are equilibria and, although the system might be stable with respect to population size, it is neutral with respect to frequency composition, just as in the constant fitness case. Thus frequency-dependence of some sort is a necessary feature of the selection regime providing stable polymorphism. It is, therefore, the only possible explanation of stable polymorphism for systems with complete or partial dominance.

Bryan Clarke has been a most vocal advocate of frequency-dependent selection as a cause of polymorphism in natural populations. In a recent paper (Clarke, 1979), he presented a complete review of different ecological mechanisms leading to frequency-dependence. Without going into the details of his paper, I would like to point out that most of these mechanisms correspond to cases of complete or partial dominance, and are therefore in agreement with my statement.

It is interesting to ask what kind of frequency-dependence is necessary to provide a stable polymorphism in our special class of systems. We will next use a simpler model to show that the frequency-dependence must be some sort of *rare-type advantage*.

Consider a model of pure frequency-dependent selection. It does not necessarily mean that the W_{ij} do not depend on population size, N. It means only that

$$W_{ij}(\mathbf{p}, N) = V_{ij}(\mathbf{p})f(N)$$

where $f(N)$ is the same function for all the genotypes. Therefore, the population size can grow logistically, but its growth does not affect the genetic composition of the population. Indeed, in system (6.15), $f(N)$ factors out and we can consider $V_{ij}(\mathbf{p})$ as new relative fitnesses. Let us assume now that we have a hypothetical equilibrium $\mathbf{p}^*$ and it is stable. The matrix of the first approximation system around the equilibrium point has the form

$$\begin{pmatrix} p_1^* & & 0 \\ & p_2^* & \\ & \ddots & \\ 0 & & p_n^* \end{pmatrix} \begin{pmatrix} \frac{\partial}{\partial p_1}(V_1 - V) & \cdots & \frac{\partial}{\partial p_n}(V_1 - V) \\ \vdots & & \vdots \\ \frac{\partial}{\partial p_1}(V_n - V) & \cdots & \frac{\partial}{\partial p_n}(V_n - V) \end{pmatrix}$$

where all derivatives are calculated at the equilibrium point. It is difficult to express the stability conditions in terms of the behavior of individual fitnesses without additional assumptions specifying the character of the frequency-dependence. One necessary condition follows from the negativeness of the trace for any stable matrix. In our case it takes the form

$$\sum_{i=1}^{n} p_i^* \frac{\partial}{\partial p_i}(V_i - V) < 0 \qquad (6.19)$$

which states the average rare-type advantage. In reality, a negative derivative

$$\frac{\partial}{\partial p_i}(V_i - V) < 0 \qquad (6.20)$$

would mean that an increase in frequency p_i benefits the population more than an increase in the ith allele fitness. Unfortunately, we have established this only on the average, (6.19), and not for every individual allele. All this is true only locally around the equilibrium point. A more detailed result can be obtained if we make additional assumptions about the shape of the fitness functions. In the case of two alleles, the result in (6.20) is true without additional assumptions, so we can be sure that local rare-type advantage of both alleles is a necessary condition of stability in a two-allele system.

Let us summarize our results. We have obtained a few necessary conditions of polymorphism for systems with complete or partial dominance. These conditions provide us with a simple rule for recognizing the presence of frequency-dependent selection in nature without actually measuring the fitnesses. If we see a genetic system with full phenotypic dominance in a polymorphism, there is frequency-dependent selection. If it is a system with partial phenotypic dominance, we should make sure that there are no reasons for over-dominance or under-dominance in fitness; if there are none, then we again have frequency-dependent selection.

If the conditions of complete or partial dominance in fitness are satisfied, we should have all genotype fitnesses equal at the equilibrium point. Lewontin (1974) has discussed at some length the problem of fitness measurement, and he emphasized that fitnesses usually do not differ by much, which is an obstacle to measurement. Could it be that frequency-dependent selection is responsible for an approximate equalization of genotypic fitnesses?

6.5 Problems and Discussion

1. Let me suggest here an example to show that frequency-dependent selection with rare-type advantage can account for stable polymorphism in a system with any number of alleles. Consider the fitness of every genotype to be inversely proportional to the genotype frequency:

$$W_{ij} = \frac{\alpha_{ij}}{p_i p_j}, \quad i, j = 1, \ldots, n$$

The obvious deficiency of this definition is an infinite advantage for the rare type when its frequency is near zero. This can easily be corrected, as we will show later. With this definition our standard equations in (6.15) will have the following simple form:

$$\dot{p}_i = \left(\sum_{j=1}^{n} \alpha_{ij} \right) - p_i \left(\sum_{i,j}^{n} \alpha_{ij} \right), \quad i = 1, \ldots, n$$

All equations are separated from each other. The unique polymorphism

$$p_i^* = \frac{\sum_{j=1}^{n} \alpha_{ij}}{\sum_{i,j}^{n} \alpha_{ij}}, \quad i = 1, \ldots, n$$

134 Chapter 6: Growth with Density- and Frequency-Dependent Selection

is clearly stable. With the choice of appropriate values for α_{ij}, the equilibrium point can be placed in any position on the simplex.

Returning to the problem of infinite advantage, note that multiplication of every equation in system (6.95) by a positive function does not change the qualitative behavior of the trajectories. By choosing this function to be, for instance, the product of all the gene frequencies, we can define our fitnesses as

$$W_{ij} = \frac{\alpha_{ij}}{p_i p_j} \left(\prod_{k=1}^{n} p_k \right)$$

These fitnesses are finite, $0 \leq W_{ij} \leq \alpha_{ij}$, and will produce qualitatively the same result as before.

I have suggested this example only to show the robustness of the model of frequency-dependent selection and to stress, again, that the problem is not merely mathematical, but conceptual. The theory of frequency-dependent selection will only progress with a deeper understanding of the mechanisms that produce frequency-dependence in nature; such knowledge would ultimately come from progress in our understanding of the biology of the species in question.

7 Ecological Implications of Natural Selection

At present, the theory of population growth and evolution is a "microtheory." It is useful for describing interactions between a few populations or a few genotypes. As we have pointed out many times in previous chapters, however, it is impossible to use this theory to explore more complicated situations. A sufficient expansion of even the simplest models would become a matter of insuperable difficulty at every step, from the collection of infinite quantities of data to the accurate identification and evaluation of all the necessary genetic and ecological parameters, from the processing of fitness matrices of astronomic size to the (perhaps most intractable) problem of correctly interpreting the multidimensional results.

A general theory to incorporate evolution into models of population growth has yet to be formulated. This final chapter is intended as a large footnote in which I raise and discuss what I consider to be the central problem: that of macroscopic description.

We already tried, in Chapters 3 and 5, to describe macroscopically the influence of natural selection on population growth. By this I mean a description in terms of macroparameters that depend on gene frequencies but can be observed directly from population growth curves. The objective is to discover whether the average fitness dynamics, and therefore the acceleration of population size, follow some simple macroscopic regularities. If such regularities exist, they may suggest a way to generalize our ecological models.

Statistical physics offers a splendid example of the kind of macrotheory we need for analyzing biological models. But the founders of statistical physics were already equipped with such fundamental notions as pressure and temperature and with an empirical idea of how they were related. We, on the other hand, still do not know what is to be measured, or which direct measurements will conform to simple relationships, or whether any such relationships might have a valid theoretical (explanatory or predictive) use.

7.1 Malthus' Law

Models of population dynamics are based on population size as the complete descriptor of the dynamic state. We can write this central assumption of the theory as

$$\frac{1}{N} \dot{N} = f(\mathbf{E}) \qquad (7.1)$$

where N is the population size; $(1/N)\dot{N}$ is the relative growth rate, or average number of surviving offspring per parent per unit of time (what we called *fitness* in Chapter 1), and $f(\mathbf{E})$ is the environmental function, in which it is understood that population size itself might be one of the environmental parameters, as in the case of density-dependence. The time intervals considered are assumed to be appreciably longer than the generation time, so that processes which occur on the order of one generation can be safely ignored (see the discussion in Chapter 1).

To construct an ecosystem model, we write such equations for each of the populations in the ecosystem. Environment E for any given population includes the sizes of the other populations affecting that environment, and thus we obtain the system of equations designed to describe the ecosystem dynamics. The differences between models are due to different assumptions concerning the forms of the function f. There is no doubt that the growth rate truly depends on the environment. Nevertheless, this dependence is so complex and multifaceted that I, naturally, wish to change the formulation of the problem.

Let me call constant all environments in which a given population increases (or decreases) exponentially, or maintains a given size. There is no external way to determine such a constancy. We cannot, for example, do it by enumerating; food is enough, oxygen is present in necessary quantities, temperature is constant, and so on. But there is no need to enumerate the separate causes. Environmental invariability *for a given population* can be established by examining the population itself, since the environment is invariable only if the population size is constant or changes exponentially.

I will write the Malthusian law $N(t) = N_0 e^{rt}$ in a slightly unusual form:

$$\frac{d^2}{dt^2}(\ln N) = 0 \tag{7.2}$$

Paraphrasing Hutchinson (1975): "Populations preserve exponential growth unless they do not." Although sounding tautological, it has, in my opinion, a meaning analogous to Newton's first law describing what happens when "nothing happens in the environment." In the suggested form (7.2), it has no parameters and requires two initial conditions: population size and the growth rate.

I would like to end this section noting that Malthus' law is the only formula in population theory to which the word *law* has been unanimously applied; all the rest were *models*. I completely agree with this usage of words, stressing exponential growth as an important background for understanding all the events and processes in population dynamics. In the next section I will try to reconstruct the principles of population dynamics based on an extended notion of the dynamic state.

7.2 Evolutionary Adaptation in Models of Population Dynamics

Classical models in theoretical ecology do not take into account genetic heterogeneity of the population. From the point of view of population dynamics, this means that population growth rates respond to any environmental change "instantaneously" on the accepted time scale of the model. One of the direct effects of genetic heterogeneity is that the population will respond to environmental change with some time-delay (that is, the population will have some inertia). The amount of this inertia is related to the intensity of natural selection that occurs in a population after the environmental change. This effect might be of considerable importance, in that a certain amount of inertia might be more adaptive than direct tracking of a changing environment. Genetic variation is important in this sense, not as a direct adaptation to environmental heterogeneity, but as a damper on consequent fluctuations in the population dynamics. Inertia works as a mechanism for averaging out such fluctuations, and thereby produces more stable behavior in varying environments. Both the total absence of inertia and a very high inertia would seem maladaptive. The amount of inertia that a population possesses should ultimately be translated into the amount

138 Chapter 7: Ecological Implications of Natural Selection

of natural selection (fitness variability) and genetic variability in a population.

As one can see from the previous chapters, most of the theoretical work done on the interface between genetics and ecology has been concerned with ecological effects on the genetic constitution of populations. I am going to concentrate here on the opposite influence. I am interested in the effects of genetic variability on population dynamics. The problems are certainly related. Macroscopically, though, different genetic systems might produce the same or similar effects on population dynamics. In such cases, a macroscopic description would be approximately invariant with respect to a specific genetic scheme.

Suppose that an environment was constant at E_1 up to the moment t_1, then changed to the better and also constant environment E_2 until t_2, and finally changed to the worse environment E_3 at t_3 (Figure 7.1). If we accept the model (equation 7.1) literally, the dynamics of the growth rate should look like the broken line in Figure 7.1. Taking into account adaptation effects, we would expect the process to look like the solid line on the same figure. Remember that we do not consider effects on the order of the generation time; this includes possible physiological, demographic, and other adaptations to the new environment which would change the character of the curves around the points t_1 and t_2. (See the classification of adaptation mechanisms with respect to their characteristic time of action in Slobodkin and Rapoport, 1974.)

Since a constant natural selection regime is assumed here as the only cause of adaptation, the growth rate in a constant environment

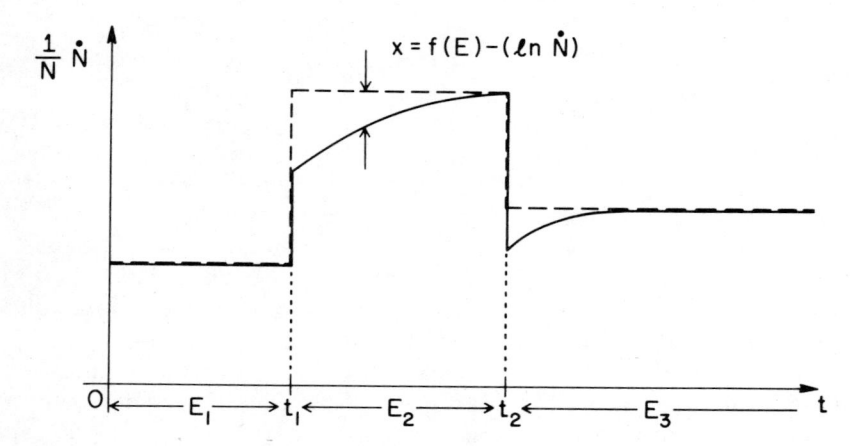

Figure 7.1 Reflective growth rate of a population as a function of time in the thought experiment described in the text.

7.2 Evolutionary Adaptation in Models of Population Dynamics

can only increase. This is certainly true for a haploid population, and it summarizes the content of Fisher's fundamental theorem of natural selection for a diploid population (Chapter 3). Of course, in the case of frequency-dependent selection, the growth rate could decrease during the adaptation process. We have assumed here a constant fitness selection only for the sake of clarity; appropriate generalization will not present a problem in our context.

In an attempt to include the adaptation process in the description of population dynamics, I will postulate the basic equation in a new form:

$$\frac{d^2}{dt^2}(\ln N) = f\left(\mathbf{E}, \frac{d}{dt}\mathbf{E}, \frac{d}{dt}\ln N\right) \qquad (7.3)$$

which describes the rate of change in the growth rate as a function of the environment, the rate of change in the environment, and the growth rate. Recall that population size may itself be a necessary component of the environment. This equation, as well as the Malthusian law in the form of (7.2), requires two initial conditions: population size and growth rate. Thus in the suggested model the dynamic state of a population is described by two numbers instead of one, as in the traditional approach.

In a fixed environment any population should eventually be able to reach its equilibrium (postselected) growth rate depending on the environment. For this growth rate, we will use the same notation $f(\mathbf{E})$ as in the old model: $d/dt\,(\ln N) = f(\mathbf{E})$. In our model, due to the Fisher theorem, $d/dt\,(\ln N) \leqslant f(\mathbf{E})$, the preselected growth rate cannot exceed the postselected growth rate. Taking into account these two properties, we can specify the form of the right-hand part of equation (7.3) as follows:

$$\frac{d^2}{dt^2}(\ln N) = \frac{\partial f}{\partial \mathbf{E}}\dot{\mathbf{E}} - g(\mathbf{E}, \dot{\mathbf{E}}) + A(\mathbf{E})\left(f(\mathbf{E}) - \frac{d}{dt}(\ln N)\right) \qquad (7.4)$$

There are three reasons for growth rate changes:

1. A change in the balanced growth rate, $(\partial f/\partial \mathbf{E})\dot{\mathbf{E}}$.
2. A new disbalance in the growth rate generated by a changing environment, $g(\mathbf{E}, \dot{\mathbf{E}})$. It follows from the Fisher theorem that $g \geqslant 0$, $g(\mathbf{E}, 0) = 0$.
3. An adaptation process that brings the growth rate towards its equilibrium value. Here it is assumed to be proportional to the imbalance in the growth rate. We call $A(\mathbf{E}) < 0$ *adaptability*.

The linearization is not essential here. It is equivalent to the assumption that the solid curves in Figure 7.1 are exponential; we use it only to clarify the meaning of the adaptability parameter. The parameter $1/A$ thus can be considered as a measure of inertia.

Equation (7.4) is basically an attempt to reduce all hidden evolutionary dimensions of a population to one variable;

$$x = f(\mathbf{E}) - \frac{d}{dt}(\ln N) > 0 \tag{7.5}$$

imbalance in the growth rate. Equation (7.4) can then be rewritten as a system of two first order equations:

$$\frac{d}{dt}(\ln N) = f(\mathbf{E}) - x$$
$$\frac{d}{dt}x = g(\mathbf{E}, \dot{\mathbf{E}}) - A(\mathbf{E})x \tag{7.6}$$

Such reduction of a complex evolutionary process to one extra dimension cannot be exact. Hidden dimensions should lead to a hysteresis (history-dependent behavior) of both the imbalance-generating function g and the adaptability A. I hope, nevertheless, that these effects will not be very important in many real cases, and that most of the qualitative features of the evolutionary process, from the point of view of population dynamics, can be sketched by the suggested model.

The traditional approach of (7.1) is a limiting case of the new model, obtained by letting $A \to \infty$. Clearly, infinite adaptability corresponds to the case of no inertia—that is, to direct tracking of environmental variations.

The idea of using second-order equations in models of population dynamics is not new. With no reference to adaptation-producing inertia as a basic mechanism, it appeared independently in Clark (1971) and Ginzburg (1972) and was criticized by Innis (1972).

7.3 Examples

Consider examples where we can apply this approach to the description of adaptation processes in cases where the "exact" genetic models have been developed. My goals here are to compare the suggested approximate macroscopic description with the detailed description and to clarify the meaning of the adaptability parameter.

Density-Independent Growth in Stationary Environment

The complete genetic model was considered in detail in Chapter 5. We obtained there an equation relating the average fitness and the

7.3 Examples

entropy distance between initial and final genetic composition:

$$\int_0^\infty [W^* - W(\mathbf{p}(t))] \, dt = H(\mathbf{p}_0, \mathbf{p}^*) \tag{7.7}$$

Let us compare this exact description with the suggested approximation. In the stationary density-dependent environment, the first two terms in the equation (7.4) vanish and we have

$$\frac{d^2}{dt^2}(\ln N) = A\left(f - \frac{d}{dt}(\ln N)\right) \tag{7.8}$$

where A is the adaptability constant and f is the asymptotic growth rate. At the beginning of the process, the growth rate $\ln N$ can only be less than f; growing monotonically, it subsequently approaches f:

$$\frac{d}{dt}(\ln N) = f - [f - (\ln N)_0]e^{-At} \xrightarrow[t \to \infty]{} f \tag{7.9}$$

We now identify the growth rate of the population ($\ln N$) with the average fitness W and the equilibrium growth rate f with the equilibrium W^*. The exact process is not necessarily exponential, so these identifications are not precisely correct. We can require, however, that the global property of the adaptation process (7.7) holds. We will then have

$$\int_0^\infty [f - \ln N] \, dt = H(\mathbf{p}_0, \mathbf{p}^*) \tag{7.10}$$

Substituting (7.9) into (7.7), we obtain the expression for the adaptability:

$$A = \frac{f - \dfrac{d}{dt}(\ln N)_0}{H(\mathbf{p}_0, \mathbf{p}^*)} \tag{7.11}$$

This represents the overall gain in the growth rate per unit of entropy distance between the initial and final genetic structures.

For the population size $N(t)$ we obtain, integrating from (7.9),

$$N(t) = N_0 \exp\left(ft - \frac{f - \dfrac{d}{dt}(\ln N)_0}{A} \exp(-At)\right) \xrightarrow[t \to \infty]{} N_0 e^{ft} \tag{7.12}$$

We see from this example that the approximate description preserves all the qualitative features of the exact description, but rather than exact knowledge of the genetic parameters, it requires only the extra initial condition for the growth rate.

Density-Independent Growth in a Time-Dependent Environment

In a purely time-dependent environment, equation (7.3) becomes a first-order equation with respect to the growth rate ($\ln N$) and can be integrated explicitly. Evolutionary inertia can only lower the growth rate compared to the traditional model of (7.1). One consequence is that in a periodic environment with period T, $\mathbf{E}(t + T) = \mathbf{E}(t)$, the inequality

$$\frac{1}{T} \int_t^{t+T} f(\mathbf{E}(t)) \, dt > 0 \qquad (7.13)$$

is no longer a sufficient condition for survival. The new condition includes the comparison of this quantity with some kind of integrated "genetic load."

$$\frac{1}{T} \int_t^{t+T} f \, dt > \frac{1}{T} \int_0^T x \, dt > 0 \qquad (7.14)$$

The other consequence is a significant modification of the amplitude of the oscillations in the population size. This modification depends on the dynamics of the newly generated imbalance, g, and adaptability, A.

The case of a randomly fluctuating environment for the suggested model was considered by Braumann (1981). An introduction of "noise" for the rate of change of the growth rate (rather than for the growth rate itself) leads to a decreased variance and strengthened autocorrelation of the process with respect to results obtained by traditional approaches.

Density-Dependent Growth

Based on the same multiple-alleles, one-locus genetic scheme, an exact density-dependent growth model was studied in Chapter 6. From the population-dynamics point of view, the most interesting effect of adaptation is the nonmonotonic character of the growth curves around the carrying capacity equilibrium level.

Let me show how this phenomenon looks within the framework of the suggested macroscopic approach. We assume that the population size itself is the only environmental parameter influencing the population growth, so that equation (7.4) will take the form

$$\frac{d^2}{dt^2}(\ln N) = \frac{\partial f}{\partial N} \dot{N} - g(N, \dot{N}) + A(N)\left(f(N) - \frac{d}{dt}(\ln N)\right) \qquad (7.15)$$

Adaptability in this case may depend on the population size, $A = A(N)$. Note that the traditional logistic-type model is a special case of (7.15) obtained by $A \to \infty$ and $d/dt(\ln N) = f(N)$. To illustrate the effect, let us linearize this equation around an equilibrium $\mathbf{N}^*$ which is the root of the equation $f(N) = 0$. Since $g(N, \dot{N})$ is always nonnegative, it will have a local extremum at the equilibrium point and, therefore, a zero term for the first approximation. Introducing $y = \ln(N/N^*)$, we have

$$\ddot{y} + (k + A^*)\dot{y} + A^* k y = 0, \qquad (7.16)$$

where

$$k = \left.\frac{\partial f}{\partial \ln N}\right|_{N=N^*} > 0$$

measures the strength of density-dependence around the equilibrium point, and

$$A^* = A(N^*)$$

is the adaptability measured at the equilibrium point.

The solution of this equation is the sum of two exponentials,

$$y(t) = \left(1 - \frac{k}{A^*}\right)^{-1}\left(y_0 + \frac{1}{A^*}\dot{y}_0\right)e^{-kt} + \left(\frac{k}{A^*}y_0 + \frac{1}{A^*}\dot{y}_0\right)e^{-A^*t} \qquad (7.17)$$

This demonstrates both of the effects noted in the complete genetic model: the overshooting of the equilibrium level and the temporary decrease in size due to adaptation followed by an increase and an asymptotic equilibrium at $N = N^*$ (Chapter 6). Once again we see that the macroscopic description using one additional parameter, adaptability, captures the main qualitative characteristics of the process.

By analogy, one can go on and rewrite the prey-predator, competition, and other ecosystem models, including adaptability as an additional parameter and using second-order instead of first-order equations for each population. This requires quite a change in intuition, since growth rates are now just initial conditions and the interactions describe environmental changes rather than environments. A general guess about the properties of such two-dimensional models is that they will show destabilization of otherwise stable equilibria, leading to oscillations (or more general bounded behavior) and possibly to extinction. It is not my goal here to go on so far, since it may only obscure the point I am trying to make.

7.4 Bimodality of Evolutionary Rates

Another application of the suggested approach is to the seemingly unrelated problem of evolutionary theory.

Chapter 7: Ecological Implications of Natural Selection

The recent controversy over whether stepwise changes (the punctuated equilibrium hypothesis, Eldredge and Gould, 1972) or gradual changes have been more common in past evolution can be rephrased quantitatively by asking whether the distribution of evolutionary rates is unimodal or bimodal. The difficulty in answering this question lies in the definition of the rate itself. This definition will depend very strongly on the time scale in which one chooses to look at evolution. Clearly, stepwise changes can be made to appear gradual if a coarse-enough time scale is selected (Bookstein, Gingerich, and Kluge, 1978; see also the discussion in Gould and Eldredge, 1977). It is a separate and interesting problem to discover at what time scales one hypothesis or the other best fits the data.

Based on the simplest model of natural selection, I will now show that the distribution of evolutionary rates may look unimodal or bimodal, depending on the time scale. This conclusion would not be surprising if one assumed that the fitness differentials themselves are bimodally distributed. In other words, some adherents of the punctuated equilibrium hypothesis implicitly assume that fitness differentials, as a result of a mutation or an environmental change, are more often low or high than intermediate. An example of this thinking is a reference to mutation in a regulatory gene versus mutation in a structural gene. The first supposedly has a strong fitness effect, whereas the second has a weak effect; another possibility for structural mutation is that evolution follows an environmental change that shifts selection pressures (Levinton and Simon, 1980).

It is our purpose to demonstrate that even an unimodal distribution of fitness differentials can generate a bimodal distribution of evolutionary rates if the time scale is chosen appropriately. This result reduces the utility of a dichotomy between punctuational and gradual change. Macromutations or sudden environmental changes are unnecessary for generating bimodality.

Consider the simplest possible scheme: survival of the fittest. Assume that a population consists of two exponentially and independently growing forms,

$$N_1(t) = N_{10} e^{\lambda_1 t}, \qquad N_2(t) = N_{20} e^{\lambda_2 t} \qquad (7.18)$$

where t is time, λ_1 and λ_2 are the growth rates of the two forms, and N_{10} and N_{20} are the initial sizes of the two groups. We assume that $\lambda_2 > \lambda_1$ and $N_{20} \ll N_{10}$. Consider the dynamics of the average fitness (growth rate of the mixture):

$$\frac{\dot{N}(t)}{N(t)} = \frac{\dot{N}_1(t) + \dot{N}_2(t)}{N_1(t) + N_2(t)}$$

7.4 Bimodality of Evolutionary Rates

It will, of course, tend to λ_2 when $t \to \infty$. Note that the population size of the mixture satisfies a simple second-order equation

$$(\ln \dot{N}) = (\ln N)(\lambda_2 - \ln N)$$

which has the general form of (7.3) and is a logistic equation in terms of the relative growth rate. What we are interested in is the gain in fitness, W, at the time t, which we define as

$$W(t) = \frac{\dot{N}(t)}{N(t)} - \lambda_1$$

This finite-time gain in fitness has the expression

$$W(t) = s \frac{1}{\theta e^{-st} + 1}, \qquad (7.19)$$

where $\theta = N_{10}/N_{20}$ is the ratio of the initial abundances of the lower and higher fitness types in a mixed population, and $s = (\lambda_2 - \lambda_1) > 0$ is the fitness advantage of the higher fitness type over the lower fitness type.

Of course, $W(t) \to (\lambda_2 - \lambda_1) = s$ when $t \to \infty$. Formula (7.19), however, gives us an expression for the finite-time gain in fitness for the mixture, which is a nonlinear function of s and θ.

We can now ask the question, What is the distribution of the finite time gains, $P_W(W[t])$, given that we know a priori the distribution of fitness advantages, $P_s(s)$? This question has a simpler answer:

$$P_W(W[t]) = P_s(s[W]) \left(\frac{\partial W}{\partial s} \right)^{-1} \qquad (7.20)$$

where $s(W)$ is implicitly defined by (7.19) and $(\partial W/\partial s)^{-1}$ is defined by the expression

$$\left(\frac{\partial W}{\partial s} \right)^{-1} = \frac{(\theta e^{-st} + 1)^2}{1 + \theta(st + 1)e^{-st}} \qquad (7.21)$$

When $t \to \infty$, $(\partial W/\partial s)^{-1} \to 1$ and $P_W(W[t]) \to P_s(W)$. In other words, the distribution of average fitness gains asymptotically equals the expected distribution of fitness differentials, $P_s(s)$.

Let us now look at what happens in a finite time. To do that, we must look at the behavior of the term $(\partial W/\partial s)^{-1}$ in formula (7.20). The graph of this function is presented in Figure 7.2 for different values of θ. It is convenient to show this function as a function of the product st so that any change in time, t, would mean only a scale change along the horizontal axis.

The curve always starts with values higher than 1, then falls below 1, and eventually climbs to level 1 again. Therefore, the low rates will always be overrepresented in the finite-time gain distribu-

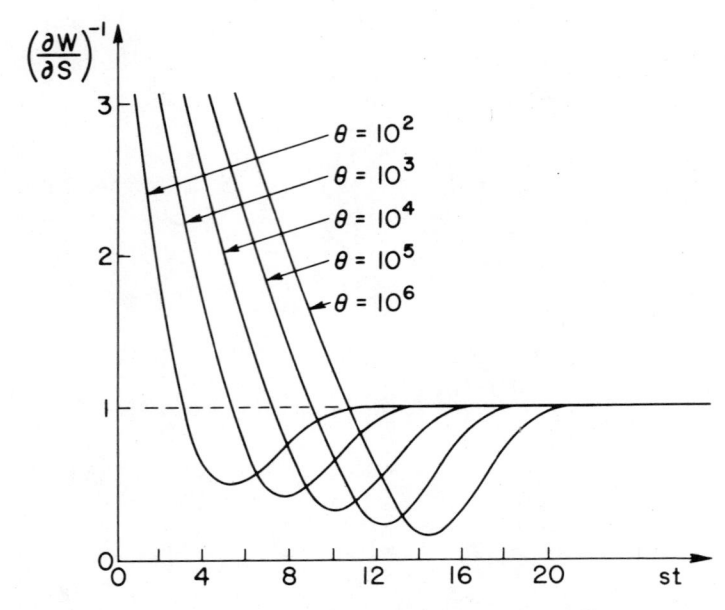

Figure 7.2 The qualitative behavior of the derivative $(\partial W/\partial s)^{-1}$ for the different values of θ.

tion, the intermediate rates will be underrepresented, and the high rates will be presented exactly as they appear in the expected distribution $P_s(s)$. Thus, depending on the shape of the distribution P_s and the time t, we may or may not observe the product in (7.2) as bimodal. We will not be able to observe the bimodality if time t is too short; in this case, $(\partial W/\partial s)^{-1}$ will reach its minimum far beyond the range of values where P_s significantly differs from zero. We will also not be able to observe the bimodality if time t is too long; here $(\partial W/\partial s)^{-1}$ will differ from unity only for a very small interval adjacent to zero. An experimentally observed histogram with any reasonable accuracy would not be capable of detecting a very small wave in the behavior of the P_W distribution around zero.

We might be able to observe the bimodality if time t is intermediate. To estimate the order or magnitude of this intermediate time, let us assume that the expected distribution of fitness differentials has a mean value of $\bar{s}$ and that it is unimodal with the mode at $s = 0$. In other words, the higher the gain, the less probable it is. Then the time t at which the minimum of the curve $(\partial W/\partial s)^{-1}$ is on the order of $\bar{s}$ should be on the order of $(\bar{s})^{-1}$—that is, inversely proportional to the average fitness differential (Figure 7.3).

Since we do not know anything about the shape or even the mean of the fitness differential distribution, we are not able to make any numerical estimates of t. The inverse statement, however, is

7.4 Bimodality of Evolutionary Rates   147

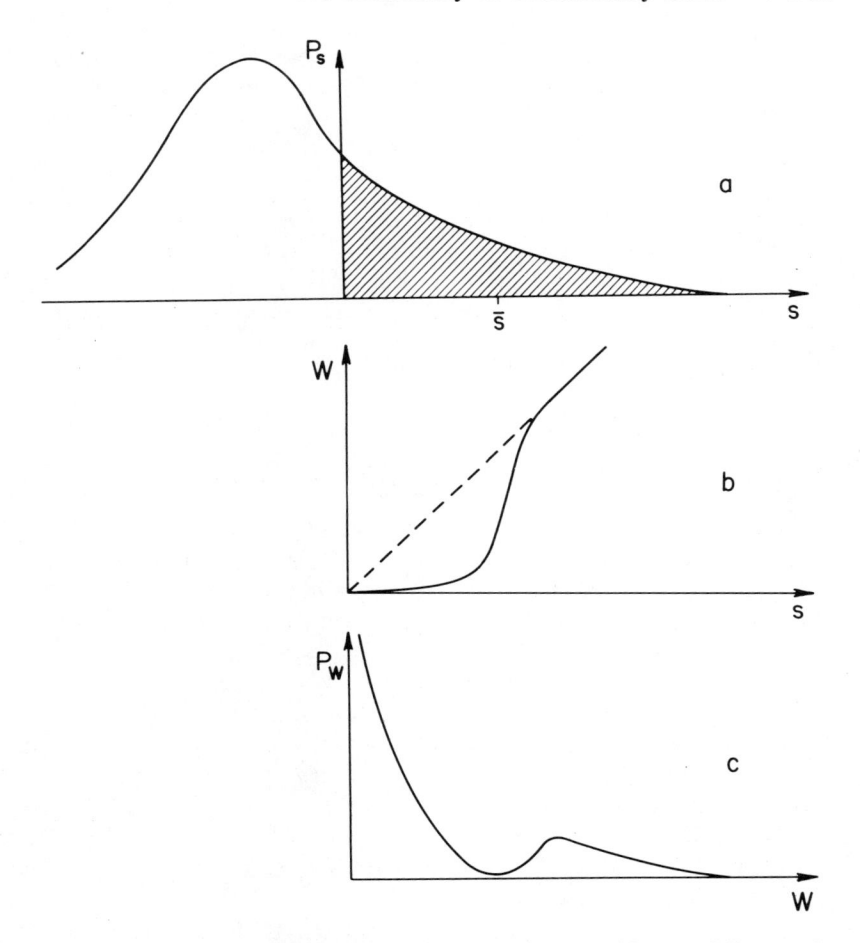

Figure 7.3 (a) A hypothetical unimodal distribution of fitness differentials, P_s. (b) Qualitative behavior of the transformation between the fitness differential, s, and the finite-time mean fitness gain, $W(t)$ for an appropriate time scale, t (formula (7.19)). (c) Bimodal distribution of the finite-time mean fitness gain, P_W, (the distribution P_S transformed by the function (7.19) and pictured by part (b)).

more promising. If we observe a bimodality of the evolutionary rate distribution on some time scale, we might be able to say something about the order of magnitude of the average fitness differential that would be required to produce such a bimodality.

Of course, we cannot observe the average fitness gains directly. The most we can hope for is that we have data on morphological trait evolution in a lineage which could be a result of selection on this trait. Assume that the first form in our model has a mean trait x_1 and the second has a mean trait x_2. Then the expression for the finite time gain in the mean trait is

$$\Delta x(t) = \left(x_1 \frac{N_1(t)}{N(t)} + x_2 \frac{N_2(t)}{N(t)} \right) - x_1 = \left(\frac{x_2 - x_1}{\lambda_2 - \lambda_1} \right) W(t)$$

Therefore, the shape of the morphological trait-change distribution depends on the extent to which it is the under control of selection. With the simplest possible assumption of a linear relationship between the trait and the fitness, the distribution of evolutionary rates with respect to the trait will copy the distribution of average fitness gains subject only to a scale change. More complicated trait-to-fitness mappings may produce a wider variety of distributions.

The model presented here is admittedly simple. In fact, it is the simplest imaginable model of natural selection. The qualitative conclusion, however, is largely model-independent. Finite-time gains in the average fitness will always be nonlinear functions of the fitness differentials; although the expression (7.19) comes from this particular model, the shape of this dependence will be qualitatively similar to (7.19) for any model, and thus could lead to a bimodality of the finite-time average fitness gains if measured in an appropriate time scale.

The main implicit assumption of the suggested model is a low enough mutation rate so that any mutant appearing in a population is fully selected (for or against) before the next new mutant appears. Advantageous mutations are assumed to be "running through" the population at a faster rate than they appear. Superficially, this assumption seems to conflict with possible applications to the evolution of quantitative traits. Under the influence of many loci, the mutation rate per trait can be quite high. But, in fact, we are speaking here only of the *advantageous* mutation rate per trait, which can be orders of magnitude lower than the overall mutation rate. In general, my argument becomes progressively weaker as the number of equally effective loci determining a trait increases. In the absence of accurate accounts of the orders of magnitude for advantageous mutation rates and selection intensities, my argument stands as a plausible hypothesis. At the other extreme, we might assume that mutation rates are always high. This would lead to the gradualistic point of view, as demonstrated by R. Lande (1980) in his summary. The collection of fine-scale evolutionary data is critical for distinguishing between these two alternatives.

Let me end this discussion with an imaginary example. Consider a population of *E. coli* cultivated in a chemostat under a fixed environment for a number of years. (For an imaginary example, we can omit the technical problems of how one might really do this.)

Assume that I sample cells from the culture at different time intervals to discover whether the culture has evolved with respect to a number of traits. If I sample, for instance, on a biweekly basis, most of the time I would find that nothing has happened. Rarely would I find changes which seemed punctuative, since the replacement time in a chemostat is typically much shorter than 2 weeks. If I made observations on an hourly basis, the details of the replacement process would be obvious, and thus the overall picture of evolution would look more gradual. On the other hand, if I made only yearly observations, the process would look gradual again, but for a different reason: I would have lumped a number of changes during the year into one yearly change. The numbers in this example are all imaginary, but not entirely unrealistic; bimodality of the evolutionary rate on a biweekly scale would in fact correspond to the typical selective advantage of the order of 10^{-3} per generation.

7.5 Summation

This final chapter has been concerned mainly with alternative approaches we might use for describing the dynamics of evolving

TABLE 7.1 Principles of the description of population dynamics

	Traditional approach	Suggested approach
Dynamic State of a Population	$N(t)$ Population Size	$\left\{ N(t), \dfrac{\dot{N}(t)}{N(t)} = \dfrac{d}{dt}(\ln N) \right\}$ Population Size Growth Rate
Malthusian Law	$\dot{N}/N = r$ With Initial Condition: $N\|_{t=0} = N_0$	$\dfrac{d^2}{dt^2}(\ln N) = 0$ With Initial Conditions: $N\|_{t=0} = N_0$ $\dfrac{d}{dt}(\ln N)\|_{t=0} = r$
General Growth Equation for Varying Environment $E = E(t)$	$\dot{N}/N = f(E)$ With Initial Condition: $N\|_{t=0} = N_0$	$\dfrac{d^2}{dt^2}(\ln N) = F(E, \dot{E}, (\dot{\ln} N))$ With Initial Conditions: $N\|_{t=0} = N_0$ $\dfrac{d}{dt}(\dot{\ln} N)\|_{t=0} = \dfrac{d}{dt}(\dot{\ln} N)_0$

populations, so that a coherent macrotheory can eventually be developed. Table 7.1 is a quick reference summary of my basic suggestions. Note that in one respect this chapter creates what we might call a Newtonian approach to population biology, in which we define the concept of environmental force as a quantity proportional to the acceleration of population growth, $d^2/dt^2 (\ln N)$. The growth rate itself is merely an initial condition here. This certainly narrows the field, but only as far as the gross idea of force is concerned. It does not mean that the analogy can be carried further; genetic heterogeneity is not mass, biological laws are not physical laws, and in any case we have no units for measurement.

The future success of the suggested approach depends on whether—and how well—we are able to discover and define the terms on the right-hand side of the environmental force equation.

Literature Cited

Armstrong, R. A.; and McGehee, R. 1980. Competitive exclusion. *Am. Nat.* 115:151–70.

Ayala, F. J.; Tracey, M. L.; Barr, L. G.; McDonald, J. F.; and Pérez-Salas, S. 1974. Genetic variation in natural populations of five *Drosophila* species and the hypothesis of the selective neutrality of protein polymorphisms. *Genetics* 77:343–84.

Bellman, R. 1960. *Introduction to matrix analysis.* New York: McGraw-Hill.

Bookstein, F. L.; Gingerich, P. D.; and Kluge, A. G.; 1978. Hierarchical linear modeling of the tempo and mode of evolution. *Paleobiology* 4:120–34.

Braumann, C. A. 1981. Population adaptation to a noisy environment: stochastic analogs of some deterministic models. In: *Quantitative Population Dynamics*, ed. D. G. Chapman and V. F. Gallucci. Fairland, Md.: Int. Coop. Publ. House.

Castilla, M. 1977. A parametric model for predator-prey interactions (unpubl. paper).

Chakraborty, R.; Fuerst, P. A.; and Nei, M. 1980. Statistical studies on protein polymorphism in natural populations. III. Distribution of allele frequencies and the number of alleles per locus. *Genetics* 94:1039–63.

Charlesworth, B. 1980. Evolution in age-structured populations. New York: Cambridge University Press.

Literature Cited

Chorick, F. 1968. Infusoria in the lakes of Moldavia. Kishinev (in Russian).

Clark, G. P. 1971. The second derivative and population in modeling. *Ecology* 52:606–13.

Clarke, B. C. 1979. The evolution of genetic diversity. *Proc. R. Soc. London.* B 205:453–74.

Costantino, R. F.; and Desharnais, R. A. 1980. Gamma distributions of adult numbers for Tribolium populations in the region of their steady states (submitted to *J. Anim. Ecol.*).

Costantino, R. F., and Rowe, P. M. 1972. Genetic analysis of a population of *Tribolium*. IV. Gene expression modified by corn oil and relative humidity. *Heredity, Lond.* 29:247–52.

Costantino, R. F.; Bell, A. E.; and Rogler, J. C. 1967. Genetic analysis of a population of *Tribolium*. I. Corn oil sensitivity and selection response. *Heredity, Lond.* 22:529–39.

Costantino, R. F.; Ginzburg, L. R.; and Moffa, A. M. 1977. An experimental check of fitness entropy versus selective delay. *J. Theor. Biol.* 68:317–20.

Costantino, R. F., Rogler, J. C.; and Bell, A. E. 1968. Genetic analysis of a population of *Tribolium*. II. Metabolic pattern of corn oil sensitivity anomaly. *Heredity, Lond.* 23:477–83.

Desharnais, R. A.; and Costantino, R. F. 1982. Natural selection and fitness entropy in a density-regulated population *Genetics* (in press).

Dobzhansky, T.; and Spassky, B. 1963. Genetics of natural populations. XXXIV. Adaptive norm, genetic load, and genetic elite in *D. pseudoobscura*. *Genetics* 48:1467–85.

Eldredge, N.; and Gould, S. J. 1972. Punctuated equilibria: an alternative to phyletic gradualism. In *Models in Paleobiology* ed T. J. M. Schopf, pp. 82–115. San Francisco: Freeman, Cooper and Co.

Ewens, W. 1979. *Mathematical Population Genetics*. New York: Springer-Verlag.

Falconer, D. S. 1971. *Introduction to Quantitative Genetics*. New York: Ronald Press.

Feldman, M. W.; Franklin, I. R.; and Thomson, G. 1974. Selection in complex genetic systems. I. The symmetric equilibrium of the three-locus symmetric viability model. *Genetics* 76:135–62.

Feldman, M. W.; Lewontin, R. C.; Franklin, I. R.; and Christiansen, P. B. 1975. Selection in complex genetic systems. III. An effect of allele multiplicity with two loci. *Genetics* 79, 333–47.

Fisher, R. A. 1930. *The genetical theory of natural selection*. Oxford: Clarendon Press.

Franklin, I. R.; and Feldman, M. W. 1977. Two loci with two alleles: linkage equilibrium and linkage disequilibrium can be simultaneously stable. *Theor. Pop. Biol.* 12:95–113.

Franklin, I. R.; and Lewontin, R. C. 1970. Is the gene the unit of selection? *Genetics* 65:333–47.

Gantmacher, F. R. 1959. *The theory of matrices*, vol. 2. New York: Chelsea Publishing Co.

Gause, G. F. 1934. *The struggle for existence*. Baltimore: Williams and Wilkins.

Gillespie, J. 1977. A general model to account for enzyme variation in natural populations. III. Multiple alleles. *Evolution* 31:85–90.

Gimelfarb, A. A.; Ginzburg, L. R.; Poluektov, R. A.; Pykh, Y. A.; and Ratner, V. A. 1974. The dynamical theory of biological populations. Moscow: Nauka (in Russian).

Ginzburg, L. R. 1971. The diversity of fitnesses and the generalized fitness. *Zhurnal Obshchey Biologii*. Vol. XXXIII, no. 1 (in Russian).

———. 1972. The analogies of "free movement" and "force" of concepts in population theory. In Coll. *Studies of theoretical genetics*, pp. 65–84. Novosibirsk (in Russian).

———. 1975. Equations of the theory of biological communities. In *Mathematical Models in Biology*, pp. 53–91. Moscow: Nauka (in Russian).

———. 1977a. A macro-equation of natural selection. *J. Theor. Biol.* 67:677–86.

———. 1977b. Local consideration of polymorphisms for populations coexisting in stable ecosystems. *J. Math. Biol.* 5:33–41.

———. 1977c. The equilibrium and stability for n alleles under the density dependent selection. *J. Theor. Biol.* 68:545–50.

———. 1979. Why are heterozygotes often superior in fitness? *Theor. Pop. Biol.* 15, 2:264–67.

Ginzburg, L. R.; and Braumann, C. A. 1980. Multilocus population and genetics: relative importance of selection and recombination. *Theor. Pop. Biol.* 17:298–320.

Ginzburg, L. R.; and Costantino, R. F. 1979. On the rate of genetic adaptation under the natural selection. *J. Theor. Biol.* 77:307–16.

Ginzburg, L. R.; Goldman, Y. I.; and Railkin, A. I. 1971. Mathematical models of interaction between two populations. I. Predator-prey. *J. Gen. Biol.* 32:724–30 (in Russian).

———. 1972. Mathematical models of interaction between two populations. II. Competition-symbiosis. *J. Gen. Biol.* 33:450–55 (in Russian).

Ginzburg, L. R.; and Konovalov, N. Y. 1974. Mathematical models of ecological genetical interactions. In *Cybernetic Models in Biology*, pp. 99–112. Novosibirsk (in Russian).

Ginzburg, L. R.; Konovalov, N. Y.; and Epelman, G. S. 1974. Mathematical models of interaction between two populations. IV. Theoretical and experimental data. *J. Gen. Biol.* 35:613–19 (in Russian).

Gould, S. J.; and Eldredge, N. 1977. Punctuated equilibria: the tempo and mode of evolution reconsidered. *Paleobio.* 3:115–51.

Literature Cited

Hardy, G. K.; Littlewood, J. E.; and Polya, G. 1934. *Inequalities*. Oxford: Clarendon Press.

Harris, H.; Hopkinson, D. A.; and Robson, E. B. 1974. The incidence of rare alleles determining electrophoretic variants: data on 43 enzyme loci in man. *Ann. Human Genet.* 37:237–53.

Hastings, A. 1981. Disequilibrium, selection, and recombination: limits in two-locus two-allele models. *Genetics*, in press.

Hedrick, P.; Jain, S.; and Holden, L. 1978. Multi-locus systems in evolution. In *Evolutionary Biology*, vol. 11, pp. 101–84. New York: Plenum.

Hutchinson, G. E. 1975. Variation on a theme by Robert MacArthur. In Coll. *Ecology and Evolution of Communities*, pp. 492–521, Cambridge, Mass.: Harvard University Press.

Innis, G. 1972. The second derivative and population modeling: another view. *Ecol.* 53:720–23.

Karlin, S. 1975. General two-locus selection models: some objectives, results and interpretations. *Theor. Pop. Biol.* 7:364–98.

———. 1977. Selection with many loci and possible relations to quantitative genetics. In *Proc. Intl. Conf. Quantitative Genetics*, pp. 207–25. Ames, Ia.: Iowa State University Press.

———. 1978. Theoretical aspects of multi-locus selection balance, I, In *Studies in Mathematical Biology*, ed. S. Levin, vol. 16, pp. 503–87. New York: The Mathematical Association of America.

———. 1979. Principles of polymorphism and epistasis for multi-locus systems. *Proc. Nat. Acad. Sci.* 75:541–46.

———. 1980. The range of stability of a polymorphic linkage equilibrium state in a general two-locus two-allele selection model. *J. Math. Biol*, in press.

Karlin, S.; and Feldman, M. W. 1981. A theoretical and numerical assessment of genetic variability. *Genetics* 97:475–93.

Karlin, S.; and Liberman, U. 1979a. Central equilibria in multi-locus systems. I. Generalized monepistatic selective regimes. *Genetics* 91:777–98.

———. 1979b. Central equilibria in multilocus systems, II. Bisexual generalized monepistatic selection regimes. *Genetics* 91:799–836.

Kimura, M. 1968. Evolutionary rate at the molecular level. *Nature*, 217:624–26.

King, J. L.; and Jukes, T. H. 1969. Non-Darwinian evolution: random fixation of selectively neutral mutations. *Science* 164:738–98.

Kingman, J. F. C. 1961. A mathematical problem in population genetics. *Proc. Camb. Phil. Soc.* 57:574–82.

Kolmogorov, A. N. 1936. Sulla teoria di Volterra della lotta per L'esistenza. Giorn. dell'Istituto Italiano degli attuary, anno VII, no. I, pp. 74–80.

———. 1972. Qualitative analysis of the mathematical models of population dynamics. *Problems of Cybernetics*, vol. 25, pp. 100–106. *Nauka* (in Russian), Moscow.

Kostitzin, V. A. 1938. *Biologie mathematique.* Paris: Armand Colin Collection.

Kullback, S. 1960. *Information theory and statistics*, New York: John Wiley.

Lande, R. 1980. Genetic variation during allopatric speciation. *Am. Nat.* 116:463–79.

Levin, S. A. 1970. Community equilibria and stability, and an extension of the competitive exclusion principle. *Am. Nat.* 104:413–23.

Levin, S. A.; and Udovic, G. D. 1977. A mathematical model in coevolving populations. *Am. Nat.*, in press.

Levins, R. 1974. The qualitative analysis of partially specified systems. *Annals of N.Y. Acad. of Sci.* 231:123–38.

Levinton, J. S.; and Simon, C. M. 1980. A critique of the punctuated equilibria model and implications for the detection of speciation in the fossil record. *Syst. Zool.* 29:130–42.

Lewontin, R. C. 1958a. A general method for investigating the equilibrium of gene frequency in population. *Genetics* 43:419–34.

———. 1974b. *The Genetic Basis of Evolutionary Change.* New York/London: Columbia University Press.

Lewontin, R. C., Ginzburg, L. R.; and Tuljapurkar, S. D. 1978. Heterosis as an explanation for large amounts of genic polymorphism. *Genetics* 88: 149–69.

Lotka, A. J. 1925. *Elements of physical biology.* Baltimore: Williams and Wilkins.

Mandel, S. P. H. 1959. The stability of a multiple allelic system. *Heredity* 13:289–302.

May, R. M. 1974. *Stability and complexity in model ecosystems*, 2nd ed. Princeton, N. J.: Princeton University Press.

Maynard Smith, J. 1976. What determines the rate of evolution? *Am. Nat.* 110:331–38.

Moffa Scully A. M.; and Costantino, R. F. 1977. Genetic analysis of a population of *Tribolium*. VI. Polymorphism and demographic equilibrium. *Genetics* 87:785–805.

Nagylaki, T.; and Crow, J. F. 1974. Continuous selective models. *Theor. Pop. Biol.* 5:257–83.

Ohta, T. 1973. Slightly deleterious mutant substitutions in evolution. *Nature* 246:96–98.

———. 1975. Statistical analysis of *Drosophila* and human protein polymorphisms. *Proc. Nat. Acad. Sci.* 72:3194–96.

———. 1976. Role of very slightly deleterious mutations in molecular evolution and polymorphism. *Theor. Pop. Biol.* 10:254–75.

Literature Cited

Ramshaw, J. A. M.; Coyne, J. A.; and Lewontin, R. C. 1979. The sensitivity of gel electrophoresis as a detector of genetic variation. *Genetics* 93:1019–37.

Rescigno, A., and A. Richardson. 1967. The Struggle for Life. I. Two species. *The Bull. of Math. Biophys.*, vol. 29, no. 4, p. 377.

———. 1968. The Struggle for Life. II. Three competitors. *The Bull. of Math Biophys.*, vol. 30, no. 2.

Roughgarden, J. 1976. Resource partitioning among competing species: a coevolutionary approach. *Theor. Pop. Biol.* 9:388–424.

Roughgarden, J. 1979. *Theory of population genetics and evolutionary ecology: an introduction.* New York: MacMillan.

Scully, A. M. M.; and Costantino, R. F. 1975. Genetic analysis of a population of *Tribolium*. V. Viability of the unsaturated fatty acid sensitive mutant. *Can. J. gen. Cyt.* 17:585–90.

Slatkin, M.; and Maynard Smith, J. 1979. Models of coevolution. *The Quarterly Review of Biology* 54:233–63.

Slobodkin, L. B.; and Rapoport, A. 1974. An optimal strategy of evolution. *The Quarterly Review of Biology* 49:181–200.

Strebel, D. E.; and Goel, N. S. 1973. On the isocline methods for analyzing prey-predatory interaction. *J. of Theor. Biol.* 39:211–39.

Turelli, M; and Ginzburg, L. R. 1982. Should individual fitness increase with heterozygosity (submitted to *Genetics*).

Turner, J. R. G. 1971. Wright's adaptive surface and some general rules for equilibria in complex polymorphisms. *Am. Nat.* 105:267–78.

Volterra, V. 1931. *Leçons sur la théorie mathématique de la lutte pour la vie.* Paris: Cauthier-Villars.

Wangersky, P. J. 1978. Lotka-Volterra population models. *Annual Review of Ecology and Systematics* 9:189–218.

Watterson, G. A. 1978. The homozygosity test of neutrality. *Genetics* 88:405–17.

Whittaker, R. H.; and Levin, S. A. 1976. *Niche theory and application.* New York: Halsted Press.

Index

Adaptability, 139–143
Adaptation curve, 101, 106, 109
Age structure, 7, 14
Allele frequency
   defined, 3
   spectrum, 88–95
Amensalism, 18
Artificial selection, 70
Attraction zones. See Wrights's adaptive topography

Balanced growth, 30–32, 35, 41, 50, 139
Basic population growth model, 6–9
Bimodality of evolutionary rates, 143–149
Biomass, 16, 45, 128–129

Carrying capacity, 45, 121, 142
Changing environment. See environmental changes
Classification of the interaction types, 18–22, 27–28, 35, 41, 115
Coevolutionary models, 4, 30, 48, 121–129
Coexistence
   of multiple alleles. See polymorphisms

of populations. See ecosystems, equilibrium states
Commensalism, 18
Competition, 14, 18, 20–22, 28–30, 34–35, 37, 41–45, 78, 83, 115, 126–129
   coefficients, 37, 41–44
   equations, 14, 29–30, 42–43, 143
   models. See competition, equations.
Competitive
   ecosystems. See ecosystems, competitive
   exclusion principle, 14
Conservation of allelic fitnesses, 52–53, 77, 104

Demography, 2–3, 107–108, 138
Density-dependence, 4, 25–27, 29–31, 42–43, 45–46, 136
   in selection models. See natural selection models, density-dependent
Didinium nasutum, 45–46
Dirac delta function, 92
Dominance, 69, 88–95, 97, 130–133

157

Index

Drosophila
  equinoxalis, 89
  heteroneura, 89
  tropicalis, 89
  willistoni, 89

E. coli, 148–149
Ecological stability. *See* ecosystem, stability
Economic models, 30
Ecosystem(s)
  boundaries, 17
  competitive, 20–22, 28, 35, 126–129
  conservative, 20–21
  dynamics, 7, 12–48, 121–129, 136
  equilibrium states, 31–48, 123–129, 143
  extinction, 39–42, 44, 47, 143
  fitness. *See* fitness, ecosystem
  inhibited, 19–20, 25
  limited, 31–41, 43
  matrix, 123–129
  mixture of, 19–20, 24–25
  modeling, 4, 6–8, 12–48, 121–129, 136, 143
  mutualistic, 20–22, 28, 35, 127
  neutral, 15, 19–21, 24, 30–45
  noninvasibility condition of, 36, 40
  prehistoric, 39
  size, 16–25, 27–34, 36–41, 43
  size spectrum, 38–39
  stability, 15, 31, 35–36, 39–47, 123–129, 143
  state, 7, 19–23, 27, 39
  state vector, 16–17, 19–20, 25, 27, 29, 37–38, 40
  stimulated, 19–20, 25
  structure, 17–41
  two species, 8, 13–15, 18–19, 41–48, 121–129, 143
Effective population size, 88, 92–94
Electrophoretic data, 74, 88–89
Entropy distance, 101, 111, 141
Environmental
  changes, 7, 16, 22, 28, 70–71, 136–144, 149
  force, 136, 139–140, 149–150
  function, 136–140
  parameter(s), 6–7, 13, 16–18, 22–23, 25, 27–28, 136–139, 142
Epidemiological processes, 14
Epistasis, 67, 70–71, 97
Euler identity, 116

Evolutionary
  inertia. *See* population, inertia
  models. *See* natural selection models

Feedback coefficients, 126–129
Fisher's theorem, 53–55, 58–59, 64–71, 101, 105–106, 112, 118, 120, 139
Fitness
  absolute, 4, 9–10, 53, 108–109
  allelic, 4–6, 50, 52–54, 56–58, 64, 71, 77, 103, 108–109, 113, 118, 122–125, 130
  average, 4–6, 9–11, 15–19, 22–23, 25, 27–29, 31–32, 36, 39–43, 45, 50, 52–58, 64–73, 77–82, 97, 100–109, 113–126, 128, 130, 135–136, 140–141, 144–149
  depression. *See* inbreeding, depression
  differentials, 144–149
  ecosystem, 17–25, 27–31, 35–36, 39–41
  genotype, 3–6, 9, 29, 50–52, 56–59, 64–65, 67, 70–72, 76–97, 113, 118–126, 129–134
  heterozygote, 56, 59, 72, 76–93, 96–97, 117, 130–131
  homozygote. *See* fitness, heterozygote
  matrix, 4, 49–52, 54, 56, 66, 70–72, 75–79, 83, 86, 96, 113–125, 135
  peaks, *See* Wright's adaptive topography
  population. *See* fitness, average
  relative, 9, 90, 132
Frequency dependence, 29, 70
  in selection models. *See* natural selection models, frequency dependent
Frobenius theorem, 37

Gametic selection. *See* selection, gametic
Generation time, 2, 5–6, 28, 108, 136
Genetic
  drift, 3, 89–90, 94–95
  load, 142
  variability, 3, 74, 137–138, 150 (*see also* polymorphism)
Gradualism, 144–149
Group selection, 71

Heterosis. *See* heterozygote superiority
Heterozygote superiority, 69, 75–96, 117
  chromosomal, 96

Index

Homogeneous density-dependence, hypothesis of, 25–27
Homo sapiens, 89

Imbalance-generating function, 140, 142
Inbreeding, 3, 72
  depression, 81–82

Kolmogorov models, 7–8, 12–13, 15–16, 41, 47

Limit-cycle behavior, 14–15, 45, 46
Limiting factor(s), 14, 26, 43, 118
Linkage. *See* linkage disequilibrium
Linkage disequilibrium, 56–59, 64–65, 67, 69, 72, 95–96, 111
  function, 56–59, 64–65, 11
Logistic growth model, 26, 29–31, 37, 44, 122, 132, 142, 145

Lotka-Volterra
  competition, 14–15, 29
  hypothesis, 26
  models, 5–8, 12–16, 26, 29–30, 41, 45, 47–48
  predator-prey, 13–14, 29

Macaca fuscata, 89
Malthusian
  growth, 30
  law, 136–137, 139, 149
  parameter, 4, 30, 53, 104, 107
Mandel-Kingman stability condition, 51
Mating, preferential, 3
Measure-concentration effect, 60–62, 69, 71–72
Microbial systems, 7, 28, 148–149
Migration, 14
Morphological trait evolution, 147–148
Mutations, 3, 70, 88–96, 144, 148
Mutualism, 18, 20–22, 28, 34–35, 115, 127

Natural selection. *See* selection
Natural selection models
  demography and, 3
  density dependent, 4, 30, 96, 109, 112–131, 140–143
  equilibrium states, 49–53, 56–57, 69–73, 75–83, 91–97, 99–111, 113–134
  frequency dependent, 88, 96–97, 109, 112, 123–125, 129–134, 139

multiple loci, 6, 49, 55–73, 82, 95–97, 109, 111
one locus-multiple allele, 2–6, 8, 18, 29–30, 47–59, 67, 70–72, 75–95, 99–111, 112–134
  stability of, 49–53, 56–57, 69, 71, 75–87, 96–97, 111, 113–134
  with exponential growth, 99–111
  within one population, 2–6, 8, 11, 49–121, 129–150
Neutral theory, 3, 74, 88–96
Newtonian physics, 53, 137, 150
Nondecomposition, 37
Nonoverlapping generations, 2–3, 6

Optimal life-history strategies, 3
Oscillations, 14–15, 70, 112, 142–143

Pair interactions, hypothesis of, 24–25, 30
Panmixia, 3, 87
Paramecium
  aurelia, 44–45
  caudatum, 44–46
Perron-Frobenius theorem, 117
Poincaré-Bendixon theorem, 46
Polymorphism, 50–52, 56–57, 69–98, 106, 111–134
  complete. *See* polymorphism, fully stable
  fully stable, 50–53, 56–57, 71, 75–87, 96–97, 113–134
  probability of, 91–92
Population(s)
  equilibrium, 31–48, 54, 96, 99–111, 114–131, 137–143
  extinction, 14, 143
  fitness. *See* fitness average
  frequency, 17–18, 20, 22–25, 27, 29–31, 33–36, 38–43, 45
  genetic structure of, 100–111, 113–134, 138–143
  growth dynamics, 1–2, 4, 11–49, 52, 55, 99–145, 149–150
  interactions. *See* species, interactions
  natural, 3, 14, 67, 74, 130–131, 134
  number of, 6–7, 15–16, 33–36
  relative growth rate. *See* fitness, average size, 3–4, 6–8, 13–16, 19, 26, 29, 32–33, 37–47, 50, 55–56, 59, 69, 88–89, 91–94, 96, 99–101, 104, 109, 113–129, 135–145, 148–149

Index

Predator-prey relationships, 4, 13–15, 18, 29, 41–47, 127–129, 143
Punctuated equilibrium, 144–149

Quantitative genetics, 70

Random effects. *See* stochastic effects
Rare alleles, 88–89, 94–95
Rare-type advantage, 132–134
Rate of adaptation, 105–106, 108–109
Recombination, 6, 55–60, 64–70, 72–73, 82, 95, 97, 111
   intensity, 66–69
Resources, 14

Selection
   gametic, 49, 71
   intensity, 2, 6, 56–58, 66–70, 91, 101, 137–138, 148
   models. *See* natural selection models
   theory, 49–95
   zygotic, 49, 54, 71–72
Selective delay, 99–101, 104, 106–109
Sexual structure, 3
Simplex. *See* standard simplex

Spatial structure, 3
Species
   interactions, 2, 4–8, 12–48, 121–129, 135, 143
   list, 35–36, 48
Standard simplex, 17, 24–25, 35, 38, 50, 55, 60–69, 72–77, 102–103, 111, 114–120, 125, 134
Stochastic effects, 3, 8, 88–95, 142
Survival of the fittest, 54, 144
Sybiosis, 18

Taricha rivularis, 89
Time scale, 2, 4–7, 28, 136–137, 144–149
Triangle inequalities, 75–79, 83, 87, 95, 103
Tribolium castaneum Herbst, 106–109
Turner's principle, 69

Volterra mechanism, 14

Wright's adaptive topography, 53, 55, 70, 72

Zoarces viviparus, 89
Zygotic selection, *See* selection, zygotic